Brazil, Lyric, and the Americas

UNIVERSITY PRESS OF FLORIDA

Florida A&M University, Tallahassee
Florida Atlantic University, Boca Raton
Florida Gulf Coast University, Ft. Myers
Florida International University, Miami
Florida State University, Tallahassee
New College of Florida, Sarasota
University of Central Florida, Orlando
University of Florida, Gainesville
University of North Florida, Jacksonville
University of South Florida, Tampa
University of West Florida, Pensacola

Brazil, Lyric,
and the Americas

◇
◇
◇

Charles A. Perrone

University Press of Florida
Gainesville · Tallahassee · Tampa · Boca Raton
Pensacola · Orlando · Miami · Jacksonville · Ft. Myers · Sarasota

15   14   13   12   11   10   6   5   4   3   2   1

Library of Congress Cataloging-in-Publication Data
Perrone, Charles A.
Brazil, lyric, and the Americas/Charles A. Perrone.
p. cm.
Includes bibliographical references and index.
ISBN 978-0-8130-3421-8 (alk. paper)
1. Brazilian poetry—20th century—History and criticism. 2. America—
In literature. 3. Brazil—In literature. 4. Literature and globalization—Brazil.
5. Brazilian literature—American influences. I. Title.
PQ9571.P46 2010
869.1009'989–dc22   2009034635

The University Press of Florida is the scholarly publishing agency for the
State University System of Florida, comprising Florida A&M University,
Florida Atlantic University, Florida Gulf Coast University, Florida Interna-
tional University, Florida State University, New College of Florida, Univer-
sity of Central Florida, University of Florida, University of North Florida,
University of South Florida, and University of West Florida.

University Press of Florida
15 Northwest 15th Street
Gainesville, FL 32611-2079
http://www.upf.com

Contents

Illustrations

Preface and Acknowledgments

This book has taken shape over the last ten to twelve years and, given its temporal focus and themes, contemporary and current, the research and writing could easily continue to grow for another decade. Yet here it is now, *hic et nunc, aqui e agora*. Looking back, I can situate early incentives to commence this enterprise in an invited presentation at the Segunda Bienal Internacional de Poesia de Belo Horizonte (Minas Gerais, Brazil, November 1998) and in conversations that ensued. Early in 1999, while working on a collection of essays about popular music and globalization, I received an inspiring inquiry regarding an initiative in the study of poetries of the Americas. A first working title for my projected participation was something like "An Island Called Brazil: Outreach and Isolation in New World Lyric." As ideas evolved and the undertaking grew in scope and depth, a longer name for the project emerged—"Interfaces: Insularity, Invention, Brazilian Lyric in/and the Americas"—in complement to the title of my previous monograph on twentieth-century lyric, *Seven Faces: Brazilian Poetry since Modernism* (1996). In this twenty-first century, the "In-" words in the extended working title ended up being used for the introduction to the present volume and remained as guiding tropes of the study. The pivotal word *interfaces* comprises as well a crystallization of the transamerican poetics developed since the 1990s and applied here. In a nutshell, this book is about how recent Brazilian lyric (since about 1985) has engaged with counterparts and other heritages in the Americas, essentially the United States and so-inclined countries of Spanish America. It is informed, as a friend has observed, by a "generous assumption" that studying poetry in comparative perspective can help to answer concerns about the inequalities of globalization and to imagine a utopian hemispheric solidarity. The introduction will broach those issues, set forth the concepts of interface and the other guiding tropes, and explain the purpose of each chapter.

The book is distinctive both in what it covers and in how it does so. This is the only full-length English-language study of Brazilian poetry since the 1980s; it applies, moreover, hemispheric principles throughout. While decidedly not a survey of trends and tendencies in the genre, these reflections do employ poetry to contemplate aspects of the Brazil of the late second millennium, both artistic scenes and experiential situations. The present study addresses several gaps in literary scholarship. As compared to fiction or other discursive genres, lyric has been the subject of much less critical explication with geocultural positioning in mind. Related interest has certainly grown in the past twenty years, and tracking that concern in the case of Brazil is one of the prime burdens here. Within Luso-Brazilian and inter-American studies at large, poetic discourse remains rather understudied and merits scrutiny from a number of angles. While the approach here cannot pretend to be exhaustive, I have attempted to document and demonstrate extensively.

In bringing this project to fruition, I was fortunate to be able to count on the assistance of numerous people. Personal thanks in a book of this extent could cover pages, and the names of many who helped out appear in the notes and bibliography. In Rio de Janeiro, I was privileged to enjoy the cooperation of poet-professors Adriano Espínola, Paulo Henriques Britto, Antonio Carlos Secchin, and Suzana Vargas, as well as the courtesy of the publisher 7Letras (formerly Sette Letras). In São Paulo, Editora Iluminuras provided me with all pertinent works from its catalogue, and the magnificent arts institution Casa das Rosas, which houses the Espaço Haroldo de Campos de Poesia e Literatura, received me in exceptional fashion. Longtime director Frederico Barbosa and 2008 director Claudio Daniel are paragons of poetic diplomacy. Horácio Costa and Moacir Amâncio have lived and shared transamerican poetics for decades. At the intersection of visual and verbal arts, I recognize the genius and generosity of Arnaldo Antunes and Augusto de Campos. Expressions of gratitude are also due to colleagues in other cities, such as Ricardo Corona (Curitiba), Maria Ester Maciel (Belo Horizonte), and Amador Ribeiro Neto (João Pessoa). In North America, the project was improved by the suggestions of colleagues who read portions of the manuscript, Leopoldo Bernucci and Alicia Genovese, and gracious judges who examined the whole, Severino Albuquerque, Luiza Franco Moreira, and William Calin who contributed beyond the call of duty. Odile Cisneros, Luiz Fernando Valente, and Frederick Williams share interest in the topics treated here, including translation, and they demonstrated solidarity at professional meetings and through correspondence. In addition to material and artistic support from so many, I recognize the intellectual models, professional encouragement, and moral support of, in alphabetical order, Gordon Brotherston, Christopher Dunn, Ana Paula Ferreira, Earl Fitz, David William Foster, Roland Greene, Randal Johnson, and Vicky Unruh. I am grateful for the chance to present parts of the book-in-progress at universities including UC–Berkeley, Stanford, UC–Santa Cruz, UCLA, UC–Irvine, Arizona State, Texas, UMass–Dartmouth, North Carolina, Minnesota, Georgetown, Brown, and Florida, where the very first public revelations were made in the collegial colloquium Entre Nous. At the University of Florida, work on this project was facilitated by awards and assistance from the Department of Romance Languages and Literatures, the Center for Latin American Studies, and the Humanities Research Enhancement Fund of the College of Liberal Arts and Sciences. Thanks go to the University Press of Florida for showing interest in my work across the millennial divide, and to Ann Marlowe for sensitive copyediting. Again, *muito obrigado*, much obliged, to all concerned.

Portions of chapters 1, 2, and 3 appeared in *Luso-Brazilian Review* and *Chásqui: Revista de literatura latinoamericana*. In Portuguese, portions of chapter 3 appeared in *Revista iberoamericana* (Pittsburgh), a section of chapter 4 appeared in *ArtCultura* (Universidade Federal de Minas Gerais Uberaba), and a summary of its conclusions was included in *Via Atlântica* (USP). Chapter 6 is based on an essay that first appeared in Rio de Janeiro and has since appeared in an edited volume in Brazil. A section of chapter 7 appeared in *Graphos* (Universidade Federal da Paraíba, João Pessoa).

For these previously published works, recognition is made of the publishers:

"Resource and Resonance: A Story of Transamerican Poetics and Brazilian Song in Global and Cultural Perspective," *Luso-Brazilian Review* 38, no. 2 (2001): 75–85. Portions used here by permission of the University of Wisconsin Press.

"Insular Outreach Moveable Outlook: Transamerican Currents in Brazilian Lyric," *Chásqui* 33, no. 1 (2004): 66–94. Cooperation of the journal is hereby acknowledged.

"O sopro do *jazz*, o lamento do *blues*, e a eletricidade do *rock* na atual poesia brasileira," *Revista iberoamericana* 173 (2006): 919–32. Copyright by the journal.

"A poética da criação novo-mundista em *Toda a América*," *ArtCultura* 8, no. 12 (2006), 117–29; "Três séculos, três Américas: Irmandades épicas e imperativos hemisféricos," *Revista Via Atlântica* 11 (2008), 153–63; "Do *bebop* e o Kaos ao Chaos e o *triphop*: Dois fios ecumênicos no escopo semimilenar do tropicalismo," *Linha de pesquisa* 1 (2001): 155–70, revised in Nelson Barros da Costa, ed., *O charme dessa nação: Música popular, discurso e sociedade brasileira* (Fortaleza: UFEC-SECULT, 2007), 283–301; "*Harpas farpadas*: Casos singulares de interlocução interamericana," *Graphos* 11, no. 1 (2009).

Repeated good-faith efforts have been made to contact all poets, editors, and heirs in the United States and in Brazil in order to request permission to use lines, stanzas, or whole texts of poems or song lyrics.

Introduction

◇

Interfaces

Insularity, Invention, Brazilian Lyric in/and the Americas

Interfaces may connote any number of aspects of encounter, exchange, communication, and especially technology, all of which are relevant to the international inquiry that I have undertaken here. The word normally signifies a point of contact and conversation for two or more processes, between human or other physical entities. It denotes a shared boundary, a surface connecting two units, subsystems, or devices, often defined by specific attributes, whether functional, material, or related to signs and signals. If a dominant sense of *interface* concerns computation and e-devices, the meanings of the term also relate integrally to the making and dissemination of poetry in Brazil and neighbors in the last decades of the twentieth century and the beginning of the twenty-first. *Interface* is a new word belonging to an old prefixal paradigm that includes such verbs as *interact*, *interview*, *intersperse*, and *interfere*, such nouns as *interlocutor*, *interplay*, *interrogation*, *interpellation*, and such adjectives as *interlocking*, *intersecting*, *intervening*, and just plain *interesting*. More to come as things progress toward the (in-)conclusion of this study.

As for the "in-" terms in the subtitle of this introduction, they too may take multiple turns. The first component, *insularity*, refers to the literal and/or literary state of being an island, real or imaginary, as well as to isolation or separateness of the cultural variety. What I present here is partially hypothesized as a response to such situations in Latin America's largest yet only Portuguese-speaking nation. The notion of insularity encompasses a lot. It relates to medieval and Renaissance imaginaries and histories of expansion, and vestiges thereof. In the Americas, it is especially important in the Caribbean because of its geography. In the case of Brazil, there is an associated folklore, and insularity has entailed to a greater degree separation in terms of culture. Cartographies and chronicles of navigation figure throughout, from start to finish. Today the second element, *invention*, is normally associated with its younger meaning, which is contrivance, the making of something new, in industry or art, as in innovative products or inventive poetry, clearly quite pertinent to Brazilian aesthetics since modernism. Equally important, *invention* has signified coming upon something already there, the act of finding, discovery, as in the years 1492, 1500, and beyond in the New World, the (West) Indies, Brazil, America. *Invention* and *insularity* can claim both deep historical roots and modern currency, as critical metaphors in hemispheric approaches and as tropes in actual poems, which may appear in any of the segments that follow. Various kinds of interfaces are explored in the successive chapters. Still within the subtitle of this introduction, the preposition *in* continues and harmonizes with the "In-" pattern of Invention, Insularity, and Interfaces, while the cofeaturing of the conjunction *and* is meant to suggest the existence of different vantages on Brazil, as a stand-alone entity, side by side with neighbor countries, and within the hemisphere as a whole. The plurality of *Americas* relates to overriding concerns with this nomenclature and interconnectedness between genres, languages, and nations. *Lyric* is intended in the broadest sense of genre and poetic composition, whether conventional strophic or free verse, visual or material poetry, or song.

The guiding word *interfaces* is also a homage to a unique creative writer and prematurely departed cultural agitator, Waly Salomão (1943–2003), who bridged the counterculture of the early 1970s and the artistically polymorphous initial years of the new millennium. In one of the poems of his last (posthumous) book, entitled "Interfaces," he links our classical heritage to the age of hypertext and Web portals, alliteratively designating himself as "o demiurgo / o domador / o designer / o diagramador" (*Pescados vivos*, 27) [the demiurge / tamer-trainer / designer / layout artist]. The concluding three-item flourish of the book in which Salomão's short lyric appears represents the hemispheric spirit underlying the present critical study. On facing pages (74–75) the Brazilian poet reproduces a marked-up paragraph from Ralph Waldo Emerson's essay "The Poet" and the most celebrated universal linguistic truth at the center of that piece: "Language is fossil poetry." The second item is a translation from the Spanish of a celestial-toned text by Chilean avant-garde poet Vicente Huidobro, which ends in "silence." The third item, on the final page (79) of Salomão's last book, is a translation of Walt Whitman's "Once I Passed through a Populous City," which celebrates togetherness, memory, and wordless farewell. Emotion, engagement, and multilingual geography remain as an open message in a lyrical design left by an ecumenical artist who at the time of his death was working for the pop-star minister of culture, Afro-Brazilian singer-songwriter and community activist Gilberto Gil, in the capacity of national secretary of books and reading. Salomão also inspired parts of chapter 2 and its title. Viva.

The organization of content here is thematic, not chronological. The fundamental criteria for selection of writers and primary material are their articulating a bi- or multilateral disposition and/or manifesting hemispheric spirit, which, as seen in the differently motivated chapters, can lead to any number of paths and assume diverse forms. Discussion encompasses heterogeneous corpora of texts from successive generations and contrasting tendencies, only occasionally articulated movements. Some important contemporary poets may not be cited simply because no specific poem of theirs conveniently demonstrates a given point. With a few exceptions, poematic exemplifications are from the late 1980s onward, and most poets cited were born no earlier than the mid-1940s, some as late as 1980. During the current period covered in this study, unlike most of the twentieth century, there are no named movements per se in Brazilian poetry, and examples brought to bear here may come from the work of individuals or coalitions with their own priorities, whether formal experimentalism, subjective expressivity, positionality, or identity.

Chapter 1 sets out general notions to situate lyric phenomena, principally transamerican poetics, as cultural actors in the age of globalization, and it includes a discussion of the operative geographical term *America* plus variants. In addition to the terms of this introduction's title, *deterritorialization* is presented as a flexible concept with continually instigative applications to poetry. "Americanization" is often associated with an insalubrious worldwide spread of fast food, fashion, consumer goods, electronics, and the like, but it may also relate, in a less pernicious manner, to the accelerated circulation of such cultural artifacts as film, song, and literature within regions such as the Americas. Chapter 2 concerns Brazilian engagements with USAmerican English and poetry, analyzing a spectrum of micro- and macro-intertextualities, from early letters (the Emerson above) to contemporary repertories. The appropriations of English inevitably suggest associations with a postcolonial perspective. Chapter 3 examines an

"America-scape" in Brazilian poetry involving expressive media other than literature: comics, film, popular music (including the troubadours of rock), icons of tourism, and USA-born digital worlds. Chapter 4 examines in detail neo-epical works written by Brazilians but envisioning the Americas as a whole; therein one might see celebrations of "American ingenuity" or denunciations of imperialism, pre-Columbian glories or present-day sports. Poets of the Americas may have elected neo-epic as the form best suited to ponder historical residues of the centuries-long conquest and domination of the hemisphere, as well as expansive geography; the very size of North America and the Brazilian territories amplifies further if one considers the entire hemisphere, as the three Brazilian texts examined in this chapter do. Chapter 5, with fewer readings of poems and greater attention to the documentation of activities, is wholly about Brazilian–Hispanic American relations, with a special focus on contemporary lyric and efforts to cultivate commonalities. Chapter 6 applies the modernist notion of *poetry for export* and hemispheric ethics to popular music, from the sixties' Tropicalism to its revival in the USA, and especially the hybrid phenomenon known as *mangue beat*. This segment draws a performative inter-American arc from the late 1950s to the 1990s, focusing on the role of an author never before examined in criticism published in English. Chapter 7, as its title conveys, is a conclusion in the sense that it is the last segment and considers terrain traversed, but the subject matter is contemporary, current, still unfolding, and active; thus it remains open to greater appreciation and further thought or rethinking.

Throughout the largely repertory-driven chapters, there is an orienting concern with New World consciousness, linguistic craft, and humanistic understanding which writers in Brazil may share at any given turn with peers in North America, Spanish America, or the Caribbean. Poets in any land can present, given historical realities, critiques of overbearing or less-than-democratic conduct on the part of the United States, usually by barons of industry or ambitious politicians. In the case of contemporary lyric from Brazil, there has developed a noteworthy tension between cultural fraternity and situationally justified discontent vis-à-vis the USA—a tension seen, in one way or another, throughout. Textually and socially rich considerations of ever-evolving affinities and relations with Spanish America also appear in each chapter. What will prove to matter most, it is hoped, are constant factors of inducement and surprise.

1

◇

Insular Outreach, Moveable Outlook

Transamerican Currents in Brazilian Lyric

Can one be at once more oneself and more a national being through poetic appeals to the selves and signs of potent Others and their locations in the same hemisphere? Do poets feel that they expand the reach of their craft by using nonprint vehicles, by composing in different languages, or by redefining spaces in relation to alternate territories? Is the substantiation of mass media and electronic technology as cornerstones of contemporary existence worldwide antithetical to lyric or a source of revitalization? Can poems open fresh perspectives on the experience of cybernetic environments? Is the perception of place, with the changes it undergoes, a topic for all genres of present-day literature? Such are some of the questions that motivate the present study of threads of poetry in Brazil in the context of the Americas, that is, in relation to the United States, Spanish America, and the hemisphere as a whole. Both historical and ongoing connections in lyric between Brazil and the USA, two countries of continental proportions, enfold not only national languages and letters per se but tourism, film, music, and other aspects of popular culture as well. Latin American matters in song and verse involve shared mythologies and histories, contrasting and converging styles, and present-day activism. This nuanced nexus—of Brazilian resources, recourses, and discourses in the Americas in the circumscribed domain of contemporary poetry—forms its own part of the encompassing array of processes and situations that comprise globalization.

If an overriding concern of intellectual inquiry and critique in the 1980s was to assess the nature and limits of epochal phenomena subsumed under the rubric of postmodernism, from the 1990s into the early twenty-first century the imperatives of analysis of human endeavor, and the priorities that continue to drive critical agendas, have been shaped by the subjects of globalization, understood in the most basic sense to mean widespread transnationalization and intensification of the integration of different parts of the planet. When this topic came to the fore of public discussion, the predominant perspectives were those of economics and geopolitics. Considerable attention has now been paid as well to institutional implications and the ramifications for communities. Cultural dimensions of globalization have been the focus of incisive integral studies in social anthropology and of collections of essays by humanists and theoreticians of discourse. *Culture* in such approaches most commonly operates according to a "conventional social scientific sense" summarized as "the beliefs, values, and lifestyles of ordinary people in their everyday existence" (Berger, 2). Given the central role of mass media in the planetary spread of ideas and products, investigations of expressive culture most often refer to electronic means of communication and the impacts of technology, from film, radio, and television to the ever-expanding Internet. The late 1990s are generally considered to be the years when the Internet truly took hold not only in North America but in such nations as Brazil as well. Even before the definitive assertion of the World Wide Web, Arjun Appadurai distinguished himself both for having shifted emphasis from the accustomed configuration of culture in nation-states to a series of dimensions of cultural flows termed "-scapes" (ethno-, media-, techno-, finance-, and ideo-) and for having relativized fears of rampant Westernization and cultural homogenization. In the account of Fredric Jameson, globalization presupposes essentially a confluence of economic and cultural factors in a "communicational concept" (55) based on technologies and their implantations. Interrelations of local and globalized behaviors also concern analysts of cultural globalization in a fundamental way, especially with respect to counterpractices (protest, resistant discourse, alternative modes of expression) and issues of identity.

There is limited published research directly related to globalization that ponders *culture* understood conventionally as (elite) aesthetic production ("high culture," if you will), including painting, sculpture, concert music, drama, fiction, and, of course, poetry. While on an understandably lesser scale compared to varied social-science domains, turn-of-the-millennium literary scholarship indeed began to consider imaginative writing under transnational rubrics, to seek means by which a discipline attuned above all to national formations could respond to the challenges of the age of globalization.[1] To make a transition from a worldwide focus to area studies, there is a useful allied theory of regional, continental, or hemispheric *subglobalization* (Berger, 14–15). In this approach, focus can be directed to areas of the world as opposed to the globe as a whole. Like Persian Iran in the Arab-dominant Middle East, Portuguese-speaking Brazil in Latin America is an interesting case of a nation that is the largest and most economically influential in the region but not central in cultural terms because of linguistic singularity.

With respect to polynational study of literatures of the Americas, colleagues in the relatively recent (sub)discipline of American studies have made eloquent appeals for the expansion of outlooks, some limited to immediate neighbors of the United States, others imagining America, as the Mexican muralist Diego Rivera did, as "the territory stretching between the ice-caps of the two poles."[2] With purposeful inclusion of writing in Portuguese and French, comparative scholars in North America have posited such fruitful critical positions as inter-American literature, New World studies, and transamerican poetics. The first, posited on the integration of "different languages, cultures, and historical experiences" and recognition of "very real differences between the American states," explores commonalities and similarities in Pan-American literatures.[3] As developed by Earl Fitz, this method can encompass topics as diverse as New World identity in the novel, appreciation of indigenous heritage, the widespread influence of Walt Whitman, and, as seen in chapter 4 here, neo-epic poetry. Roland Greene explains that New World Studies "takes for its object the making of American cultures and of a transamerican culture from an interdisciplinary perspective" and "can be understood as a set of practices that investigate the givenness of local, national, and transamerican worldviews through the collation of literary representation and social fact."[4] Whether brought to bear to relate early-modern writing in the Americas to metropolitan letters or to illuminate varieties of modernism on this side of the Atlantic, this kind of study wholly enriches appreciation in different contexts.

Transamerican poetics is more specifically related to the genre of lyric. Not a platform per se, but the combined views of various scholars, working for the most part in North America, the transamerican way eschews a planetary point of view and posits a hemispheric approach, one that pursues praxis and attitudes that cross national boundaries from Canada to Tierra del Fuego. Interest lies in efforts to surpass ingrained geolinguistic limits on the assertion of local/regional outlooks when making and disseminating poetry in the final decades of the twentieth century and beyond. A point of departure was established by Charles Bernstein, who wrote that the cultural space of an "impossible America is transected by innumerable overlaying, contradictory or polydictory, traditions and proclivities and histories and regions and peoples and circumstances and identities and families and collectivities and dissolutions—dialects and ideolects, not National Tongues; localities and habitations, not States." He complexifies this configuration with a reminder that "everywhere the local is under fire from the imposed standard of a transnational consumer culture and undermined by the imperative to extract it and export it as product."[5] A problem with the initial application of this stirring proposal was that it was not wholly transamerican, as it really examined only varieties of English, leaving French, Spanish, and Portuguese aside. Bernstein's special issue of *Boundary 2* was worldwide in scope, including two Brazilian contributions. In the new millennium, in a São Paulo venue, the critic set forth a broader New World vision:

> A poetics of the Americas would be less concerned with analyzing the themes and cultural narratives produced in Spanish and English fiction than in listening for—and composing—a collage of distinct language practices across the Americas. . . . I am suggesting that we conceptualize our Americas as a hypertextual or syncretic constellation, with alphabetic, glyphic, and a/oral layers. A constellation is an alternative model for understanding what is often characterized as fragmentation, parataxis, isolation, insularity, atomization, and separate development. Hypertextuality maps a syncretic space that articulates points of contact and that potentiates both spatial connections among discrepant parts and temporal overlays that merge or melt into one another. ("Our Americas," 87)

Where directions of cultural flows are concerned, the modifier *transamerican* means within Latin America as well as from North to South America and from South to North, including Central America and the Caribbean. One of the assumptions is that overall globalization and specific regional plans, such as NAFTA, Mercosul (see the final part of chapter 5), or the proposed "free-trade zone" of the Americas, affect changing circumstances in aesthetic production too. Greene ("Transamerican") specifically hypothesizes that lyrical identities and poetries of countries "are being refashioned under the external pressures of hemispheric transnationalism and the intrinsic logic of a turn-of-the-new-century cultural interdependence."

Given relative translatability and the spatiotemporal expansiveness of narrative, prose fiction seems to be the literary genre best suited to study in terms of globalization. Lyric is naturally problematic here since it is the most idiosyncratic of aspects in a national, regional, or linguistically-defined transcontinental culture (one example being Portuguese-speaking or Lusophone).[6] Some scholars have suggested that "world" writers actually compose and modify their words with an eye to translatability and English-language markets, especially the USA.[7] Respondents often note that considerations of market are much less relevant in the art of poetry. Issues of globalization and poetry are further complicated if one factors in peripheral status or isolation that may motivate new stylizations, vehicles, and content. If it is somewhat trickier to update assessments of interrelations of poetries and of planetary or subglobal linkages, there are profitable modes to imagine transnational aspects of lyric of a nation or region which get beyond the received wisdom of comparative literature and/or such conventional analytical devices as "influence," though these certainly cannot simply be set aside. As this book sets out to explore, present-day poets in nations such as Brazil carry on textual, practical, and diplomatic conversations with foreign interlocutors as never before, most notably within the hemisphere. Moreover, efforts to overcome lyric's constitutional or generic interferences with expanded communications have resulted in manifestations that merit scrutiny from national and extranational standpoints. Most significant in the late-twentieth-century phase of global expansions, elements of varied provenance league Brazil, neighbor nations, and the United States in the domain of lyric, as suggested in the very prospect of transamerican poetics, with its interrogations of perimeters, provinces, and mutations in space. A spatial or territorial paradigm runs through the present deliberations via the concepts of deterritorialization and insularity.

Deterritorialization has been applied variously in studies of culture and globalization. The idea originates in the collaborations of philosopher Gilles Deleuze and psychiatrist Felix Guattari, who used it in a geopsychological sense of transference with reference to processes involving movement away from structures in the mind or society that control or coerce. The complementary term *reterritorialization* involves movement toward another destination or location. In social-scientific applications, deterritorialization comes to mean detachment, dislodging or disassociation of behaviors from specific places, especially nation-states and their "typical" cultures. As a basis for cultural reproduction, Appadurai treats deterritorialization as transformations from established places (with physical borders) to spaces (dispersed and not concentrated). Néstor García Canclini defined deterritorialization simply as "the loss of the 'natural' relation of culture to geographical and social territories" (239). Tomlinson seeks to unite social theory and a cultural-studies approach to grasp globalization as an empirical condition of the modern world characterized by "complex connectivity," an "ever-densening network of interconnections and interdependences," and a widespread dissolution of links between "lived experience" and territorial location (2). In this final aspect he adopts García Canclini's basic explanation, which was tied to the concept of hybridity, focus of much subsequent debate.

Migration and other kinds of transit of people and things generate hybrid artifacts of expression. Pnina Werbner affirms the related critical value of applying a Bakhtinian idea of "intentional hybridity," a conscious deployment in linguistic and other cultural forms of a mixing intended to "shock, change, challenge, revitalize or disrupt through deliberate intended fusions of unlike social languages and images."[8] This angle makes increasing sense in the age of globalization as flows of people, languages, and goods, symbolic and material alike, increase exponentially. Deterritorialization, in sum, is a flexible instrument. Jean Franco has noted the appeal of Deleuze and Guattari in Latin American cultural critique, recognizing fruitful applications by the Chilean essayist Nelly Richard—"deterritorialization" not as "negative separation from roots and authenticity, but rather a release of energies that would otherwise be bound to institutions such as the patriarchal family, the nation, and the work ethic"—and the interest of Néstor Perlongher, the Argentine poet relocated in Brazil, a personality who will appear in chapter 5.[9]

Throughout the present pages, there will be numerous and diverse instances of creative and critical manipulation of such (de-)(re-)territorialized concepts. Indeed, this cluster can be (re)deployed to uncover aesthetic lines on the face of globalization and to tease out meanings for poems that reflect or implement, sometimes quite explicitly, interconnectivity or changing perceptions of place. There are myriad ways in which turn-of-the millennium lyrical repertoires transcend boundaries and overcome old prejudices, incorporating different sorts of neighborly wisdom but also eyeing and commenting on, without stricture, the present and new realities in play. Poets can witness surface thematic paradigms of globalization, subglobalization, hemispheric sway, and bi- or multilateral relations, incorporating their signs, altering matrices, and adjusting horizons of expectation. Witness the brief lyric "Cacofonia social" (Social cacophony): "Com a globalização / dá-se dos pobres / a exclusão / acima dos médios / a inclusão / e destes—se ricos— / a reclusão" [With globalization / what occurs for the poor is / exclusion / for the above average / inclusion / and for these— if rich— / seclusion].[10] Seven facilely rhymed lines and an unbecoming bunch of nouns are enunciated to broach socioeconomic stratification and segmentation (even gated communities) exacerbated by new economics, with sly irony.

Analysts and observers in Brazil have portrayed states of affairs in ways that support multidisciplinary and multinational interpretations of lyric output. For Heloísa Buarque de Hollanda, Brazilian poetry of the 1990s was being "produced under the most recent form of dictatorship imposed by the logic of consumption and the processes of globalization" and within "a situation dominated by the logic of an extremely competitive cultural market guided by an accelerated process of massification, transnationalization, and specialization in the production and commercialization of products." Poets are "more invested in the search for strategies to enable critical and innovative positions in the face of the challenges of the new Zeitgeist."[11] For their part, the informed editors of a lyricocentric arts review in Brazil specifically note that globalization, consumer culture, and other mass-mediated aspects of today's world inexorably affect artistic contexts, the language of poetry, and aesthetic desire: "there arise poets interested in exploring the power that poetry, as a form of visionary knowledge, still has to affect the exterior world, instead of being merely affected by it."[12] In this declaration, *exterior* denotes external in a general way but also connotes *abroad* in a geocultural take. As we shall show, such positioning often moves into a transamerican circle. After citing "elective affinities" with North American dictions, an exuberant anthologist of turn-of-the-century lyric comments upon the "open and critical dialogue with other cultures and the transformed (miscegenated) appropriation of forms" and upon moves to "share (or exchange) visions, life modes, colors and sounds of other geographical or temporal latitudes, in an era where there are no more frontiers."[13] Elsewhere, a poet-professor and guest editor expresses his belief that "the force of the poetic—dismantling frontier garrisons and dislocating axes held to be fixed—is to be found in an opening up to the other, to the outside, that insist on, in a healthy and intense fashion, intervening."[14] For his part, situating the 1990s generation in Brazil, and alluding to practices common in the 1960s and 1970s (and somewhat beyond), a widely recognized young poet stresses New World links:

> It's a generation, or at least a group within a generation, that, more than responding to the proposals and issues of previous generations, evolved out of the turbulence caused by contact with foreign poetries. The new North American poetry of Creeley, Frank O'Hara, of the languages poets and, for those somewhat younger, the Latin American neobaroque . . . the newest poetry of Argentina surely has more impact on this generation than fundamental issues of earlier generations, such as nationalism, utopian humanism, experiments with visual aspects of words or the belief in spontaneity.[15]

In wider temporal perspective, similar vantages and operations in lyric of the Americas must indeed include not only what is current but also essential legacies, such as colonial writing, romantic impulses, nation-building ethics, this-side-of-the-pond perspectives on linguistic revitalization, and New World modernist finds and rediscoveries, including local applications of avant-garde aesthetics. With reference to postconquest and expansion periods, Gunn asserts boldly that "the basis of virtually all of the imaginative, and many of the discursive, arts in all of the countries of the Americas would subsequently be furnished by the way these hybrid American societies would eventually undergo a revolutionary break with the colonizing power and then reconstitute themselves as something self-consciously different from European parents" (*Beyond Solidarity*, 3). Stressing genre per se, Greene underscores that lyric, as opposed to epic, "is a widely adaptable literary technology in the early modern period, offering an outlet to any number of formed views and inchoate reactions" and argues for the "extraordinary vitality of lyric as the carrier of social and political reflections."[16] He brings his arguments forward to examples of *modernismo*, concrete poetry, and innovative Brazilian popular music, three phenomena essential to the Brazilian arts and transamerican poetics.[17] What Greene claims for early modern lyric should, for different reasons, be taken into account in approaches to late modern or globalized postmodern lyric. Configurations modified and contested by more than one team are of more immediate interest in Pan-American contexts. One basic way of "rethinking a poetics of the Americas would be, then, in the intersection of common issues and different languages. Instances in which some concerns, not their outcome or resolution, could be recognized as a shared moment."[18] Here stand out the multinational endeavors of Brazilian concretism in the 1950s and beyond, as well as subsequent North/South American vanguard differentiations from Europe in the 1970s.

In the case of Brazil, a point of departure for a transamerican focus is the existence over time of a certain insularity, both real and metaphorical. Efforts at energizing articulations within the hemisphere come against a historical backdrop of isolation or separateness that is configured geographically, culturally, and linguistically. Brazil's internationally acclaimed singer-songwriter Caetano Veloso, recognized at home as one of his generation's leading poets, wrote with respect to the European discovery of the New World, Brazil among the nations of the Americas, and otherness:

> As children we learned that Brazil was discovered by the Portuguese navigator Pedro Álvares Cabral on April 22, 1500. All other American nations consider it enough to have been discovered by Christopher Columbus in 1492. It was only Brazil that had to be discovered later, separately. . . . they say Brazil appeared as an independent continent, a huge island in the middle of the South Atlantic, a surprise for those Lusitanian sailors who, aiming to follow the coast of Africa to reach the Indies, sailed too far west. That such a vaguely defined event should be situated so precisely in the middle of the second millennium serves to force upon Brazilians a sense of themselves as a nation both unsubstantiated and exaggerated. The United States is a country without a name: America is the name of the continent where, among others, the states that were once English colonies united. Brazil is a name without a country. The English seem to have stolen the name of the continent and given it to the country they founded. The Portuguese seem not to have founded a country, but managed to suggest that they landed in a part of America that was absolutely Other, and they called it Brazil.[19]

One of the aims of Tropicália, or *tropicalismo*—the 1960s musico-poetic movement led by Veloso and the point of departure for chapter 6—was "an unveiling of the mystery of the island of Brazil." Among the many other expressions of intertwined conceptions of problematic place, language, and new art, an active poet-diplomat, tying together several contingencies, states clearly: "The Portuguese language needs to expand much more, and I don't doubt that a good part of that expansion will be by way of experimentalism. Portuguese is isolated in its continent."[20] In the same vein of insularity qua isolation, a proverbial image is imagined in a title by a cosmopolitan poet-critic: "Brasil: entre la espada atlántica y la pared andina" [Brazil: between the Atlantic sword (rock) and the Andean wall (hard place)].[21] The reference to the Atlantic brings up a deep history in Western civilization that, as we shall see, may vibrate even in turn-of-the-millennium lyric. The association of insularity with Brazil stretches back many centuries into myth, legend, and primitive cartography in Europe, preceding the age of maritime discoveries.

For the words *island* and *mystery* to be wed in Veloso's above-cited metaphor of archival discovery or writerly uncovering almost at the turn of the twenty-first century means that they are potent figures with remarkable staying power. The meanings of the pair of terms relate to a wondrous place called Brazil, or something similar, harking as far back as medieval times. European consciousness fancied a marvelous isle called Brazil more than half a millennium before the Portuguese fleet of Cabral landed at a spot now called Porto Seguro. The notion of an elusive, yet-to-be-discovered, and specially endowed or blessed place had multiple manifestations in the late Middle Ages and Renaissance. Maps as early as the ninth century have an island of Saint Brendan or Brazil of Saint Brendan, for the canonized Irish monk who claimed to have visited a land called Hy Bre-sail, meaning Fortunate Isle, where, to quote a transcript of legend, "bells tolled over the old sea and the island seemed to vanish in the horizon every time the sailors tried to reach it."[22] Another curiosity is that the saint claimed that this Garden of Delights was full of parrots, an element reflected on several maps many years later and certainly relevant to any exotic Brazil-scape since. Other ancient Irish tales spoke of a phantom island of Brey-zil believed to lie off the south-west coast of Ireland. The place was named after Bres, son of a Fomorian sea god, Elatha, and of Ériu of the Tuatha Dé Danann. This fantastic location Bresil was a magical realm—neither sea nor land, yet both—known as the Isle of the Living, the Isle of Truth, of Joy, of Fair Women, and of Apples. Related early Celtic lore also says that the island appeared only at sunset in the mists of the Atlantic, and they called it, according to one source, "the blessed stormless isle, where all men are good and all women pure and where God retreats for a recreation from the rest of us." This legend also entered the Anglo-Norman realm.[23]

Scholars of mapmaking record abundant assertions of the toponym *Brazil* starting in the fourteenth century. The mythical island of Hy-Brazil appeared on charts as early as 1325, and on numerous maps for the next two hundred years, or more than five hundred if we count locational shifts and reconceptualizations. From 1351 up to about 1730, the specific name Hy-Brazil could be found on most European sea maps, showing it as an island in the Atlantic Ocean. Insula Sancti Brandani "migrated" from north of Europe to the west. Insula de Brazi shows on the Venetian Biano map of 1436 as one of the Azores, which established a Portuguese connection. Both name and island moved westward, eventually being transformed into a landmass and recognized as such by Duarte Pacheco Pereira in his *Esmeraldo de situ orbis*, circa 1505, after the historic voyages of Columbus and Cabral.[24]

As for North American links, well before 1494 fishing ships from Bristol went out "in search of a mysterious island called Brazil," assumed to exist somewhere west of Ireland. In 1494 "John the Venetian, Sebastian Cabot the native of Bristol, and other Bristol mariners saw the coastline" of North America but did not make a chart anywhere near accurate, since they remained too distant. "Bristol seamen called it Brazil for the mythical island they thought it was" (Kelsy, 250–51). This is a little-known cartographic curiosity but potentially a fruitful symbolic tie between South and North America. The first mapmaker to use the term *America*, in 1507, placed it in the tract of land that would become Brazil, which name was assigned on that map to a river. A rich interpretation of the emergence of the designation of the future country in relation to insularity correlates very profitably with a superb treatment of nominalization of the land and cartographic representations of Brazil.[25] Historical curiosities and exegeses can be brought to bear in the imagining of US-Brazilian relations in literature in the present age.

The idea of this grand New World location as a specially endowed island persisted and still contributes to the international imaginary. In 1998 Rio de Janeiro hosted a multinational summit. Brazilian president Fernando Henrique Cardoso, former professor of sociology and prolific author, opened his address to world leaders with reminders about the history of colonization and, with their scriptural and cartographic predecessors, about common representations of his nation abroad, especially in the so-called First World. In Portuguese, such associations are reflected in the rhyme of *ilha* (island) and *maravilha* (marvel). Clichés of Brazil as lush, sensuous, privileged, unique, and mysterious are today maintained by touristic image peddling and die-hard stereotypes. Vestiges of this whole element exist even in the erudite domain of poetry. Following a 1996 visit to cosmopolitan São

Paulo, the prominent USAmerican poet Robert Creeley wrote to his hosts: "I am sure that there is much the same sense there, often, of that other part of one's world which stays as its decisive complement and yet still seems shadowy and undiscovered. So it had been for me, that this huge and historic parallel to my own 'New World' stayed all too unreal, at most a transforming if inchoate river of vast proportion and an ancient yet vulnerable forest of primal order."[26]

Brazil, and especially Brazilian writers, have constantly had to deal with issues of place, register, and participation in hemispheric cultural affairs in ways distinct from those of the hegemonic cultural behaviors of North America and the linguistically unified spheres of Spanish America. Insularity remains an issue, and its status is double edged. On one hand, there are the flattering connotations and implications of blessedness, uniqueness, self-sufficiency; on the other, those of deprivation, lack of recognition, misunderstanding. Toumson (47–48, 125) explains how the isle was a geo-oneiric representation, a dream of restarting the world; insularity, being cut off from bad outside influences, was one of the functions of utopian discourse. The isle became ambiguous, however, "a place of oscillation and indecision where are conjugated salvation and perdition." In the realm of lyric in the late twentieth century, a transamerican outlook can be seen as a way to counteract or overcome insularity, as a method, spoken or unspoken, of integration. In wide historical perspective, a key vocabular interrelation is indeed with utopia: "holding these elements together in an early modern ideologeme, Brazil is long imagined to be an island—which is to acknowledge, however implicitly, the fictionality of the entire construction around the name. Within the first years of Brazil's establishment, Thomas More was to argue implicitly in his *Utopia* for the congruence of the epistemological category of fiction with the conceit of island."[27] The etymology of the contrived name—from Greek *eutopia*, good place, and *outopia*, no place (Levitas, 2–3)—clearly relates to the mythology of Brazil over the centuries. *Utopia* (1516), one of the most influential books in the Western tradition, posited an ideal good place, a nonplace or nowhere; these senses will emerge in select creative moments later in our explorations.

Insular motifs manifest variously in lyric throughout the late twentieth and early twenty-first centuries, especially since the panoply of activity surrounding observations of the five hundred years of Brazil. Vogt's title piece "Ilha Brasil" (65) is pregnant with presentified history:

Quando descoberto
no atacado,
o Brasil avulso
já estava nu
com diversidade.
Vestidos pelo descobrimento,
seus habitantes
que por aqui viviam,
os que antes vieram,
durante, depois e já
mais
os que nasceram desse intercurso
rasgaram na avenida
a fantasia
da igualdade.

[When discovered / in wholesale, / Brazil set loose / was already nude / with diversity. / Vested by the discovery, / her inhabitants / who lived around here, / those who came before, / during, after, and now / plus / those who were born of that intercourse / tore up on the avenue / the fantasy-costume of equality.]

In a comparative situation, the poem pits multiethnic and mixed populations—very much the focus of so much current discussion worldwide—against the tired stereotype of Brazil as the quintessentially carnivalesque location. The popular classes who have made fame with their Carnival have been used and abused by profiteering since time immemorial. This poet's language has been heard as an instrument of uncovering and revisualizing in a complicated present of geopositioning: "It is in the intrigue of this language of today, interwoven with those inherited from poets of other times and other latitudes, that the poems of *Ilhas Brasil* become an archipelago."[28] This particular poem also proves to serve as an updated illustration of the thesis elaborated by Greene under the title "For Love of Pau-Brasil: Objectification in Colonial Brazil" (chapter 2 of *Unrequited Conquests*) by which commodification and commercial (more than cultural or religious) interest mark Portuguese imperialism in the New World as compared to that of the Spanish. Even in the *modernismo* of the 1920s, for some artists "the problem of objectification—a founding article of Brazilian society that had never disappeared—was especially urgent" (131). And that feeling may have filtered its way to the beginning of the next millennium, when love and lyric have suffered so many unforetold impacts.

Further to the conceit of isle and its linkage with on-the-ground experience, bodily reality, a visual poem by multimedia artist Arnaldo Antunes is wholly congruous. "Ilha" (figure 1) consists of the superimposition of a map fragment, depicting a large island (*ilha*) and surrounding accidents, on an anatomical drawing of a human side, or flank (*ilharga*). The leglike cartographical slice is of the grand isle of Marajó at the mouth of the Amazon River, encompassing such contiguous islands as the suggestively baptized Ilha dos Macacos, or Isle of Monkeys. There is some basic wordplay—the unprinted but absolutely present word *ilharga* sounds similar to *ilha larga*, wide island—but more compelling is all the implied interrelation of tropical geography and human form, the engagement (interface) of science and nature, an embodiment of insular being and thought. The territorial paradigm invoked, with its instinctive ties to the continuity of the utopian idea, will be seen to recur and vary in scope.

In a more general way, aesthetic acts with the potential to comprise a counterpoint to notions of mystery, isolation, or problematic difference may take several paths or change tack. Lyric in Brazil has developed characteristic dialects as well as dialectics of self-affirmation and outreach, a search that moves from the individual and the local to combined sensibilities, common ground, contact, and exchange with/within the Americas. There are a series of activities and textual outputs that are relevant to the affirmation of a contemporary stance that could be called "transamerican," which are symptomatic of the urge to accept variance and to attempt forms of extension of the university of lyric, as it were. As elsewhere in the Americas, present-day Brazilian poets are preoccupied with national and purely literary heritages, but currents that target convention and flow beyond frontiers constitute their own significant aspect of contemporary poetics, in and of themselves and as responses to insularity.[29] Peculiar attitudes of ecumenical tenor became more evident in the final decades of the twentieth century. Brazilian poets published in Spanish or English, at times making border dialects, Anglophone leverage, or linguistic Luso-distinctiveness themes unto themselves. Active writers also promoted bilingual binational anthologies, procured articulations with USAmerican circles, appealed to visual and/or electronic means, sought inter-American dialogue, and marked a "share-aware" presence. Several Brazilians have published directly in Spanish, in

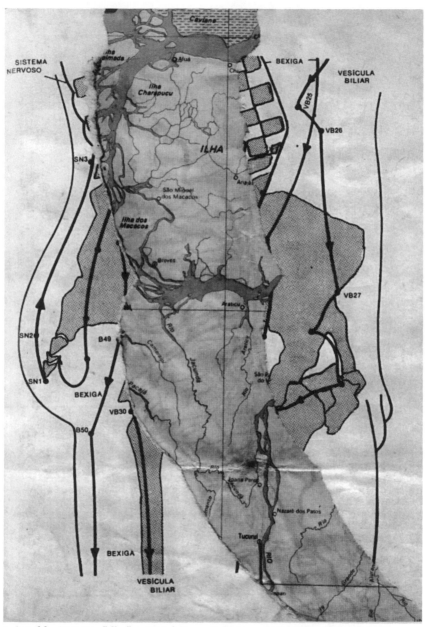

1. Arnaldo Antunes, "Ilha," material poem in *Dois ou mais corpos no mesmo espaço*, 1997. Courtesy of the artist.

print and on the Internet. Efforts to join with Spanish American colleagues multiply, through sponsorships, events, reviews, anthologies, studies, bilingual Internet journals, and travel. Such relations are examined at length in chapter 5.

Creating versions of works of imaginative literature by one's neighbors may well have diplomatic implications too. As a scholar of cross-border culture observes, "when they venture into transamerican thinking by travelling or translating other American poems, writers perform an act of cultural ambassadorship."[30] The reference here is to pathbreaking nineteenth-century instances of US-Hispanic interchange, but a similar spirit also orients more contemporary activity. In the case of Brazil, there are important antecedents in the stay of sui generis late Romantic poet Sousândrade in New York and his unique epic of a South-to-North-American periplus (1876), as well as in Ronald de Carvalho's *Toda a América* (1926), as detailed in chapter 4. A well-known case in the mid-twentieth century was the long-term residence of Elizabeth Bishop in Brazil, her related poems, and her influential anthology of Brazilian poetry.[31] The second volume of that project featured the theorists and makers of concrete poetry in São Paulo.[32] They did much in the 1950s and 1960s to expand creative and critical horizons in Brazil with the introduction, promotion, and/or explication of a select group of authors "of invention" including such North American figures as Ezra Pound and E. E. Cummings. Both Haroldo and Augusto de Campos traveled to the United States and made indispensable contributions to the fundamental publications of concrete poetry in the Anglophone sphere (Solt; E. Williams). In the 1970s, continuations of such efforts took in numerous others, including Emily Dickinson, semiotician Charles Sanders Peirce, and a special guest who performed in Brazil and inspired a placard by Augusto de Campos.[33] This visual poem (figure 2) is a homage to a sui generis artist of invention and a vehicle of interface, between complementary media—music (sound/notation) and the devices of the I Ching—and between Brazil and the United States. The intrahemispheric journey, in short, appertains physically and figuratively to a poetics of making and interpretation.

At the turn of the new millennium Ernesto Livón-Grosman, an active proponent of vanguard poetics, also believes that "traveling and translation are instrumental for the dialogue that ultimately constitutes key strategies in the ongoing effort to create a different kind of exchange within globalization, one that could subvert the hierarchical relation between North and

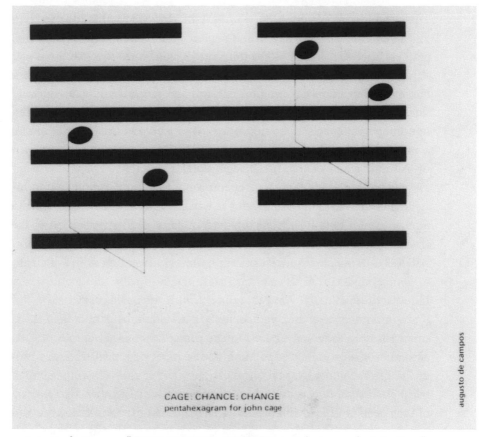

CAGE: CHANCE: CHANGE
pentahexagram for john cage

augusto de campos

2. Augusto de Campos, "CAGE: CHANCE: CHANGE, pentahexagram for John Cage," visual poem placard, 1977. Photograph courtesy of the artist.

South, as we know it."[34] Empirically, activity picks up considerably on the Brazilian front in the 1990s. Pursuit of inter-American communication and articulations with USAmerican circles has been evident in invitations, events, publications, and subtending attitudes, as seen in further detail in the next two chapters. In experimental graphics and later cyberspace, appeals to optical and electronic means are eminently transamerican, and Brazil is truly prominent in Internet posting, Web design, and digital-art congresses. As for publication, in the postdictatorial New Republic of Brazil, several important new translations of leading USAmerican poets have appeared. In the 1990s, poet-translators such as Régis Bonvicino and Rodrigo Garcia Lopes actively sought links with key North American figures. The former hosted and translated Robert Creeley and Michael Palmer, also enlisting Charles Bernstein and two dozen others to write a trilingual renga tellingly dubbed *Together*.[35] The journal *Sibila: Revista de poesia e cultura*, edited by Bonvicino and others since 2000, has decidedly transamerican content linking Canada, the USA, Brazil, and the rest of Latin America. For his part, Lopes resided on three occasions in the United States, studying Jerome Rothenberg's ethnopoetics and Laura Riding. He published a series of (translated) interviews with US art-world luminaries and a volume of Whitman's *Leaves of Grass*; he also coedits an innovative new-century arts journal with an Americanist inspiration, *Coyote*.[36] Transamerican intentions were overt and purposeful in events organized by Horácio Costa in São Paulo. A view he has expressed of *comparativismo* embodies the transamerican wholly; what matters is to discern "translinguistic and transnational movements that unify a current of works and authors . . . synchronically in many Latin American countries, Brazil—also in the United States, Canada, the Caribbean—and that cover a wide temporal spectrum."[37]

The twentieth-century Brazilian author who has most attracted the kind of comparatist attention desired in the foregoing is assuredly Oswald de Andrade (1890–1954), playboy and poet-provocateur of Brazilian modernism, prose fictionist, polemical essayist, and author of two celebrated manifestos that have, during the rise of postcolonial studies, been joined to the international roll of propitious aesthetic statements. Oswald has had a wide influence on different classes of antinormative Brazilian poetry after *modernismo*, from the theoretical refinements of concrete poetry and the justifications of *tropicalismo* to informal youth verse of the 1970s and constructivist verse of the late twentieth century.[38] Some of the ideas of his two landmark declarations can be related to transamerican poetics and the economy of lyric around the turn of the millennium. An axiomatic position in the primitivist "Manifesto of Pau-Brasil Poetry" (1924) is the reversal of cultural flow from the metropolis to the (former) colony in the making of "poetry . . . for exportation" (185). Seven main factors are advanced for the nationalistically aware and technically avid program: "Synthesis / Equilibrium / Automotive finish / Invention / Surprise / A new perspective / A new scale" (186). The first and second items involve integrated use and balancing of folk and scientific matter, while the fifth is wholly reminiscent of shock-hungry shouts of the European avant-garde. The most important term, in broad historical perspective, is the fourth.

In modern times, *invention* connotes contrivance, original fabrication, making something new, thus its logical application to change in the arts and watershed creative writing. In article nine of the Brazilwood Manifesto, Oswald puts forth "Agile novel, born of invention. Agile poetry" (184). He imagines agility akin to a candid child, which may imply the fresh world-view possible in the Americas, born of romantic desire in the early years of independent American states but reconsidered with modernist eyes. Oswald's is an antinaturalist attitude and practice "against copy, through *invention* and *surprise*" (186). The former keyword, further back in history, meant discovery or finding; it takes one back to the age of maritime exploration, the first encounter of Iberian navigators with the lands and peoples of the New World. The initial article of the manifesto casts "cabralin blue" (184), a particularly Lusitanian chromatic apperception of the sea, where Portuguese explorers such as Cabral earned such fame. The third asserts outright "All the pioneering and commercial history of Brazil" (184). The descriptor in the title of the manifesto, and of the book of poetry soon to follow, is in fact taken from the product of native extraction that would so heavily influence the naming of the colony and that, gathered to send back to Europe, would first signify export. Interrelations of essential terms in these textualizations of Oswald demand close attention, as the conceits of the manifesto "directly engage with the legacy of objectification," in Greene's apt words.[39] Invention, linked to discovery and all that ensued during colonization, inexorably carries tremendous loads of baggage, and disengaging from cultural imperialism via artistic inventiveness proves to be quite the challenging task. Madureira (28) corroborates: "Oswald would later call this ostensibly 'natural' label (brazilwood) 'a factory brand' . . . 'a patent of invention' . . . perhaps suggesting that in its very desire 'to write the world anew,' the collection inevitably reiterates not only the very fifteenth- and sixteenth-century 'discovery' claims whose historical primacy it seeks to displace, but colonial extraction itself." If the meaning of invention as creativity is, for both Oswald and those whom he influences, the preferred emphasis, discovery, extrapolated onto experience in general, can also be related to lyric: "Poetry for poets. The happiness of those who don't know and discover" (184, article eight).

Cultural semantics surrounding *invention* (*invenção* < Latin *inventio*, the act of coming into or upon) reach back even further, to classical antiquity. In the 1920s and the contemporary period, the term reverberates with multinationalism and centuries of specialized uses of language. For Cicero, in the first century BC, *inventio* was one of the five fundaments of rhetoric, involving the pursuit and finding of the right mental path or material sources, and, in oratory, arguments toward persuasion. In late medieval and Renaissance poetics, invention may comprise finding or making poetic content, thus implying independent original production. Some Romantics would conceive of invention as a superior capacity of endowed creative beings. As early as the mid-sixteenth century, there had been utilizations of the word to mean pioneer contrivance, mechanical or artistic.[40] In modern times, the ability to fabricate new structures or forms is what characterizes invention, whether in studies of antiquity or of the present. In his early didactic prose, Ezra Pound referred to the "inventors," those who established new models in poetry, "melodic invention" in Homer (fresh, previously unused sound patterns), and "the key invention, the first case or first available illustration" of an artistic device or form.[41]

This position—parallel to the technological or scientific sense of new contrivance or device, groundbreaking process—is what so appealed to the Noigandres group of poets in São Paulo who founded *poesia concreta*. In the late 1950s and 1960s, they actively promoted an agenda of invention linked to the legacies of Pound and Oswald. The former is invoked to open a theoretical pondering of "criticism and works of invention" by Haroldo de Campos, who shares Pound's advocacy for the "truly creative and pertinent text from the point of view of the evolution of forms and of invention."[42] In this instance, the Brazilian poet-critic essentially assumes that the reader understands the keyword as innovative, revolutionary, neoteric form. In 1960 the Noigandres team joined other like-minded poets to form a collective. From January 1960 until February 1961 in the *Correio paulistano* they maintained an arts section dubbed "Invenção." Following this newspaper adventure, a fine-press journal (see figure 3) was produced, intending to avoid affiliation with any specific proposal or group. *Invenção: Revista de arte de vanguarda* (1962–67) would promote "new signs," experimental poetry, music, and graphic art, with supporting essays. The first issue, in fact, consisted solely of two position papers (about the current situation of poetry and its ties to *modernismo*) and a brief initial presentation. This foreword explained that the "point of encounter" of the different contributors was "precisely invention," which was glossed as "a gamut of tendencies, less and more radical, but all useful in the configuration of the profile of a civilization in evolution and in the production of works that contribute to its artistic definition."[43] This statement reflects the effects of sociopolitical activism of the period on the arts, as further seen in number 4 (1964), which has a telling self-characterization—"criar coisas realmente novas é criar liberdade" [to create really new things is to create liberty]—eight months after the right-wing military coup that so repressed opposition and shaped socioeconomic conditions for twenty-one years to follow. Independent of difficult circumstances, the concrete poets anticipated having their own publishing venture—with the name Invenção—that could produce such titles as *Antologia de poesia brasileira de invenção*, a collection of cutting-edge lyric since baroque times, based on the idea of "text" characterized by its "informative content (its inventive components)."[44] The 1964 issue of *Invenção* was dedicated to the "inventor" Oswald de Andrade, who himself enjoyed posing the word *invenção*. In his penetrating analysis of the leading modernist's most experimental work of fiction, Haroldo de Campos calls it a *romance-invenção* or invention-novel, noting that on the title page of the copy he received from the author the word *romance* had been lined out by hand and replaced with *invenção*.[45] The revival of the writings of Oswald by the São Paulo poets should be counted among their most notable achievements as purveyors of invention and shapers of contemporary taste.

If both main senses of the term *invention* resonate in the Brazilian arts, in one way or another, from the modernist decade of the twentieth century to the turn of the new century, from Oswald's pages and concretist adoptions of him to a series of engaged endeavors in poetry, it remains demonstrable and meaningful that writerly desire for admirable novelty is what most endures. The 1974 collection *Bahia invenção: Anti-antologia de poesia baiana* (Risério) applies Haroldo de Campos's idea of a syntagmatic slice of formally innovative, canon-challenging lyric across the centuries. Technical newness and forward-looking volition motivate the name and purpose of an e-poetry gathering called "Invenção: Thinking about the New Millennium" (1999).[46] Indeed, in the digital age, inventors (in the Poundian sense) would be those who crafted modes of poetry with emerging media (such as holography or computer animation), as Augusto de Campos understood as early as the 1950s. The turn-of-the-century anthology *Na virada do século: Poesia de invenção no Brasil* banks somewhat on the semantics of its title, and the preface considers (or implies) some of the meanings of "poetry of invention" circa 2000: finding ways to integrate modernist advances and a certain postmodern permissiveness, transformative (re)construction of worn language and relationships between words, postconcrete syntactical disarticulation and semantic mixing, metaliterary consciousness applied

REVISTA DE ARTE DE VANGUARDA
N.º 2   ANO I   2.º TRIMESTRE 1962

SUMÁRIO
POEMAS DE HAROLDO DE CAMPOS, AUGUSTO DE CAMPOS, DÉCIO
PIGNATARI, RONALDO AZEREDO, JOSÉ LINO GRÜNEWALD, CASSIANO
RICARDO, JORGE DE SENA, PEDRO XISTO, EDGARD BRAGA, AFFONSO
ÁVILA, PAULO MARCOS DE ANDRADE

CARTA DO SOLO — POESIA REFERENCIAL   AFFONSO ÁVILA
MAX BENSE SÔBRE BRASÍLIA
PRÉMIÈRES NOTES SUR LA POÉSIE CONCRÈTE   PHILIPPE JACCOTTET

MÓBILE: DRUMMOND DÁ LIÇÃO DE COISAS — JORGE DE SENA SÔBRE
OS QUATRO SONETOS A AFRODITE ANADIÓMENA — NOTAS

MASSAO OHNO EDITÔRA

3. Front covers of *Invenção* 2 (1962) and 4 (1964). Used by permission of Augusto de Campos.

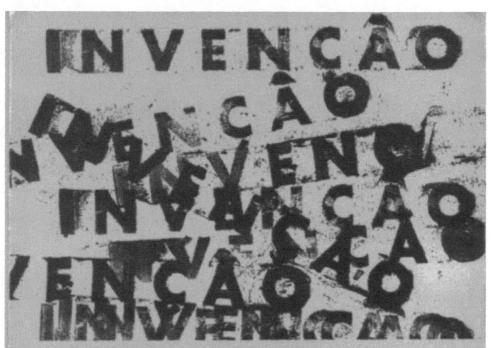

REVISTA DE ARTE DE VANGUARDA

N.º 4   ANO 3   DEZEMBRO 1964

to linguistic materiality—in sum, understanding poetry as an elaborate artifice of language.[47] A city-specific anthology in the same spirit, *Invenção Recife*, confirms an approach defined by visuality and transgressive idiom aware of multiple sources.[48] In a wider critical perspective of transamerican pedagogical reasoning, in a Brazilian venue, Bernstein ("Our Americas," 90) underscores invention as a key feature of syncretic poetics: "A syncretic poetics of ingenuity and invention, of collage and palimpsest, is averse to the accumulative and developmental model of literature still reigning in the U.S. literary academy (and elsewhere in the Americas)."

To verify how *invention* as linguistic artifice can weigh heavily in Brazil, it is worthwhile to register the conclusion of an individual book by the coeditor of the turn-of-the-century anthology cited above. In *Louco no oco sem beiras: Anatomia da depressão* (Crazy in the edgeless hollow: Anatomy of depression), Frederico Barbosa forges a supposed twenty-first-century discourse on melancholy. In a postscript to the self-absorbed sequence, the persona-speaker, almost mocking his own facile rhymes, poses as an aesthete for whom "impression" is both mental (as in "it seems to me") and physical (the act of (im)printing), and for whom expressing (feelings, one assumes) does not match up to contrivance and imagination:

> entre a expressão
> (banal)
> e a invenção
> (genial)
>
> fico com a impressão
>
> invento
> no leitor
> a expressão
> do meu horror
>
> imprima-se
>
> FIM.

[between expression / (banal) / and invention / (ingenious) // I'm left with the impression // I invent / in the reader / the expression / of my horror // imprint it // The End.] (83)

This is in fact the conclusion of a tag section, the very end of the add-on poem, and of the collection as a whole. And the mental condition? Does it matter? Amador Ribeiro Neto (12–13) notes that the poet's pose here is melancholic, that the subject seems lost in a hostile world and seeks escape in writing. In the short book, "intertextualities and intratextualities remain as interfaces of a cultured poet, interlacing different artistic codes and diverse linguistic resources." Among those sources are the sense of invention advanced by concretism and the questioning cosmopolitan heritage of *modernismo*.

Returning to the inventor of "brazilwood poetry" as a point of departure for late-century work, the second aesthetic declaration by Oswald de Andrade, "O manifesto antropófago" ("The Cannibalist Manifesto," 1928) is less beholden to early modern ideology and has greater aptitude to be disruptive. And as it is not specifically limited to poetry, this tempestuous writing has generated considerably more national and international response.[49] Much more daring, its elaboration of the metaphor of cultural cannibalism has become the signature song of an aggressive Brazilian practice of appropriating, absorbing, and reformulating foreign matter. The author borrowed from a revenge-minded Hamlet and coined an enduring pun of artistic being—"Tupi, or not tupi that is the question"—to help anchor this document and the sense of New World valorization (to what extent should one favor a native orientation to counteract Old World inheritance?). That modernist cannibalization is an important precursor of a well-developed twist of the figure of Caliban—the brutish yet bright island-bound indigenous slave in Shakespeare's *The Tempest* (1611)—to affirm a stance of proud defiance. Roberto Fernández Retamar's *Calibán: Apuntes sobre la cultura en nuestra América* (1971) has been usefully described as "simultaneously a discourse of resistance, a problematization of metropolitan paradigms, and a criticism of neocolonial power structures; and a discourse of unification, continental solidarity."[50] In revised editions of the landmark essay, the respected Cuban critic acknowledges the importance of Oswald, who had been overlooked in the original exposition.[51] A crucial aspect of Caliban as a trope of cultural critique is making the language of the master one's own tool to talk back. In some cases, Brazilian poets' use of the language of today's lone superpower may comprise its own figurative breed of Calibanization, as seen in chapter 2. There are two other phrases in Oswald's second manifesto with particular New World spice. Artful connections abound in the last line of the seventh paragraph: "O cinema americano informará" [The cinema of (the) America(s) will inform]. And article thirteen reads "A idade de ouro anunciada pela América. A idade de ouro. E todas as girls" [The golden age announced by (the) America(s). The golden age. And all the girls], which again brings up objectification and New World prospects, while hinting at something about an influential English-speaking nation. Implications of these lines will be taken up in chapter 3.

Throughout this first chapter the appellations *America* and *American* have been used without specific definition or explanation. Given the hemispheric reach of the present study, a targeted discussion of the principal geographical names, labels, and regional identifiers would certainly be in order. Most of the many variations of *America/American* do, in fact, prove to play some role in contemporary repertories examined here, sometimes explicit and purposeful, sometimes more insinuative. This is not the place to review in depth the evolution of what Mignolo calls "several names signifying a lengthy multilayered and complex politics of labeling," but the contours of basic issues of naming and some particulars merit attention in advance of the production-focused chapters.[52] The main difficulty that arises when discussing cultural or political phenomena in the (far) Western Hemisphere is that the very terms *America*, its adjectival forms (in the European languages of the hemisphere), and regional specifiers carry such historical weight and are so replete with overtones, often ambiguous. For so long, most in the Northern Hemisphere have associated *America* with the United States, while for Spanish and Portuguese speakers the singular term already encompasses all of what must be expressed in English with the pluralization: the Americas. The hegemonic reach of the USA has been such that Spanish, to some degree, and Brazilian Portuguese, to a more evident extent, also concede the singular use of their equivalents of *America* and *American* to designate what can conveniently be simply *USA* and *USAmerican*.

The name *America*, as noted above, made its first cartographic appearance in 1507 to indicate what would today be South America. Spanish conquerors used different names for the New World (Indias, Indias Occidentales, Nuevo Mundo), the Portuguese chose names for the lands they came to (Veracruz, Santa Cruz, Brasil), and the French used *Amérique* for a general term and *France antarctique* in the mid-sixteenth century for an attempted colony in what is today Rio de Janeiro.[53] The name *America* spread north and south, coming to embrace all the colonial territories of Spain, Portugal, England, and France. Only one nation incorporated the continental designation into its name, the United States of America. By virtue of synecdoche, among other factors, that incorporation led to usage of the last part to refer only to itself, especially after the declaration of the Monroe Doctrine (1823), which claimed to shield the hemisphere from European interference. It seemed to many south of the Rio Grande in the 1800s, however, that "America for the Americans," the associated slogan purportedly for all, really meant for the USA alone. The geographical names were in effect usurped, but postindependence historical developments led to the consolidation of notions of multiple Americas.

As early as 1836, the enterprising French diplomat Michel Chevalier remarked in his travel writing, *Lettres sur l'Amérique du Nord*, that he perceived two Americas, one in the north, Anglo-Saxon and Protestant, and another in the south, Latin and Catholic, these serving as adjectives, not as any sort of proposed new terminology to supplant the north-south divide. In an 1856 lecture in Paris, the Chilean statesman Francisco Bilbao Barquín posited the concept of *América Latina*, including México and Central America. For his part, the Colombian intellectual José María Torres Caicedo pushed the term *América Latina* (including Franco- and Ibero-America) in opposition to Anglo-Saxon (plus Danish and Dutch) America. In practice, since the new compound term was employed in concert with efforts by several factions to promote unity among the former colonies of Spain, especially to form a common state as Bolívar had imagined, it essentially meant Spanish America, as Brazil was still an empire.[54] In the 1860s, the regime of Napoleon III harbored renewed imperial designs in the New World, hoping to compete with the United States, and there was an organized undertaking to promote the geopolitical notion of Amérique Latine to join all the former colonies whose national languages descended from Latin. Especially with the French adventure in Mexico (1862–67), there was an urgency to influence attitudes toward fellow Romance-language states and to legitimize intervention in the land of Juárez. In conjunction, the cultural idea of *latinité* was elaborated. As a contemporary French scholar has it, "Latinity had the advantage . . . of giving France legitimate duties concerning her American 'sisters,' Roman and Catholic."[55] After the 1860s, the existence of multiple Americas would be a given.

So briefly, from circa 1860 forward, both Spanish American and French contingents promoted acceptance of Latin America as a unitary block of one form or another. Ibero-America clearly meant Brazil plus Spanish America, but Hispanic America was still a little less certain, since the ancient Roman sense of Hispanic meant both Spanish and Portuguese, which would transfer to New World holdings. Just after the first, and clearly commercially oriented, Pan-American conference in Washington, José Martí penned from New York his famous essay "Nuestra América" (Our America, 1891), which calls for cultural awareness, self-assertion, and resistance to Yankee dominance. While he did not mention the republic of Brazil (1889) by name, the poet-diplomat did refer to "the romantic nations of the continent," and he was, of course, perfectly cognizant of multilateral relations in the hemisphere. Further to the Iberian connection, decades later the prolific anthropologist Gilberto Freyre wrote a series of essays on "the Brazilian amongst the other Hispanics," noting that certain behavioral and attitudinal affinities descend from the period of Spanish dominion over Portugal, and her colonies, 1580–1640. The relevance of these nomenclatural positionings to transatlantic, New World, and postcolonial studies is more than evident, as is the potential bearing on transamerican poetics.

In the early twentieth century, the French state updated awareness of the importance of science and culture for international relations. Specifically, the Groupement des Universités et Grandes Ecoles de France pour les Relations avec l'Amérique Latine (established 1907) targeted university cooperation, leading to the establishment of French institutes in Latin American capital cities. The *Revue d'Amérique Latine* promoted anew *latinité* against North American Pan-Americanism. The most significant French involvement in a Latin American institution was at the University of São Paulo (founded 1934), where visiting professors included a young Claude Lévy-Strauss, future author of the widely influential *Tristes Tropiques* with its famous depictions of New World natives. He and other scientists and intellectuals shaped the central unit of what would become the region's foremost university.[56]

In the early twentieth century the terminologies of identity were still slippery. An apt illustration of this linguistic state of affairs in relation to a more general pondering of the unity of regional thought can be found in a declaration by the penetrating Peruvian essayist José Carlos Mariátegui, who prefers to refer to affinity thinking as "inteligencia indo-ibera." In the immediately following paragraph his idea of spirit-in-formation is applicable to his key geo-cultural terms: "Hispanic American thought is being elaborated. The continent, the race, are being formed as well. [In] Western floods . . . the embryonic Hispanic American culture is developing."[57] This same thinker provides a clear indication of the unfavorable associations of "Pan-American" that last to this day, of why it cannot be an ideal for the continent: "Pan-Americanism . . . does not enjoy the favor of intellectuals. It cannot count, in this abstract and inorganic category, on estimable and sensible adhesion . . . only on a scarcely masked sympathy. Its existence is exclusively diplomatic. Even the slowest mind easily discovers in Pan-Americanism the tunic of North American imperialism." What is important in this positioning is the express separation of poets and governors; opposition to the USA—as echoed in various Latin American poetries of subsequent decades of the twentieth century—is opposition to economic empire, not to the "noble cases . . . intelligence and spirit [of] Thoreau . . . Emerson, William James . . . Walt Withman [sic] . . . strong masters of continental idealism."[58] The Brazilian literary critic who devised the diplomatic document "Plano Cultural Interamericano" in the 1950s expressed belief in "pan-americanismo," like "pan-europeísmo . . . pan-asiatismo . . . pan-africanismo," as a "continental spirit," a transition between the spirits of nationality and universality.[59] The continent is held to be a social and geographical reality, and, even if the national clearly has the strongest affective mark, the continental is real and merits cultivation in the interests of peace. This temperament, though unavoidably tied to the US-dominated politics of the Organization of American States, should also be kept in mind when a hemispheric grasp of poetry is in play.

As for *Latin America*, following a hundred years of vacillation in terms, the dominant definition worldwide and across disciplines today, though far from universally applied, is the inclusive variant. A Brazilian historian asserts that this definition "gained force when multilateral institutions adopted it after the Second World War."[60] A current specialist in comparative literature from Rio de Janeiro notes that in some instances even Québec is included in the scope of Latin America, an inclusiveness that makes sense given the existence of several nuclei of comparativism involving the literature of French Canada and that of southern Brazil.[61] Mignolo, while exposing massive Indo- and Afro-descendant gaps in conceptions of the region and thus bracketing the exclusionary modifier in (Latin) America, also points to the option of "l'Amérique latine du Nord" in his in-depth analysis of the matrix of colonial power behind the names discussed here,[62] clearly advantageous to any truly transamerican approach. What remains to be understood in a pervasive way is the extent to which *America* came into being as an ideological construction. Mexican philosopher-historian Edmundo O'Gorman challenged the givenness of the New World in *The Invention of America*. Totally bypassing the classic meaning of the keyword as "discovery," which for him implies that the basic nature of the thing found was previously known, he argued that America was "the inspired invention of Western thought,"[63] a process of formation of ideas of Europeans "less interested in determining, in all their empirical distinctiveness, the reality of New World conditions than in reimagining those conditions as forms of alterity against which they as Europeans might redefine themselves."[64] Thus, the particular sense of *invention* in this historical interpretation is actually closer to the conceptual contrivance of imaginative literature.

Just as essayists have parsed and sought to destabilize hegemonic geocultural vocabularies, Latin American poets may intervene in the contemporary discourse of reading and follow vanguard impulses to unsettle received notions of communication via the page. In a comparable move of aesthetic bearing, the ever-relevant Paulo Leminski (1944–1989) utilized the historical syntagm of New World discovery to conclude his own lyrical counterversion in "Ler pelo não" (To read through the "no," or, To read by what's not), with its advocacy for variegated discernment and reversals of apprehension that insinuate rethinking the longest legacies of European letters in the New World, Brazil, America:[65]

> Ler pelo não, quem dera!
> Em cada ausência, sentir o cheiro forte
>   do corpo que se foi,
> a coisa que se espera.
>   Ler pelo não, além da letra,
> ver, em cada rima vera, a prima pedra,
>   onde a forma perdida
> procura seus etcéteras.
>   Desler, tresler, contraler,
> enlear-se nos ritmos da matéria,
>   no fora ver o dentro e, no dentro, o fora,
> navegar em direção às Índias
>   e descobrir a América.

To read by what's not, so much better!
To sense, in each absence, the strong smell
    of the body unfettered,
the thing so awaited.
    To read by what's not, beyond letters,
to see, in elevated rhyme, prime stone setters,
    there, where the forms gone astray
go seeking their etceteras.
    To un-read, counter-read, read-err,
to get reentangled in these rhythms of matter,
    outside see the inside, and inside the out,
to set sail toward the Indies
    and discover America.

There is here, as a fellow Brazilian poet would have it, a confluence of different elements that, when combined, disguise what they are in order to appear to be absolutely new. To read via negation, the voyage to the Orient that leads to the unknown Extreme Occident, is a "reading adrift" by someone not at all concerned with common ways but rather with hitting upon unblazed paths, possibilities, extensions, "etcéteras." The governing "no" is a "yes" to divergence, to linguistic deformation in the literary text (T. Melo). In the play between physical and nonphysical realms in these thirteen lines, they emerge as metaliterary, engaging both the making of poetry—with its functions of sound, rhythm, image, symbol, idea—and the act(s) of consumption, cognition, reading. In the original, the unusual verb *tresler*, meaning to read backwards or to dote from too much reading, also rings of trespass, solidifying an antinormative stance alongside the pair of neologisms *contraler* and *desler*, which may evoke, for the conversant in literary theory of the period, Bloom's theory of misreading.[66] Overall, the poem endorses not just reading between the lines, submitting to the suggestiveness of sound or other sensual stimuli, and turning perspectives around, but an ethics of refusal of the received. (Re-)processing language and its set configurations may be quixotic, but it is productive; venturing out driven by curiosity and a questing resolve may lead to unimagined realms. There is an allegory of epistemic shift, linked to the sea change provoked in Western civilization by finding, unexpectedly, a set of islands and another continent inhabited by other beings. Leminski uses *America* as a complex metaphor for surprise and invention, as discovery and artistic creation alike, including, one can imagine, detection and encounter of diverse bodies, texts, lands, people in his own time and hemisphere. Writing in the last quarter of the twentieth century, what he figures, while it may hark back five hundred years or more, casts light in all directions in a wide open present. In the realm of poetry in the current age, conceiving (of) America—the region(s), the nation(s), the continent(s), the etceteras—involves an exciting range of expected and unexpected moves.

2

◇

Allusive, Elusive

Brazilian Reflections of/on USAmerican Literature

Welcome, Brazilian Brother—thy ample place is ready;
A Loving Hand—A Smile from the North . . .

Thus begins a poem written by Walt Whitman upon the birth of the republic of Brazil in 1889.[1] The topic is especially apropos for Whitman, as a seer who celebrated self, difference, and the Americas, and who influenced poets of *modernismo* and beyond. Not until a century after this verse of welcome, however, did a significant rapport begin to develop in the realm of poetry. In the context of the modern Americas, the most important relationship of any given nation is with the United States, and Brazil is no exception. If historical vincula in lyric are relatively few, recent and ongoing connections between these two countries of continental proportions are noteworthy. During and following World War II, the USA courted the nations of the hemisphere, especially, given its size and resources, Brazil. Literary ties became closer via such interfaces as the sponsored cultural tours of writers like novelist Érico Verissimo and poet Cecília Meireles in the 1940s, the residence of Afrânio Coutinho (1911–2000) at Columbia University in the late 1940s and his subsequent advocacy of New Criticism in Brazil, and the promotion of Pound and Cummings by the concrete poets in the 1960s.[2] Appreciable numbers of Brazilian artists viewed the United States antagonistically or with suspicion in the wake of the Cuban Revolution and during the years of authoritarian military dictatorship in Brazil (1964–85). Since then, one of the notable aspects of poetry is the enjoyment of common New World poses, which may comprehend change—diminution, reconsideration, evanescence, reversal—in anti-imperialist sentiment. A transamerican ethic of a different stripe manifests in Brazilian lyric in several ways, especially in the use of English (titles, isolated words, keywords, phrases, passages, entire poems) and in a spectrum of intertextual gestures (dedications, epigraphs, homages, quotations, thematizations, full structural allusions) that both link literary domains and point to other artistic realms.

Conventional endeavors of recent literary cooperation between the United States and Brazil include the promotion of bilingual binational anthologies. *Nothing the Sun Could Not Explain* (Ascher et al.), with Michael Palmer as noteworthy coeditor, reached a second edition. *Outras praias / Other Shores* (R. Corona) was published in São Paulo with an eye to international readership. The public presentation of an anthology of contemporaries contained in an issue of *New American Writing* elicited an optimistic local response, with the assertion of "many reasons" to turn to Brazilian poetry, "each reason expressive of a latent desire, or expectation, or wish from our own poetry," and of an element of "resistance to globalization," which can be traced back to concrete poetry, Oswald de Andrade, and Cinema Novo (Whitener, 91–93). A Brazilian feature in *Rattapallax* included important names born since 1960 and young hopefuls residing abroad; the journal, moreover, had a publishing partner in Brazil.[3] Another bilingual volume of Brazilian poetry in the first decade of the twenty-first century featured even younger voices.[4]

Some items in these samplings of Brazilian lyric are not translated from Portuguese but rather written directly in English. Since such concrete poems as "LIFE" in the late fifties, Brazilian poets have occasionally composed in the tongue of Pound and Cummings.[5] One of these chance-takers ventures to say that the previous common preoccupation with *brasilidade*, or Brazilianness, in national letters has passed, in deed and idea, to a "transnacionalidade comportamental"—behavioral transnationality.[6] This passage sets up strong North American frames of reference, as opposed to the historically dominant prestige of things European, especially French. In her discussion of nineties lyric, Heloísa Buarque de Hollanda sees mindsets shaped by such historical events as the fall of the Berlin Wall, AIDS, the increasing exclusion of the masses, and the ethos of globalization; she underscores plurality and the identity imperatives of gender, race, Jewish heritage, gay life, and class.[7] Each of these concerns naturally spurs circumstantial conjugations and inflections of the local, yet all are linked, it is fair to say, to international movements centered in the USA. Even poetic acts in Brazil are inseparable from those unavoidable emanations, be they political, economic, cultural in general, or linguistic more specifically. By way of illustration, Amador Ribeiro Neto specifically notes that his poem "Até que um dia" (Until one day) "expõe comportamento (sexual) advindo de costumes (ou moda?) norte-americanos" [displays (sexual) behavior coming from North American customs (or fashion?)].[8] In this regard, a noticeable polypositionality of lyric selves in poetic output is certainly more than local. Buarque de Hollanda further notes that nineties poets produced in a period marked by technological and code-related novelty: "tempos de hipertexto e novos *inputs* translingüísticos."[9] In fact, of the twenty-one poets in her anthology, the selections of all but two employ a language other than Portuguese, and two-thirds use English or allude to English-named habits. The multiple belongings exercised in such demographics are a facet of transamerican poetics that grew demonstrably as the turn of the millennium approached.

Even in literature, the use of English can be construed variously: as an indication of Anglo-American imperialism and cultural penetration, as a manifestation of mental colonization, as an act of negotiation for symbolic capital and prestige, as a demonstration of erudition or fashion consciousness, as a pragmatic insertion into international schemes, as a sign of aesthetic solidarity, as an expression of artistic respect and admiration, as a context-driven gesture, as an ironic retort to any number of common assumptions or mainstream common sense. From whatever angle one approaches utilizations of US-based keywords or Brazilian poetry in original English, this polyvalence adds singular substance to lyric's presence in the cultural landscape, local, regional, global. In advance of an examination of myriad repertoires where English plays a role, it is instructive to listen to Caetano Veloso and his comments about composing pop songs in the dominant language of the late 1960s:

> English was becoming more and more international. . . . since we were being bombarded with it all the time, we had the right to use it as we could. If Brazilian radio stations played more songs in English than in Portuguese, if products, ads, stores used English in their packaging, slogans and windows, we could certainly answer with our own poorly learned English, making it the instrument of protest against the very usage being imposed on us. At the same time we wanted to establish a dialogue with the "world outside." (*Tropical Truth*, 277)

Despite the differences in reach and nature between mass-mediated popular music and sometimes seemingly clandestine poetry, this commentary illustrates both an emerging Calibanesque temperament in the global village imagined by McLuhan and a writerly urge to commune on an artistic level. Further, it suggests some of the ways English may filter into poetic texts, via internationalism, commerce, advertising, musical lyricism, political discourse, or foreign literature. Not just to curse, but also to play, to pay, to parse, to salute.

In creative works that travel, a transamerican verve may be unspoken yet inextricably woven into verbo-optical fabrics, such as those contrived by poet-musician Arnaldo Antunes. Three appearances he made in the USA illustrate a polyvalent art that destabilizes borders. An installation in South Florida—a wall plastered with red and white posterings of **NOW / NOWHERE / HERE**—stood as a simple yet powerful presentification and deterritorialization of art via, if you will, sun, fun, and pun.[10] A much more elaborate actuation was achieved in a single-channel video piece dubbed "Wherever" in which a voice-over broadcasts the text "Once upon a time.... / / / / And they lived / together / for ever / and ever, / wherever and everywhere."[11] The piece unfolds in four frames that display shadowed superfont spellings of **NOW** and **HERE**, a reduction of distance between them, their merger into **NOWHERE**, and a final emptying of the foreground. The English-language micronarrative may be formulaic, and the enabling paronomasia phonemically imperfect, yet the result is a gesture of paradox with a utopian thrust—etymologically for the no-place and contentwise for the ideal life projected. The implied and exercised relativizations of idiom, temporality, and territoriality provoked by this *hic et nunc* work are inescapably circumscribed by turn-of-the-millennium speculation about the globalization of culture. A similarly open-ended piece was featured (with white letters on a red field) at a festive Brazilian Visual Poetry exhibition.[12]

This dystic—alluding to stories in general and films in particular (see examples in chapter 3)—leaves in an indeterminate space the common expectation of narrative closure and prompts, with the benefit of global and cultural contextualizations, both an inclusiveness appropriate to transnational address in art and a terse confirmation that upon entry into the twenty-first century the story of Brazilian aesthetic identities operates across and defies boundaries of genre, language, and even nation. Antunes achieves such extensive exposure for these telling moments because his vehicles are varied: the stage and recordings of popular music; the images and projections of visual media, now including the Internet; and the old standby of print literature. An illustration of the heritage to which he writes is the conclusion to a colleague's modest lyric: "sonho com encontros impossíveis / na sala escura da imaginação: / submundo onde alegorias platônicas / roubam sempre o beijo do THE END" [I dream of impossible encounters / in the dark room of imagination: / underworld where platonic allegories / always pilfer the kiss of THE END].[13] The symptomatic epigraph of the volume from which this romantic statement is taken—"From this hour I ordain myself loos'd of limits and imaginary lines" (Walt Whitman)—affirms liberation from constraints, borders, unique languages, and sets up an advantageous position of awareness, an interface.

One of the ways English has been used by Brazilian poets with conspicuous frequency around the turn of the millennium is titles, individual lyrics written in Portuguese but given an Anglophone title. The inscription or name of a poem has numerous particular expressive possibilities, not the least of which is being (assuming conventional linear reading) the first enunciation that may shape response to the body of the text. The title sits autonomously before reading (or hearing) per se commences, and then gains meaning in association with what follows in verse, as it works in the volume where it appears, in wider relation to poems by the same author or others. A title can create expectations or intimate something about the poem, being selective or secretive, straightforward or obtuse. And, most relevant with respect to using a foreign-language header, "titles that seem extravagantly unrelated to the poem make a more violent assault on the kinds of authority claimed by the presence of a title." Since Romanticism, poets have shown with "growing urgency the need to escape the authority of generic and other traditional classifications, which are specially visible in the compressed and relatively circumscribed conventions of title formation." Overall, titles are "inherently interesting verbal constructs working according to subtle and complicated laws virtually unique to their forms and status," which is true not just for "idiosyncratic or attention-getting titles" but even for the seemingly neutral or merely informative instances.[14] Modern titles reveal the influence of myriad applications of language: labels, advertising, business and scientific writing, manifestos, street signs, visual arts, and of course the whole history of literature. Such considerations are complicated further when the title in question is written in a foreign language, carrying cross-cultural codes or built-in enigmas. In the present study, interest in English titling of poems may be two-pronged: what might the title denote/connote for native readers of the text so christened? and what points of curiosity, or awareness of difference in perspective, might be provoked in English-speaking readers?

Recent harvests of Brazilian lyric provide ample material to pursue such intriguing questions. There are countless books with a title or two in English, while some sport half a dozen or more Anglophone inscriptions on Lusophone poems. In a collection called *Coisas que o primeiro cachorro na rua pode dizer* (Things that the first dog in the street can say), among the six English titles by Caio Meira, ones such as "Close to the Bone" and "The Odd Lady" may link to the endearing book title. Of the seven English entries in Eudoro Augusto's *Olhos de bandido* (Bandit eyes), some point to the appropriation of popular culture, its technologies and ambiguities: "Close," "Detective Story," "Home Movie," "Rick's Café." When there are a great number of non-Portuguese lines in a table of contents, they may be seen to represent a sort of urban landscape, a cosmopolitan take, a scan of the mind of a typical educated person, who, as Veloso observed of the 1960s, may be inundated with English at many turns, by films and pop music, international news, business, commerce, tourism, etc. Among the many other examples of oddity, wordplay, seizing of opportunities for irony, and/ or reflections of thematic critical concerns, there are the vague haze of a "Smoke Poem," a "Day-Stripper" that puns on the Beatles song "Day Tripper" and on diurnal X-rated entertainment, and a section called "A Flurry of Amnesia," a trio of poems about possible impulses for writing (the subconscious naturally implicated).[15]

Repertories of poets who have resided abroad may logically reflect actual experience and greater linguistic diversity. While several others will be seen in the course of this chapter (see especially the New York motif below), a particularly germane case is that of poet-anthropologist Janice Caiafa. Her title "Kool Man in Williamsburgh" names a "cool" place (presumably the Brooklyn neighborhood) and perhaps the value-sharing consumer of a tainted product (drug or menthol cigarette).[16] Historical location and event are straightforward in "The Midnight Ride of Paul Revere," an alliterative celebration of the legendary episode, the response of a foreign visitor to the lore of the land. In turn, "The Weeders" simply identifies a painting in the Museum of Modern Art, while more obtuse connections exist between body of poem and title in "O'Clock" and "Bail Jumper," examples of very English-specific vocabulary.[17] The most transamerican instance, in terms of ecumenical attitude, is "Sweet Virginia," entirely based on the interplay of feminine names of southern states—"a certa saga das mulheres / e das amigas" [the certain saga of women / and (girl)friends][18]—with sisterly connections between US entities and a friend from abroad.

Turning now to the use of English words within poems, it is useful to repeat that such uses in contemporary Brazilian lyric range from simple one-item borrowings, a couple of convenient phrases, or short objects of observation to lexical fulcra and full-length texts. The utility, or broader significance, of a given English adoption are poematic subjects themselves. In a typically provocative poem, "Novíssimo Proteu" (All-new Proteus), the persona of Waly Salomão is versatile, agile, adaptable. Invention (discovery) of an English word seems so promising, but other words, especially a similar one, prove more apt:

Pensei ter pisado solo firme
quando descobri
no texto *What is Zen*, de D.T. Suzuki
que a palavra inglesa *elusive*
poderia solidamente me definir de uma vez por todas.
Qual o quê.
Vou onde poesia e fogo se amalgamam.
Sou volátil, diáfano, evasivo.

[I thought I was on solid ground / when I discovered / in the text . . . by DTS / that the English word "elusive" / could wholly define me once and for all. / No way. / I go where poetry and fire amalgamate. / I am volatile, diaphanous, evasive.]

That Portuguese had the verb *eludir*, to elude, but did not commonly use the adopted adjectival form, with all its connotations in English, enabled this stance.[19] This step of the unfolding poetic episode offers a metaphor for a certain creative process of growth in which single words can serve as bridges to wider linguistic and artistic awareness.

The wealth of the English-item repertory may depend on the degree of levity, variety, and scope. Shared and resituated words can certainly say more than their mere definitions. A visual poet in Brazil, for example, takes the all-caps word **CRIME**, rotates it counterclockwise to stand vertically, and separates the first letter with space: **C RIME**.[20] Thus, the linguistic feature most commonly associated with poetry (rhyme) becomes "criminal" (the object, say, of modernist derision), possible associations with other codes arise with the isolation of the letter-symbol "C" (Coincidence? C-note? Circa? Copyright?), and modern Portuguese is tied to old English (via French). Further by way of illustration, consider two examples in a small-press series from the state of Minas Gerais. One contributor updates the laconic and epigrammatic early style of the leading modernist poet Carlos Drummond de Andrade with a bilingual homophone in "Influência estrangeira" (Foreign influence): "Tudo o que / eu fiz / foi porque / eu **kiss**" [Everything / I did / was because / I (wanted to)].[21] Placing her utterance on the same page as a poem called "Beijo" (Kiss), the young poet achieves a sort of Oswaldian *poema-piada*, or joke poem, for the age of pop music, teen magazines, TV soap opera, and other vehicles of facile romantic content often attuned to cosmopolitan imagery. In this placement, however, one may hear more a statement of agency than of victimization. In a less evident manner, another feminine voice insinuates the Brazilian penchant for creating names from English sources and for adopting practical words. In "Sobre Viver" (About living, or, Sur-viving), a twenty-four-part variation on the ABC folk form, there is a free association of female names, places, and emotive symbols for the English-origin letter K, beginning "Kits necessários:" and concluding "'Well'mara, Cléo'nice' ou 'bed', **elos** . . . . / **'forever.'"**[22] The enunciations of names isolate positive words (well, nice) and the conclusion is ever affirmative. Semantemes of necessity, linkage (*elos* = links), and permanence suggest not only friendship (perhaps lesbian) but a relationship with the other language. The details, not offered for their eloquence, are indeed emblematic of attitude and naturalness.

In other articulations, English keywords are the foundation of a discourse of questioning. Dolhkinoff pens a challenging "Loa à toa a um *loser*"; the rhyming title of which merges a word (*loa*) for medieval dramatic prologue and laudatory discourse, especially sung, with an adverbial/adjectival phrase (*à toa*) meaning aimlessly, at random, in vain, for nothing, or worthless, careless. The poem critiques advanced (US)American capitalism, personified in "will gates," and takes global issues to an interface with personal desire and self-definition: "desejo que todos sejam / *winners* // porém / como para haver *winners* / é preciso *losers* / no mesmo *game* /

4. Arnaldo Antunes, "Céu-Hell," calligraphy, 2000. Courtesy of the artist.

ofereço-me / não em sacrifício / nem tampouco em desdém" [I want all to be / *winners* // but / for there to be *winners* / there must be *losers* / in the same *game* / I offer myself / not in sacrifice / nor in disdain]. For his part, Salgado Maranhão structures an effectual short poem over two imported words. The unabashedly titled "Via-Crúcis" in *Sol Sangüíneo* begins "Ondas de ruídos / urdem / o *script* / das ruas" and ends "Rondam / —os autos / e os bípedes— / no *drive-in* / da via-crúcis" (67) [Waves of noise / machinate / the *script* / of the streets / . . . Cars / and bipeds / make the rounds / at the *drive-in* / of the Via Crucis]. What most counts here, clearly, is poetics of space. The utterance of observation conveys modern urban noise pollution, synaesthesia of sound-sight-touch, and a sensation of destiny or inevitability. With the word *script* this poem participates in an ongoing metaliterary strain in the encompassing collection, here floating inklings of a relation to film in urban planning and present-day civil construction. Traditionally framed Christian suffering and sacrifice now imply a foreign element in a site overrun with automobiles, car culture, anonymity, aloneness, and consumer-attracting architecture. In this setup, life is more commerce-driven than ever before and a US-based global culture is signaled by language. English lexical items are signs, markers, add-ons, intensifiers, well-placed weighted vocables. A related item is the bilingual calligraphy of Antunes in "Céu-Hell" (Heaven-Hell) (figure 4), which plays within a territorial paradigm with the recurrent notions of (anti)paradise, here inverting the positions of the "underdeveloped" world and the supposedly more desirable, because advanced, Anglophone domain.[23]

In the title piece of *Sol sangüíneo* (Bloody sun), Maranhão builds an eight-section sequence of self-situating and existential examination via acute awareness of speech and writing. The operative poetics lends prime importance to a conflation of land and body in an autoimaging that invokes language, to borrow the deft phrase of Kenneth Burke, as "equipment for living." The beginning of the third section (19) contains studied usage of boilerplate words to widen the stage:

Reconheço-me no branco
que agasalha o rastro
das palavras. No rumor
de sílabas que lavram
minha urdidura: o parto

a granel sem sigla
ou *made in* . . .

I recognize myself in the white
that welcomes the trail
of my words. In the murmur
of syllables that work
my woven cloth: a birth
like gathered grain without a monogram
or *made in* . . .[24]

Up to this point, the poet's contemplation has preferred telluric organic imagery, especially soil and crops. In this section, the polyvalence of pivotal words enriches the whole further. The verb *lavrar* means to cultivate the earth, to plow or till, but also to embroider, or to work with wood, stone, or metal. Metaphorically it can imply to face heavy work or difficulties, and for linguistic craft, it can mean to draw up and fine-tune a document. Language likewise weighs heavily in the modification of "birth." While *a granel* signifies large quantity or in bulk, stand-alone *granel* denotes granary, as well as galley proofs and printer's composing stick. As for *sigla*, it usually indicates an institutional abbreviation, often the initials of a commercial outfit, but it also designates, as in English, signs standing for words on ancient manuscripts, coins, or medals, or letters used to indicate manuscript or other source of edited text. The translation as "monogram" suggests (lack of) social status and, in conjunction with "made in," helps imagine a mere person "in bulk," a common man without privilege, influential family name, special seal, brand name, or mark of fashionable place of fabrication. In this reading, the subject is in a humble position but keen to the values and effects of words. The verbal weaving also may tender the prospect of an ultimately restrictive circumscription—labeling, ID-ing, categorization, boxing—attributable to the (dehumanizing) world of commodity, commonly with an English-named product of the UK, USA, any global outpost, even Brazil itself. If the speaker can avoid that sort of mercantile limitation, he can enjoy greater freedom, an ideal origin without corporate or bureaucratic associations. While hope, desire for a cleaner authenticity, and fortification of organicity remain, the identifier of an international consumer item ("made in") may prove to be most realistic. In any case, the microfeature in English inserts the discourse into an exchange-valued exterior open to discussion.

The impact of the English tongue itself is a most appropriate theme in the age of globalization, in planetary or hemispheric modes. As Maranhão shows, in pertinent Brazilian poems dispositions range from the phenomenological and the existential to the iconic, the ironic, and the skeptical. It is edifying to observe both the anxiety and the unaffectedness that poets may exhibit in the calculated use or interjection of English lines, phrases, or words. "No centenário da Av. Paulista" (On the centenary of Paulista Avenue) bespeaks such manners: "Enquanto após o *rush*, / na *happy hour*, o *stress* / das horas de *brain storming* / dissolve-se *on the rocks*, / estende-se, através / das fendas da camada / de ozônio, a contra-céu, um arco-iris negro" [while after the *rush*, / at *happy hour*, the *stress* / of the hours of *brainstorming* / melts *on the rocks*, / extends itself, through / the cracks in the ozone layer, / against the sky, a black rainbow].[25] If English is global, its presence in the centenary of the grand avenue of Brazil's megalopolis São Paulo lends it particular weight in this short poem. The colorful spread of words sets up the appearance of the black rainbow, clearly a dark symbol of the gross pollution that comes with the progress associated with the development models of hegemonic Anglophone nations. While the eruptions of English here suggest not just convenient use but inevitabilities that must be confronted, its presence, both textual and actual, shows regard for the acclaimed agility and mobility of the language.

Nowhere are those qualities more evident than in digital worlds, for and against which lyrical language is available and ductile. For self-assertion and relative distancing from the cultural hegemony of computers and Internet, how convenient the title "Non line" by Rosane Carneiro:

Dá-me da miséria do mundo
e da solidão da vida em gomos
Existência *on-line*
em tomos

Mas meus *frames*
somente eu decido
mais torto que direito
ou bonito

A vastidão do viver
ainda vejo
em cada
pedaço

Sobrevôo sem deriva
e desfaço:
não necessito
de mosaicos

Give me of the world's misery and
of the solitude of life in parted pomes
On-line existence
in tomes

But my *frames*
only I shall decide
More crooked than straight
or good-looking

The vast lift of living
I still see
in each and
every piece

I fly over without drift
and I undo:
I've no need
for mosaics

This poem of user interface begins with Biblical tone and assigns a measure of salvation to extensive connection to the World Wide Web.[26] Yet the use of *tomes* inevitably alludes back to the conventional world of books, literature. Most importantly for the devious speaker, control of the new learning and communication environment rests with him (masculine gender assuming the adjectives at the end of the second strophe are self-referential). There may be life in the e-machine, but vivacity is still to be seen in a vast array, in each element. Broad vision and ability to effect change persist without *mosaics*. These might be imagined as virtual communities and screen glitter, sets of navigational software, browsers (including the mid-1990s product Mosaic, predecessor to Netscape). "Non line" figures a mischievious empowerment via technology, and the component of resistance to cyberculture hinges on the foreign-language paronomasia. With information technology at the fore, the 1990s are marked in a general way by neoliberalism and globalization. Those megaphenomena, in the focused view of a Brazilian analyst, affect all artistic representations, including poetry, which, wandering from literary nationalism, definitively affirmed "hybridism" as the "artistic aesthetic" of the period.[27]

In chapter 1, a connection was made between Oswald de Andrade's cultural cannibalism and Fernández Retamar's figuration of Caliban. One could allege that, strictly speaking, the mandate of "talking back" in the language of the metropolis ought to entail overtly resistant or emancipatory discourse in conversions and/or subversions of English in full-length texts with some access to wider domains of communication. In reality, various strategies are employed, some of which complexify what a continental vantage might be. A text like "Thinking Back American Culture"[28] is entirely composed of English phrases of regulation and support—"supposed to be," "born free," "blue skies"—but works toward debunking the illusion of "an earthly paradise," where "American landscape" can only mean the USA. If this is a resistant poem of realization, numerous factors obtain in a specimen such as Horácio Costa's "The Practical Poet." This is one of four poems in English in a mostly bilingual Spanish-Portuguese book first launched in Mexico, and thus eminently transamerican. If the author and his speakers offer themselves as citizens of the world, it is willfully within a hemispheric condition. The poem of four dozen lines (*Quadragésimo*, 127) counterpoises classical Greek to software language, the slang of Vietnam, and other (Yankee) constituents to construct a parallel lament about the currency of pragmatism, a very USAmerican mode of thought, and the fate lyric in postmodernity:

Oh   he conveys urns are not his cup of tea
The poet is practical takes his car's keys from the lower pocket
    of his Argentinian leather jacket
And ignites his membership in the fraternity/sorority of
    flames

Some poems with in-text or framed examples of English merit citation on their own for their humor, self-assertiveness, and geographical watchfulness. Beginning with the title, "Poema Jet Lagged" by Waly Salomão fits into the travel paradigm delineated in chapter 1; the text is emphatically peripatetic and international, incorporating multiple other Romance tongues. However, the speaker bellows such Anglophone items as "duties free, shoppings, scanners, junk food, seven types of ambiguity, full of bullshit, motherfuckers, handycams, jigsaw puzzle" and has a ready-made full territorial locution in English:

SCREEN SIGNALS
Use the information at the top of your screen
to plan your fighting strategies and
keep track of your progress
. . . .
—Indique-me sua direção, onde você se encontra agora?
—Estou exatamente na esquina da Rua Walk com a Rua Don't Walk.[29]

The speaker's disorientation under the luminous pedestrian signals ["Tell me your location, where are you now?" / "I am exactly at the corner of Walk Street with Don't Walk Street."] corresponds well to the book's title, *Algaravias*—Algarve talk, or gibberish, in ironic Arabic self-deprecation. The poem crystallizes moments of egocentric struggle, indeterminacy, and spatialization within expressions of transnational awareness, above all of codes and power. This deterritorializing is done with evident jocularity and, ultimately, metaliterary concerns that question sentiments of vengeance and recovery from perceived slights, which are relevant to tropes of domination and resistance, yet within the range of outreach as well.

English phrases may simply flag intentions to display erudition and prestige, but in texts such as those considered above, the issue of usage transcends simple maneuvering in the field of production: it underscores the necessity of English as an instrument for commerce, technology, travel, socialization, aesthetic discourse, for situating oneself as an individual subject and as a public citizen within local, national, regional, and global domains. Ringing true, Veloso's ambiguous Tropicalist song "Baby" concludes provocatively with the lyric voice commanding his ideal listener to read on his T-shirt that he loves her.[30] In song or page poetry, contrasts of centers and peripheries, of mainstreams and margins are persistent. In late-century lyric such apposition can be realistic, mocking, or even critical, without being oppositional per se or isolationist. Rather, it may be dialogical in both new and conventional ways, and transamerican in its ties with other lands in the realm.

Intertextuality in all its forms is a constant reflection of transamerican poetics. Contemplation of North American cultural spheres and representative topoi take place in Brazilian lyric in an abundance of dedications to US poets and epigraphs taken from their work, as well as in respectful nods or homages in titles, line-long allusions or whole poems, structural allusions or metatexts. Epigraphs and dedications, of course, are no novelty; what distinguishes current activity is the degree of intensity. Skepticism has been expressed about globalization circa 2000 based on the semimillennial history of European expansionism; the Portuguese reached India, after all, before 1500. Important differences at the end of the twentieth century are the rapidity and extent of communication, multipolarity, increased travel, multidirectional migration, economic integration, and new cultural flows. Taking this down to a very particular reflection in the arts, there are, similarly, both unprecedented interconnectedness and a new feeling on the part of the community of poets in Brazil in relation to USAmerican referents. Eliot Weinberger (15–16) recalls how anti-imperialist sentiment kept Latin American poets away from North American counterparts for most of the twentieth century (despite poets' separation from the state), but hails a late-century change whereby new Latin American poets write under the influence of USAmerican poets who themselves may have absorbed Latin American influences. In Brazil, such expanded interest in pertinent repertories is signaled as well by a rising frequency of references to USAmerican sources, as opposed to the historically dominant European names. There is a willingness—some would say of postmodern character—to cite the classical canon and modern Old World canons in conjunction with less established New World names. This citational posture is exemplified in the wry modesty of Antonio Pereira: "Não, não sou Ginsberg nem / ouviram meus berros na fria / da mais fria madrugada. Ainda não li Dante até / ficar rouco. Ainda não morri. . . . Rosno feito bicho solitário e / não sei o que é escolher." [No, I am not Ginsberg, nor / did they hear my howls in the cold / of the coldest dawns. I have yet to read Dante until / I get hoarse. I have not died yet. . . . I growl like a solitary creature and / I know not what it is to choose.][31] While only mildly in evidence here, contemporary lyric also exercises a dissolution of a historical prejudice against popular culture, largely constructed in the Americas, as seen more fully in chapter 3.

An urge to link gestures of recognition and one's own craft leads to serial intertextual highlighting. While some citations may appear ostentatious or demonstrative of authority and command of repertoire, more positive and effective implementations are disinterested professional or aesthetic identifications, or of combined motivation. Choice illustrations confirm varieties of contact, contagion, and collusion. With respect to titles, excellent examples of transamerican sentiment are "Jovens rugas de Pound" (Young wrinkles of Pound), as well as the vigorous lyrics that Salomão named "Carta aberta a John Ashbery" (Open letter to JA) and "Um legado de Wallace Stevens" (A legacy of WS).[32] Stevens is a distinct stimulus who elsewhere provided musical impulses for an internal rubric (a sectional epigraph), two lines from "The Man with the Blue Guitar" that refer to alterations of current phenomena via the colorful instrument.[33] A passage of Ashbery's is used as an overall epigraph by Lopes for his collection *Solarium*, a word from the quotation itself. This Brazilian book—with twelve titles in English, including the trio "América #1," "América #2," and "América #3," and four poems composed in English—is ambassadorial. Lopes also uses the titles "Betty Blue" and, in an up-front "after" gesture, "Como se eu fosse Creeley" (As if I were Creely).[34] A philosophically oriented verse maker prefers an interdisciplinary epigraph: "Language is a virus from outer space. Listen to my heartbeat. / William Burroughs apud Laurie Anderson."[35] On a similar edge of things, a musically focused Corona opens his poem "Na margem de todas as coisas: uma canção" (On the margin of all things, a song)[36] with a quotation of the eminent author of "I Hear America Singing"—"I heard the hissing rustle of the liquid and sands as / directed to me whispering to congratulate me"—from the section "Calamus" of *Leaves of Grass*.

In an ode with a title that betrays its commemorative temporal angle, "1892–2002," a present-day Brazilian poet repeats commonplaces of admiration of the "Voz das vozes de toda a América" [voice of the voices of all the Americas] in advance of a concluding image of caressing rose petals as if they were the face of the admired one.[37] For his part, novelist João Gilberto Noll perceives in a poet of the nineties generation a personality that can be updated: "at times, he resembles, say, Whitman, in the sacrifice of rarefaction, as if the North American had lost, in the streets of the labored breathing of this our century, his nearly glandular rhetorical nobility, only to come up against the fulminating estrangement of the affects of the present."[38] The subject resembling is Italo Moriconi, who is somewhat explicit in his "Poeta em Nova Iorque" as he first utters "Debruçado sobre tanta água / Uma estátua lá, ao longe" (41) [Leaning over so much water / A statue there in the distance] and proceeds to:

> Dizer os nomes, como fontes.
> A mão de Whitman suave
> Sobre meu ombro
> Brisa leve
> Alma descompassada
> Cidade viril
> Nem sei o que mais amo—tua biografia teus poemas
> Calamus . . .

[To say the names, like founts. / The soft hand of Whitman / on my shoulder / light breeze / out-of-step soul / virile city / I don't even know what I love more—your biography your poems / Calamus . . .]

This worldly lyric borrows its title, of course, from the landmark collection of (murdered homosexual) Spanish poet Federico García Lorca, *Poeta en Nueva York*, a transnational referent of some impact in Brazil as well. The last word in the quoted poem, Calamus, names a rich natural image (botanical symbol of mingling, writing instruments) and one of the most discussed sections of *Leaves of Grass*. This personal Brazilian poetic experience in New York is very corporeal, sensual, and sexualized. There is an evident desire for insertion into a gay context in league with literary recognition.

One of the most developed bodies of text with territorial contours in contemporary Brazilian lyric is the New York or Manhattan experience. The cosmopolis becomes an almost obligatory spatial presence, like Paris in years gone, and confronting the urban site of sites is a sort of rite of passage for ambitious poets. Each author adds an individual angle—poetic, personal, national, generational—to an ever-in-progress anthology. Looking back as far back as 1970, Silviano Santiago offered a homage cum critique of the iconic central city in "MAN" via fragmentation à la E. E. Cummings, such as *man-hat-tan* and elaborations, multicultural diversity, and a thematic constant, the island-ness of the borough.[39] Pertinent works may express both local identification and transnational emotion, notably the entirety of the lyrical epic by Adriano Espínola, *Táxi, ou Poema de amor passageiro* (*Taxi, or Poem of Love in Transit*), which opens with a quote of T.

S. Eliot that partially inspired the title and draws out scenes in New York. The poet, moreover, has specifically indicated *Poeta en Nueva York* as his "personal classic."[40]

Historically aware Brazilian authors, as seen repeatedly, take to insularity. Of the sixteen lines of Caiafa's "Nova York esta ilha" (New York this isle), those that most suggest a different cultural angle are "Esta ilha soa / ouvi-la a milhas" [this isle sounds / hear it miles away]. She also penned "Na Barca de Staten Island" (On the Staten Island ferry), where she is reminded of colossal aquatic junctions in the Amazon River and sees the waters around New York as "a mistura a relança aos ares / linha acima, skyline / retoma como ilha a cidade" [the mixture launches it anew to the skies / a line up top, skyline / retakes as island the city].[41] Perceiving a similar North-South image, Nicholas Brown explains the effectual copresentation of Amerindian and cosmopolitan sensibilities in the words of "Manhatã" (1999) by Caetano Veloso, in which the songwriter discovers (via a line by Sousândrade; see chapter 4) the poetic possibilities of enunciating the name Manhattan, originally Native American, as if it were a Tupi name.[42] A legendary goddess in a canoe and the island city of barons of finance coexist in melodious verse that implies multiple historical categories.

The New York component, or Manhattan motif, in current Brazilian lyric can be read within an encompassing USAmerican topos. The most distinguished section would be "american impromptu" by Haroldo de Campos in his award-winning *Crisantempo*, which includes such titles as "Renga em New York," "Manhattan's buildings" (with a remembrance of Pound), and "Taxi driver." Another poet's appurtenant set is the trio "Some American Woodcuts" with a multipart lyrical narrative of demystification, "Renata em Nova York."[43] The metropolitan group is joined in the new millennium by André Gardel, whose unabashedly discursive sequence is overtly concerned with the accessibility of language and with multiculturalism vis-à-vis the very idea of "América" as USA. Joca Wolff playfully tries everything from pseudoconcrete, readymades, and graffiti to Spanish-language tirades and imitations of ghetto-speak. Via Lorca, his title *Pateta em Nova Yorque* parodies the author himself (pathetic, silly one, moron, Disney's Goofy). Before this series of more recent examples, the venerable scholar of experimental Lusophone lyric E. M. de Melo e Castro acknowledged the long-standing interest of Brazilian poets in New York but, underscoring an ongoing emphasis on linguistic materiality, speculated that technology was throwing all expectations about writing out of whack, including the previously sure point of North America's metropolis as a sort of artistic mecca. In this light can be heard the odd English original "Before the Dream"— "I'm followed by four geese / whenever I say paradise. // I've never seen Manhattan; / thus, I learned how to fly"—which, riffing on the mythemes of Eden and Big Apple travel, suggests new modes of advancement.[44]

The first internationally puissant author from the United States of America in the nineteenth century was Edgar Allan Poe. Perhaps no other countryman has elicited more varied response in Brazil. The first of several Portuguese translations of "The Raven" was done by the doyen of Brazilian fiction Machado de Assis. Related reception of Poe and interest in his essays, short stories, and poems has been considerable.[45] In North America, specialists have proposed viewing the topic "Poe and Translation," which they define as "transference of . . . a form of energy, from one point to another," "removal from earth to heaven," and "turning from one language/medium to another (OED)."[46] Criticism, national and international alike, should indeed take note of Brazilian implementations of Poe in original verse and visual poetry, where there may occur energetic translocation, celestial conveyance, and generic interrelations. For instance, with the facing-page title "Nunca mais" (Nevermore) in 72-point font, a veteran experimenter writes: "Uma corva / meio à Allan Poe / pôs seus ovos de ferro / neste amor" [A lady raven / half à la EAP / laid her iron eggs / in this love].[47] Abiding admiration for a beacon composition is expressed in Minas Gerais and related to self in "O corvo nunca morre" (The raven never dies): "e só um pássaro, / O CORVO, / segue os meus passos" [and only one bird / THE RAVEN / follows my steps].[48] Following a discursive all-caps quasi-concrete poem in English about Eve and the serpent, another poet of that state pays this allusive and elusive homage, "POE": "game is over / same score / our name out of seven / never more."[49] A third *mineira*, operating in the mode of late sixties *poema-processo*, mixes the visual atmosphere of superhero comics, especially sound effects, and the nominal plane of song and poetry, ballooning and emphasizing exclamations of PIAF-POUND-POE.[50] A pertinent intersemiotic creation is a musical setting of "Minha vida sem saída em Edgar Allan Poe" (My life with no exit in EAP), a visual poem with different font sizes, spread over two pages in the fashion of Mallarmé's *Un coup de dés*, linking antinormative behavior in different centuries: "curvo o corpo / eu corvo / canto / meu vazio / hardcore / eu corvo / maldito / n e v e r m o r e" [I bend my body / I raven / sing / my void / hardcore / I raven / damned / . . .].[51] Other such examples span decades and

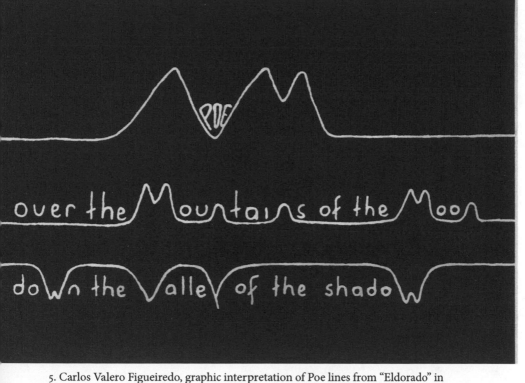

5. Carlos Valero Figueiredo, graphic interpretation of Poe lines from "Eldorado" in *Almanak 80*, São Paulo, 1980. Used by permission of Beto Borges, publisher.

locales. *Código*, a leading post-*Invenção* experimental arts journal in Salvador, featured a visual poem consisting of text scratched upon an old print portrait of Poe.[52] In 1980 *Almanak* in São Paulo featured a whole section on Poe including a translation of "Alone" and a visual rendering (figure 5), in white handwriting simulating topographical accidents on a black plane, of "Over the mountains of the moon, down the valley of the shadow," from "Eldorado" (1849). From academic study to experimental arts, in sum, Poe shines as an object of transtemporal and transamerican respect.

An especially elegant graphic merger of textual and structural interchange consists of a line from "Alone" used as a readymade reset in a vertical decompositional mode characteristic of a leading USAmerican innovator. The very top-to-bottom layout of this "Poe via cummings" is the key to all, as the interconnection of the six stacked words—**all I lov'd I lov'd alone**—is a descending column of vertical strokes: four lowercase l's and two I's.[53] Torres Filho followed the allusive visual lead with a translation into Portuguese (1993) of his own "Cumming's out (a 'stubble' poem)" (1981),[54] a work in original English that lends itself to rich transamerican readings:

> She was afraid to come out and so
> afraid to come out she said I'm not
> coming out any more
> So I looked at her uncoming out
> once more
> and there were stubbles in my
> voice as I said
>
> —Step out of that mirror
> sharply

Emily Dickinson is another nineteenth-century author appreciated anew in Brazilian environs as a North American poet who referred to Brazil, albeit obliquely, and as a stylist worthy of emulation. When she is alluded to, or something is dedicated to her, it is because *she* noticed Brazil. She wrote: "The Mighty Merchant sneered— / Brazil? . . . is there nothing else— / That we can show— Today?" (#621, circa 1862) and "A Moth the hue of this / Haunts Candles in Brazil" (#841, circa 1864). Manuel Bandeira had taken an interest in Dickinson's work before Augusto de Campos made sensitive renderings of her verse in the 1970s.[55] Sebastião Uchoa Leite poeticized her lyric likeness in his own lean way in "Duas ou três coisas" (Two or three things): "É ríspida / Respira o ar amargo / Arisca / Secreta / Nada fala / Xiita do oculto / Tal Emily Dickinson / Dura e pura / Ou insónia crítica / Da língua irônica" [(She) is gruff / breathes the bitter air / aloof / secretive / saying nothing / Shiite of the occult / like Emily Dickinson / hard and pure / or critical insomnia / of the ironical language].[56] Playing with a stereotype about masculine gaze and Brazilian preferences, another contemporary poet has quite another idea about an admirable creative process and an underappreciated lyric figure: "penso a bunda, sim, a bunda branca de / emily dickinson" [I think the buns, yes, the white buns of / ED].[57] Caiafa wrote a sequence of nine poems dedicated to Dickinson with an epigraph from her—"Tell all the Truth but tell it slant— / Success in Circuit lies / Too bright for our infirm Delight / The Truth's superb surprise"—that leads into the first, most powerful, poem (*Ouro*, 33):

O demônio tem seus delegados
Algoz ou criado—*errand boy*
Polpuda folha, proventos
Constante recrutamento

Labor é uma lida
Algo a se fazer
Não hesita, convoca
Flexibiliza—no *paper work*.

The devil has his delegates / hangman or servant—*errand boy* / pulpy leaf, pension / constant recruitment // labor is strife / something to do / don't hesitate, convoke / be flexible—in (the) *paperwork*

Expatriate Gertrude Stein has also elicited variegated poetic responses in Brazil. Guimarães (9) quotes her at length in the epigraph to what he calls "Inscriptions." Over her most celebrated phrase "a rose is a rose is a rose," Affonso Ávila composed an architecturally humorous concrete pastiche with the elements "a rose / is a / rise / ruin."[58] In one of the most celebrated debut books of the nineties, Carlito Azevedo included a Steinesque play on US critic Robert Greer Cohn's phallic interpretation of Mallarmé's "Les mots anglais": "a pen / is a pen is a pen."[59] Multimedia artist Antunes pays homage, directly and indirectly, in a series of pieces. "Act so that there is no use in a centre" (*Tender Buttons*) is the epigraph placed by Marjorie Perloff at the head of her chapter on Gertrude Stein in *The Poetics of Indeterminacy*

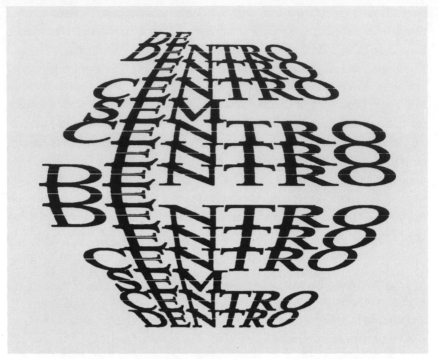

6. Arnaldo Antunes, "Dentro," concrete poem in *Nome*, 1993. Courtesy of the artist.

(67). Antunes himself "in-determinates" in the visual poem "Dentro" (figure 6) achieved on the Macintosh.[60] The rhyming words "de dentro entro centro sem centro" [from within I enter the center without center] create a phrasing that deterritorializes, making relative concepts of localization, participation, and above all valorization. "Center" implies a periphery, and their undoing, the postmodern and (sub)globalizing blurring of barriers. The audiovisual version of this composition—in which the inside is the throat of an enunciator—technologically corporifies the concept. Both the kinetic enactment and the print versions actualize a metaphor that places the Brazilian enunciation inside and outside conventional limits, a Stein-inspired noncenter, in effect. Antunes concocted a different tribute to the same artist with a graphonumerical nod to the zero degree of writing in Stein, a visual poem named "Gertrudiana" consisting of a full-page negative of a photo of roses with three quasi-anagrammatical variations of the phrase "a zero is" (figure 7). The figure of zero with which Antunes plays here dovetails with the round shape of a word image created by Augusto de

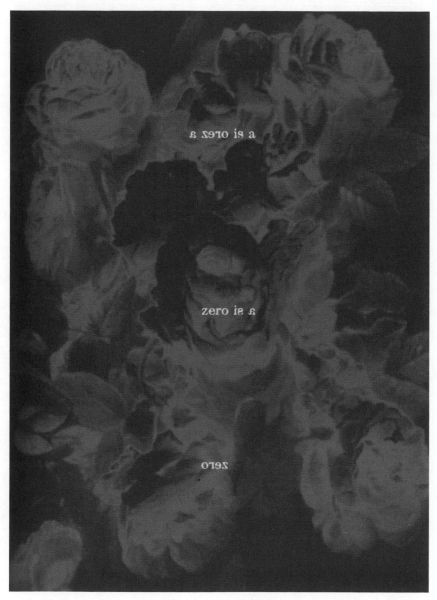

7. Arnaldo Antunes, "Gertrudiana," material poem in *Dois ou mais corpos no mesmo espaço*, 1997. Courtesy of the artist.

Campos, who had established the relevance of a visual reading of Gertrude Stein with a rendering of her most famous locution on a book cover: one, two, and three circular iterations of "a rose is" arranged concentrically.[61]

The instantaneous property of photography rings in "Steintâneos," a title-poem where the mythology surrounding Stein is used to construct a thoroughly modern metatext. Her double/triple declarative iteration, the copulative tautology of a cliché romantic symbol, antinormative ethos, and intertext itself, all conspire to aid in the underscoring of discovery and a factitious imperative: "Coisa alguma é coisa. Coisa é uma palavra. Faça-a." [No thing is a thing. Thing is a word. Make it.][62] The poem engages an ontology of maker: the poet is not just defined or determined by words used, she/he *is* the words she/he uses. Americans on different continents, again, marshal literary technologies toward ambitious ends of invention/inventiveness. Thus, an example of discursive homage such as the forty-four lines of "Após o espetáculo *Sylvia Plath* do teatro coreográfico de Heidelberg" (After the show *Sylvia Plath* at the choreographic theatre of Heidelberg) can become an integral identification. The construction makes Plath the speaker: "Meu nome era Sylvia Plath, / agora sou uma coreografia de seres improváveis / —e eu no centro" [My name was SP / now I am a choreography of improbable beings / —and I in the center].[63] Without avoiding the airs of suicide, the outsider manages to open an interdisciplinary artistic vortex.

The intertextuality generated by the work of William Carlos Williams (WCW) is truly exceptional. Whenever this prominent USAmerican modernist poet is mentioned in conjunction with Brazil, a necessary referent is Richard Morse's sage comparison with Oswald de Andrade.[64] The initial words of the WCW text therein, "The Red Wheelbarrow," serve as epigraph for Espínola—"So much depends / upon"—in a poem that understands the poeticity of objects on display: "As prateleiras" / "The Shelves."[65] The "dependent" point of departure is also used in a haiku-like piece by that implies intimate connection, "Sobre um poema de Williams" (On a poem by Williams): "tem tudo a ver / com umas folhas // saca? / dançando sobre a água / trêmula // admirada por almas / secas" [it has everything to do / with some leaves // you dig? / dancing on the water / tremulous // admired by dry / souls].[66] Such performative verses conform a paradigm along the lines of a "psychology of composition" with geo-aesthetic hemispheric content. Among all the examples of US-focused transamerican poetics in Brazil, a poem could scarcely articulate commonalities more explicitly, especially in conjunction with building, than this "Breve ontologia bilíngüe" (Brief bilingual ontology) in the tellingly titled *Xadrez via correspondência* (Chess by correspondence) (28–29) by Claudio Nunes de Morais:

Estar diante de William
C. Williams
concebido tal

qual uma natureza
comum
que é

inerente a todos
e a cada
um

Minha Jersey
lyric
avista

prédios numa estação
diante
de uma árvore

(*view of winter trees*
before
one tree)

vista de um prédio
em outro inverno
diante
de uma construção

em primeiro plano
onde
sob o neon

recente
9 pilhas de tijolos crus
aguardam
a chegada do cimento

[To stand before WCW conceived just // like a common nature that
is // inherent in all and in each one // My Jersey lyric views // buildings in a season (station) before a tree // . . . // view of a building in
another winter before a construction (site) // in the foreground where
beneath the recent // neon nine piles of raw bricks await the arrival
of cement]

Among the USAmerican modernists, WCW, with his Puerto Rican heritage,
was the poet most concerned with literature from a New World outlook.[67]
Moreover, the practice of quotation for him "contributes to an exploration
of the virtues of dehierarchization and relativism," so significant to a widening of artistic scope.[68] In the cited Brazilian example, Morais desires to
ride on the openness of WCW to others (common, all, each one) in order
to join philosophical forces. He makes a direct quotation to be followed by
a clever structural allusion that fills a pattern from one WCW poem with
elements from others. To see this, it is convenient to cite Williams's 1962
"Jersey Lyric" (2:408) whole.

view of winter trees
before
one tree

in the foreground
where
by fresh-fallen

snow
lie 6 woodchunks ready
for the fire

The "nature" of the Brazilian poem means human constitution but also
elicits botanical phenomena, and trees are among the most frequent objects
of WCW's seeing, a fitting example in this case being the similar "Winter
Trees" from 1921. In such poems, the irregular lines of free verse embody
the visual perception of bare branches. The semanteme of building is also
axial in "Breve ontologia bilíngüe," both the literal activity of constructing
an edifice for use by people and the meticulous making of a literary text, in
one language and another. The last seven lines of Morais's tribute reproduce
the syntax of the last six lines of "Jersey Lyric," but the lexical items change,

most having seemingly been patched together from other WCW poems, the model of piles or stacks of building materials (stone, metal strips, et cetera) from numerous poems of the 1930s, bricks from "The Poor" and "Classic Scene," neon from "The Attic Which Is Desire," the number nine from "Figuera's Castle" and, not coincidentally, the count of lines in "Jersey Lyric." The "bricks" function like building blocks of a verbal construct in progress awaiting the "cement," the stuff of poetic decision and fastening, in this situation the admired craft of WCW to which would aspire the author of, in effect, a metapoem about Williams. The work is done here in the spirit of WCW's characterization of the poem as "a little machine of words" and of his line "(No ideas / but in things) Invent!" from "A Sort of a Song." Morais enters into a dialogue, a common area, citing outright and rewriting, and ideally destabilizes any hierarchy of American letters in which the USA is automatically thought higher up.

Oswald de Andrade, Carlos Drummond de Andrade, and Manuel Bandeira instituted brands of Brazilian modernism that are national models that might find parallels in the imagist Americanness of a Williams or, to some degree, in the dense verse-making of a Stevens, but it would be problematic to posit any truly significant absorption of like qualities of USAmerican lyric in *poesia brasileira*.[69] However, the case of Beat Generation poetry is another story. The vanguards of Brazil and the United States in the 1950s were both influential while entirely different. *Poesia concreta* and Beat poetry each occupied a location "on the margins of the established literary system."[70] Yet their poetics moved in opposite directions: the former was wholly technophile and hardly discursive, whereas the latter was romantically rebellious, quite behavior-conscious, and effusive. Still, a penetrating transamerican comparison of Haroldo de Campos and Allen Ginsberg is able to find them "strikingly homologous, if not superficially similar: moving apart but in different directions from the gyres and vortices of modernism, they come to occupy distinctive but cognate positions."[71] In terms of attention, Beat poetry was a paragon countercurrent in North America with South American appeal and utility. If the impact of *concretismo* has been major for decades, Beat elements have been consequential in their own way.

Direct allusion to Beat authors guides an expression of a poetics of resistance in Ricardo Corona's "Tráfico de palavras" (Word traffic), which opens internationally:

estou com os novos *thoreaus*
piratas da *internet*

os poetas também engendram um rigoroso processo de
desobediência

and remember the old dogs
who fought so well
:
Bukowski, Hemingway,
Maiakóvski, Ginsberg, Leminski
. . . .
     a posição da poesia é oposição

[I'm with the new Thoreaus / Internet pirates // poets also engender
a rigorous process of / disobedience / . . . / the position of poetry is
opposition]

The poet aligns with a widely admired USAmerican tradition and quotes a
relatively well known antinormative writer of the USA to set up a conclusion taken from a fellow poet of southern Brazil of the current generation.[72]
For Salomão, exposure to other such approaches had opened up a "respi-
radouro," a vent or air shaft; Ginsberg and other US poets offered "a way to
free myself from Brazilian straitjackets."[73] He often played with his artistic
name, having used Wally Sailormoon and Waly Salut au Monde (Whitman's title), which are dialogical in themselves.[74] The author of *Howl* is
widely seen as having achieved necessary progress, as embodying a goal to
pursue. Following his passing, a Brazilian poem without title states the fact
of his death—"Morre Ginsberg"—and goes on to offer homage, to relate
synthetically what he did, and to express personal aspirations. The speaker's
last action is to kick the backyard fence, an energetic image of breaking
down barriers, of facilitating access.[75] Such a poem, one can say, performs
a transamerican act, physically and symbolically.

The apex in Brazilian poetry in the second half of the twentieth century
is João Cabral de Melo Neto (1920–1999), who flirted briefly with surrealism before 1950 and then affirmed himself as an antisentimentalist textual
architect, as a poet "of things."[76] Given this objective bias, it is no surprise
that he should most admire in USAmerican lyric, or in foreign poetry over-

all, the work of Marianne Moore, to whom he dedicates/composes several poems.[77] Whether via Cabral or any other avenue, younger poets navigate toward Moore. For example, Manoel Ricardo de Lima's "Os peixes" (51) is a sparse yet dense poem in eleven parts, taking the title from Moore's 1935 poem "The Fish" and an epigraph from its conclusion, beginning with the words "Repeated / evidence." Invocation of the admired poet of Brooklyn helps the Brazilian poet to link vivid fluid maritime imagery and a necessarily urban conclusion: "Os peixes / incorporam / a rua" [The fish / incorporate / the street].

In contemplating what makes poetry in different latitudes of the Americas alike, Paul Hoover notes that "Americans are thought to smile a lot. They are 'informal,' 'open,' 'innovative,' and 'fair-minded.' . . . Poetry has a way of considering even more puzzling things, like a rock sinking in water or the human shape of a pair of scissors." The latter suggestion finds absorbing vocalization in "MM" by Armando Freitas Filho (540–41). Attraction toward the often object-inspired Marianne Moore heads the somewhat surprising explanatory addendum to an incisive and multifarious lyric born from her initials:

> De tesoura tem os olhos
> que os dedos furam
> pois prefere o abre-e-fecha
> de lâmina das suas asas
> recortando-se ao recortar
> meio às cegas, e colando
> linhas e planos-seqüência
> de outras vozes, reunindo
> no improviso, (cf. Matisse
> *Jazz*, 1947) diversos e dispersos
> matizes: ímpares, díspares, hiatos
> o às vezes eterno, embora sopre o vento
> o que já foi dito, o por dizer
> e tudo mais que atraia o estilo MM.*
> *Aqui, mais da poeta do que da pin-up, ambas insinuantes e sinuosas.
>
> Of scissors she has the eyes
> that fingers pierce, for she
> prefers the sparrow flapping

of blades of her wings
cutting a figure on cutting out
half blindly, and pasting
lines and sequence shots
of other voices, joining
in improvisation, (cf. Matisse
Jazz, 1947) diverse and disperse
hue-shades: odd, disparate, hiatuses
the sometimes eternal, though winds may blow
what's been said, what's yet to be said
and all else that may attract the style of MM.*
*Here, more the poet than the pin-up, both insinuative and sinuous.

Though the feminine option has been preferred in the translation, the subject of the original is not actually stated, and since the final reference is to attracting the style of MM, she herself (poet or entertainment figure) should not simply be assumed to be the active agent, which, it would make sense to surmise, operates as a sort of embodied polymorphous artistic consciousness. Visual arts are projected in multiple ways, as color, line, shape, image, painting, collage, film. The interarts thrust includes the tactile, kinetic angles, synaesthesia, and a lone allusion to a European artist whose own title names a quintessential American contribution noted for sophisticated variations on theme or melody. Sound and sight in these lines inexorably invoke writing. *Jazz* was a series of cutout collages, scenes with a handwritten text of three to five pages for each image. Matisse understood jazz in terms of "chromatic and rhythmic improvisation" as well as "rhythm and meaning," order and repetition broken by the unexpected action of impromptu making.[78] This very modern act of *poeisis* is hardly spontaneous, but it proves to be thoroughly intertextual and transamerican. The curvaceous and ingratiating contours of the USAmerican modernist poet are highlighted but, given the coincidence of initials and impact, the allusion to a cutting-edge figure of a different type, the first great blonde icon of the post-WWII epoch, is inescapable.

"MM" mixes letters, pop culture, plastic arts, film, and music in one text and serves as a more than appropriate bridge to the next chapter here, which is concerned with poetry and the others arts. To close this literarily focused chapter, an affirmation by the accomplished translator of Wallace Stevens and Elizabeth Bishop.[79] Paulo Henriques Britto's confabulation with Anglophone letters encompasses both more conventional literary legacies and sixties counterculture. The shared intimacy of language is nowhere more evident than in his original English poems, as in this farewell lyric "Poema-posfácio," in a timeless mode appropriate for transamerican considerations:

> The last pages are never the best pages;
> They let nothing else be seen.
> They've failed the hope of being what
> No page could ever hope to be.
> The last pages are never the worst pages.
> At least one lie they've left untold:
> They never promised after them
> Would come a single truthful word.

This afterword is a paradoxical opening onto a horizon that extends into an ecumenical future. "Lies about the Truth" proves to be quite a well-suited name for a selection of modern Brazilian lyric prepared by a USAmerican journal.[80]

3

◇

Inter Arts Inter Alia

Film, Popular Music, and Media Lore
in the Poetic Imagination

Consumidos ídolos

. . . .

         embotamento   lua alta em gotham city

         global/ocular   tiro perdido no escuro

         senso/senhorial   a noite abrindo o zíper

            sensorial

. . . .

Consumidos

        idos

. . . .

As shown in the preceding chapter, in the late twentieth century and the early twenty-first, the scope, purvey, domain, and operational space of Brazilian poetry tended toward an expansion that increasingly considered—fraternally, critically, fruitfully—the language and literature of the United States. The lines of separation of different arts and artists appearing in lyric are not always so clear cut, as poets may ponder writers and print texts, alone or together, alongside actors, filmmakers, cinema, musical repertories, songwriters, and/or other figures of popular diversion conventionally dismissed as low or mass culture. There is much creative content and conduct in the contemporary poetry of Brazil having to do with, partially or in whole, expressive culture and media other than literature. Outreach as an antidote to insularity in lyric has had diverse manifestations, as some find near comfort with what one might call a conjunctive America-scape (with literature and other arts), while some hurl acerbic criticism. Such a dimension of interface is apparent in poetic texts in their integration of a series of mythemes, semantemes, lexemes, and real or implied graphemes related to comics, (post)modern art, and tourism, as well as, especially, cinema and popular music. Superheroes from midcentury graphic illustrations manifest throughout the decades in evolving ways. While such USAmerican plastic artists as Warhol, Lichtenstein, Sherman, Hopper, and Basquiat have been the objects of dedications and poems alike in Brazil, these will not be examined here.[1] Movies, cinematic figures, jazz, blues, rock music, and their players have been much more prominent and will be the focus of the present chapter. They may appear in any number of guises and roles, as artistic stimulants, as figurations of aesthetic affinities, as powerful vehicles of imported culture to be reckoned with, as metaphorical modes of distraction, as explicators in existential or societal situations imagined textually.

In the late 1970s, Silviano Santiago published an intriguing poetic sequence that sets the stage, as it were, for subsequent lyrical response to increased USAmerican presence in Brazil: *Crescendo durante a guerra numa província ultramarina* (Growing up during the war in an overseas province).[2] The thematically coherent volume concerns childhood and adult perspectives on the 1940s, utilizing varied stylistics, from pared-down pastiche à la Oswald de Andrade and the ironic containment of other *modernistas* to the pictographic gestures of postconcrete experimentalism (see figure 8) and the colloquialism of youth verse of the seventies. Punctuating the set of poems with English while drawing on comic books and political commentary alike, the poet-critic is able "to articulate fragments of the memory that announce a new path for the difficult history of ideologies in Brazil."[3] Indeed, the initial scene, "O rei dos espiões" (The king of the spies), recalls imported fantasy heroes and their impact on the sense of knowing: "Ninguém sabe o que se passa / por detrás dessa máscara de Batman, / por detrás dessa fantasia de Super-Homem. // Só o Sombra sabe" (16) [No one knows what goes on / behind the mask of Batman / behind the costume of Superman. // Only the Shadow knows]. This configuration affects not only youth but those who fight the World War, as in "1940": "Os manuais de instrução / do exército americano / são escritos / usando recursos / dos comic books" (38) [The instruction manuals / of the American army / are written / using resources / of comic books]. This type of bland matter-of-fact verification as poetry—likely modeled on Oswald's cut-and-paste citations of early colonial historical documents and fortified in the reading of, say, William Carlos Williams—is itself subject to self-irony, as in the readymade borrowing of "Carapuça" (Hood):[4] "Mr. Read's verse / belongs more to the history / of sensibility between the two wars / than / it does to the history of poetry. / R.P. Blackmur" (107). While the acoustic dimension of big-band music on the radio is the sequence's parting image, one of the most powerful combines suggestive names and products in a quasi-religious moment, "Comunhão" (Communion): "Em 1948 ingeria finalmente / nas Lojas Americanas / a Coca-cola da tela: / era negra e amarga. / Puseram sorvete branco dentro / e virou vaca preta" (88) [In 1948 I finally ingested / at the American Stores / the Coca-Cola of the screen: / it was black and bitter. / They put white ice cream in it / and it turned into a Coke float (black cow)]. The movies, source of this mediated libational excitement decades ago, prove to be much more poetically relevant in national and international terms.

Film is a particularly important medium to consider, since it is the focus of much anxiety and fretting about the deleterious effects of cultural globalization, Westernization, or Americanization. Fredric Jameson considers movies to be the main vehicle of cultural imperialism, purportedly destructive of traditions, and of the notorious American way of life: "alongside the free market as an ideology, the consumption of the Hollywood film form is the apprenticeship to a specific culture, to an everyday life as a cultural practice: a practice of which commodified narratives are the aesthetic expression, so that the populations in question learn both at the same time. Hollywood is not merely a name for a business that makes money but also for a fundamental late-capitalist cultural revolution, in which old ways of life are broken up and new ones set in place" (63). No one can doubt the power of film as engaging spectacle and of film industries as business, yet there are complicated overarching values and problems in the position that Jameson and other take as it applies to different places at different times. In the realm of lyric, related reaction and interpretation may incorporate political proclivity, reflect on the beauty and potency of film, forge ironic views of outsiders, or make any number of imaginative interventions.

Since before 1920, cinema has fascinated and inspired poets in the United States, who have responded to what Vachel Lindsay called "today's divine surprise" (1917), the medium itself, actors, directors, and spectatorship. Debates about the relative social and artistic merits or drawbacks of movies began early on and do not abate.[5] Whether in the Roaring Twenties or the tumultuous sixties, movies can be seen to function, on one extreme, as alienating, mass culture that cheapens literature, or, in contrast, as a socially useful and rewarding practice that merits the appellation "the seventh art." Goldstein observes further: "The ascendance of film in the hier-

8. Rogério Luz, graphic illustrations in *Crescendo durante a guerra numa província ultramarina* by Silviano Santiago, 1978. Used by permission of the artist.

archy of the arts prompted not only misgivings and jealousies but guarded
meditations by poets on the deep nature and profound consequences of
the popular newcomer in their midst" (8). As cinema evolved, the variety
of poetic responses followed suit, coming to constitute a sort of (topically
defined) genre and never succumbing to the superficial, market-driven side
of silver-screen life. From the point of view of letters, it is worthwhile to
underscore that "[m]ovie poems are *not* a form of popular culture, but bat-
teries of formal resistance to the fantasy bribes offered by the well-financed
manipulators of desire" (15). The issues that concern social critics of movies
or spur poetic interest are amplified, of course, when First World production is considered in Third World contexts of consumption, not automatically in negative ways.

Turning back to older terminology, one of the most New World phrases
in Oswald de Andrade's "Manifesto antropófago" ("The Cannibalist Manifesto," 1928) is the culmination of article seven: "O cinema americano informará" [The cinema of (the) America(s) will inform]. This line can refer, in a more liberating spirit, to the whole hemisphere or simply to the
USA, where filmmaking was already in full swing as an export industry
in the 1920s. Given the attention Oswald has commanded in Brazil since
the 1960s, it is useful to consider his quick yet significant nod to film, the
ever-strengthening novelty being produced primarily in Hollywood but
also in other countries of the hemisphere.[6] One of the principal organs
of early Brazilian modernism had made a point of highlighting the form:
"A cinematographia é a criação artistica mais representativa de nossa ep-
oca. É preciso observar-lhe a lição" [Cinematography is the most representative artistic creation of our epoch. One ought pay attention to the les-
son].[7] As for Oswald, Silviano Santiago affirmed that he could extrapolate
onto action, that the poet-provocateur had understood the "possibilities
of revolutionary human behavior" in film.[8] If this observation broaches
the wide potential of the seventh art, the pregnant line in the manifesto
has scarcely been parsed in adequate fashion by Oswaldian critics, be they
literary, cinematic, or cultural. Among other things, it merits emphasizing
that the ambivalence of the word *americano* works in concert with other
Anglophone iterations in the manifesto to relativize North-South and Old
World–New World sociolinguistic relations, not to mention narrow notions of nationalism. Article thirteen reads "A idade de ouro anunciada pela
America. A idade de ouro. E todas as girls" [The golden age proclaimed by
(the) America(s). . . . And all the girls]. Here, legends of El Dorado, lore of

gold rushes, and dreams of modern technologically-enabled capitalism all resonate. The reference to *girls* is surely show-business related, and would suggest the imbrication of entertainment personae and humor in the author's version of matriarchal cultural assertiveness that devours European heritage while remaining open to what other American locations (such as the USA) might be able to contribute (such as cinema).[9]

In philological retrospect, one might also scrutinize the seven continuous occurrences of the word *roteiros* in the manifesto. Meaning routes, itineraries, guidebooks, *roteiros* is usually taken in relation to navigation. One translator notes, germane to the present transamerican thrust, that the word "can also signify ships' logbooks or pilots' directions. Oswald can thus be construed here as referring to a rediscovery of America" (Bary, 46). Curiously, the most modern meaning of *roteiro*—only since the 1950s—is "script" or "screenplay," as one of the several recent translators actually renders the word, a mistake that may prove to be salvageable as a suggestion of Oswald's prescience with respect to the growth of film and as an extended (exported) instance of "contribuição milionária de todos os erros" [millionaire contribution of all errors], to borrow a phrase from the poet's first manifesto.[10] These various interconnected phenomena operate within a numerological, discursive, and structural logic in Oswald's most widely discussed document in a way that complements its interarts thrust.

In the final decades of the twentieth century, the sweeping influence of the seventh art increasingly figured as a rhetorical device or theme in lyric in Brazil. José Roberto Aguilar offers an advantageous jumping-off point to consider that assortment, as he does multi-mixed-media performance. His *Hércules pastiche* unfolds in five parallel parts: a brief tale, a novella based on the mythological hero, color plates of paintings, song lyrics, and page poetry. Free-form humor abounds throughout this cosmopolitan mélange where classical art meets graffiti and pondered poetry may become imbued with near total informality, in Portuguese or English. The first poem, largely about destiny, ends: "entrar no cinema / HOLLYWOOD me espera, / y la chica?" [to go into the cinema / HOLLYWOOD awaits me, / and the chick?].[11] The site of movies is associated with fate, opportunity, and interrelations; it is a full frame of reference, moving across territories (is there a Spanish-speaking maiden afoot?) and genres.

Cinematic engagements in contemporary poetic output range from titular usage and remembrances of famous personages to direct or indirect connections between artistic forms. The visuality of cinematography in its core meaning concerns Arnaldo Antunes, who thinks and views film at every turn, framing this parentage:[12]

o

olho

(fêmea)

olha

o

(

filho

)

filme.

[the eye / (female) / eyes / the / (son) / film.]

For his part, Ricardo Corona forges no less a title than *Cinemaginário*, signifying that lyric discourse of imagination draws on the cinematic, and that a sequence of poems may be filmlike in its exposition of images and of what is imagined.[13] Flávio Viegas Amoreira is a delirious postmodern writer who draws on any and all sources and whose diffuse consciousness produces thick word-image flows of marked cultural phenomena, some of which float to the top for greater exposure or proposal. Seemingly addressing an imaginary interlocutor in "O rosto de Montgomery Clift" (The face of MC), his artful speaker claims: "deviam qualquer poesia / verso em pêlo / chamar atenção / olhos pueris / Fausto / hollywoodiano, / gosto musical / abraços" [they ought to any poetry / stark naked verse / call attention / puerile eyes / Hollywoodian / Faust, / musical taste / regards].[14] Song is so often what impresses in a movie or marks a character, as in "As Time Goes By," where the speaker appeals to his amorous partner to call him Humphrey Bogart as an aphrodisiac.[15] Vocal music is also the way to closure in the whimsical development of "O amor, a literatura, e o cinema" (Love, literature, and cinema). Poet Bluma W. Vilar is clearly preoccupied with the visual and the cinematic; her collection is called *Álbum,* as in a photograph binder, and the table of contents includes such entries as "Mademoiselle Cinéma," "O sonho de Spielberg" (Spielberg's Dream), and "Drive-in" (indeed about the outdoor movie theatre). Her cited tripartite poem takes the wondering reader from Dante, Petrarch, French romantics, and the *lovesong* of Ted Hughes–Sylvia Plath to Tarzan and Jane and to Juliet singing in closing a line from a well-known Cole Porter tune: "Romeo, let's face the fact, my dear!"[16] The humorous play with the Petrarchan tradition and the high Western heritage of literature alongside a "barbarous" epoch-making celluloid *innamoramento* leads to a summation in the dominant lyric form of the American century, song. What impends at each reading (audition) is that the site of this mixed spectacle, the crossing of genres and centuries via USAmerican entertainment, is an urban cosmopolitan Brazilian setting.

European / North American perceptions of Brazil, notably as revealed in film, present a series of entanglements. A stark instance of congruous poetization, of both the international impact of film and the circulation of tropical stereotypes, is a readymade (followed by gloss) presented by Salomão:[17]

Samba
Sugar loaf
Jungle
Piranha

"Ideograma" Brazil desentranhado do filme
Crown, o magnífico (*The Thomas Crown Affair*),
USA 1968, dirigido por Norman Jewison
Falado por Steve McQueen

Familiarity with the source may add to the effect (with just these five words an upper-class thief explains to his heroine that Rio is the destination he will flee to), yet on its own the poster-poem communicates the essential matter of filmic origins and foreign impressions of the country. With two lively Brazilian words that entered English dictionaries, the minimal text achieves display of stereotypical verbal items qua veritable postcard images, crossing linguistic and mental borders.

This five-word text (not counting the gloss) is the ultimate example of what was termed English keyword in the previous chapter. Another pertinent case—for its punning with English words and its calling attention to real and cinematic violence—is Salgado Maranhão's "Moviemento"

(*Palávora*, 71) in which movement comprises changing urban landscapes, screen action, organization of weaponry, and spectatorship. The last lines remonstrate wryly:

> manhãs AR-15
> tardes AK-47
> delinqüem entre ratos
> e toletes totens.
>
> a cidade em seu afã
> a comer *hot-dogmas*
> e balas de mortelã.
>
> [mornings AR-15 / afternoons AK-47 / transgress among rats / and totem spears // the city in its bustle / eating hotdogmas / and pieces (bullets) of death-mint]

The effectiveness of the text resides in the contrast of a tough active reality (gunfire in the shantytowns of Rio de Janeiro was already notorious in the 1990s) and the eagerness to engage in passive reception of celluloid dramas and, by implication, fashionable explanations of social phenomena and establishment ideology, incarnated in frankfurters to be consumed at the theatre. The other items being eaten are, with the flip of a consonant, twisted into mortifying or mortiferous vehicles: pieces of hard mint candy (*balas de hortelã*) become bullets of death-mint (*balas de mortelã*). The abuse of *hotdog* fortifies the allusion to the international marketplace of automatic rifles.

As for actual "movie poems" and the language of Hollywood, it should not come as a surprise that Brazil has produced its share of the genre in English as well. While framing her collection with an overall epigraph from Deleuze about writing, encounter, and deterritorialization, Janice Caiafa beholds iconic figures of the silver screen in "The Empress":[18]

> Marlene was playing Garbo
> in one of her films.
> Unwilling, absolute,
> the two invincible lilies
> interchange: visibly
> images of divinity

black velvet
and Spiders.

Set decades later, "Duas línguas" (Two tongues) by Francisco Bosco casts a
reader-speaker who views a violent film that provokes discussion of levels
of language per se: "O leitor revê um filme / de David Lynch, 'Wild at Heart.'
// Logo na primeira cena, / quebra-se um crânio" [The reader sees again a
film / by DL . . . / Right away in the first scene, / a skull is busted]. The liberty to portray so much gore provokes a "pensamento-legenda" or subtitle-
thought: "(. . . Lynch recicla o cafona, / torna-o metalinguagem . . .)" [Lynch
recycles the tacky, / he turns it into metalanguage].[19] There is a constant
transit, the lyric voice goes on to ponder, not just between languages (Portuguese and English, one assumes) but between one being spoken and one
offering a critique of the other (natural language and metalanguage). Ironic
contrast—singing "Love Me Tender" during gunfire—and an open-ended
last line, "e o filme não acaba" [the film does not end], suggest the continuity between life and fiction in which this linguistic contemplation occurs.
Also using the title of the famous ballad by the worldwide icon, local poet
Fábio Weintraub pens "Love Me Tender" to wonder about interment and
odd facts about the USA, concluding: "7% dos americanos acreditam / que
Elvis Presley está vivo // Escovas de dente azuis / são mais usadas que as
vermelhas" ["7% of Americans believe / that Elvis Presley is alive // Blue
toothbrushes / are more widely used than red ones].[20]

No Brazilian poet of the last quarter century incorporates art-world and
cinematic references more pointedly than Sebastião Uchoa Leite. By way of
example, one can look to "Questões de Método" (Questions of method), in
which, it has been proposed, "the disarticulated images of social and political history as reported in the mass-media world of global capitalism have
become indistinguishable from the imaginary universe of popular mythology or cinema."[21] In terms of the hemisphere, references to El Salvador,
Tordesillas, and the State Department are harsh. Yet the finale queries most
strongly the relative potency of narratives of the moving image: "o que é
mais real: a leitura do jornal / ou as aventuras de indiana jones? / o monó-
logo do pentágono ou / orson welles atirando contra os espelhos?" [what
is more real: reading the newspaper / or the adventures of Indiana Jones? /
the monologue of the Pentagon or / Orson Welles shooting at mirrors?].[22]
This maker of questions puts himself, or his fictive poetic selves, squarely

within the bounds of entertainment media, film and popular music alike. In *A ficção vida* (The fiction life) Leite encapsulates a title "P/B" (for *preto e branco*, black-and-white) and commences (57): "Be bop & films noirs / Um gangster ri [laughs]." From such sources, the poet developed, over the course of two decades, flashes and clipped portraits of outlaws, criminality, and urban danger zones.

In Flora Süssekind's examination of cultural discourse in Brazil related to an urban existence of growing violence, instability, and segregation, Leite's turn-of-the-millennium lyric is a hub. She believes there are some "defiguration and deterritorialization processes in Brazilian contemporary poetry, which function as critical interlocutors" of that experience.[23] Leite's poems are seen to be changing the configuration of life in the city (Rio de Janeiro), both subject positions and literal locations in space, especially when the texts relay the writer's command of police-blotter and crime-page story lines. He produces "a transitional zone between inside and outside, interior-exterior, poet and landscape" in order to "reduce hierarchic distances of observation between subject and urban matter." Quite unlike (pseudo-)documentary fiction, he does not catalogue urban types— homeless, hopeless, thieves—and does not hesitate to invert the roles of observer and observed. This "constant possibility of crossing identity, social and spatial boundaries" can have a palpable reader response, to wit, intensification of an uneasiness when exposed to "liminal, ambiguous, discontinuous zones," which may include routine routes, quotidian environments, well-known tourist spots. Such writing comprises "a movement towards destabilization and deterritorialization," not just in relation to "the emergence of new urban practices . . . the intensification of the asymmetric segregation of social space . . . violence and daily uncivil acts, the inventory of Brazilian urban experience," but also with respect to the constitution of discourse itself. Such experience becomes "a fundamental element of structural indeterminacy and negativity, of a difficult process of literary formalization which, in Sebastião Uchoa Leite's work, takes advantage of the cliches of criminalization." The application of deterritorialization here is idiosyncratic and ultimately text-focused. Yet just as Leite slings insights of underworld or *bas-fonds* film, largely populated by armed USAmericans, he indeed can upset received wisdom about urban landscape, zones, mappings, inhabitants. His disruptions can be localized or expanded to include transamerican relations, of recognition and critique alike.

In the same manner that Leite manipulates the impact and pervasiveness of film to probing ends, he, some of his contemporaries, and many younger voices stage jazz, poeticizing and exploiting music and musicians to contemporary advantage. Especially in the nineties, a series of poets in Rio de Janeiro, São Paulo, and other urban centers used jazz figures and materials to forge varied lyrical texts. Besides simple thematizations or homages, this ecumenical practice offers modes to elaborate personal *ars poetica*, emotive channels, self-contemplations, intellectual exercises, geocultural localizations, and ethnosocial criticism. These late-century phenomena are better understood against an inter-American historical backdrop. In the 1920s, 1930s, and 1940s, some poets in the United States, above all such African Americans as Langston Hughes, celebrated early jazz, its roots in the blues, the swing generation, and certain standout musicians. Once jazz evolved in the 1940s to the state of bebop, with its melodic, harmonic, rhythmic, and compositional complexities, it began to make more sense to call jazz "America's classical music," a phrase employed to recognize both the unique character of the artistic form and its technical and conceptual level. Critics and aficionados in Europe, and some in Latin America, expressed strong admiration for this North American aesthetic achievement.

In the nineteen-fifties, Allen Ginsberg and other USAmerican poets allied with cutting-edge jazz (post-swing, bebop forward) in a desire to incorporate its beats, rhythms, sensuality, improvisation, and overall liberty. There emerged a manifestation of lyric called "jazz poetry," most often thought of as oralization of texts to the accompaniment of improvisational music, primarily in the Beat Generation itself. Yet this topical (sub)genre has also come to include "thematizations," poems about jazz, players, or personal response to music making. Such items constitute a vibrant multicultural and multinational anthology.[24] As a similar collection done in Portugal demonstrates, a new international section of such a collection could include numerous items from Brazil.[25] Contemplation of jazz composers, musicians, or the sensations they elicit is not at all restricted by national origin, as may be seen and heard in the series of cases to follow.

In a series tabbed "anotações" (annotations) by Sebastião Uchoa Leite, number twelve, set in an apparent train station, concentrates sensory images and has a tonal textual resolution via a major name of jazz: "Um súbito 'Giant Steps' / Subia atônito / Cego Coltrane matinal / Falsos óculos negros" [a sudden "Giant Steps" / arose astonished / blind Coltrane in the morning / false dark glasses].[26] As Scott Saul elucidates, especially the late-career Coltrane had a particular appeal to poets in the United States.[27] Such attraction in a foreign country like Brazil can lead a contemporary poet to seek to deterritorialize and, if you will, "detemporalize" unique musical phrasing; in "Coltrane às 3" (Coltrane at three) Ricardo Aleixo affirms that to hear such enunciation one time is to hear always: "roendo-a, que o vento / leva, a hora // desdobrável / em muitas, // . . . para um lugar / a esmo," [gnawing it, for the wind / sweeps away, the hour / foldable / into many, / . . . to a place / at random,].[28] Such allusions and shapings of poetic space can have several functions in lyric, from individual intimacy to collective communion. Another strategy is to strike a pose, say, as a creator of original rhythms, melodic newness, harmonic unpredictability. Thus wagers Rodrigo Garcia Lopes in the first measures of "M": "Improvisação pessoal. / Essa noite sou um jazzman / com dentes de ouro & swing / pra raiar o dia" [Personal improvisation. / Tonight I am a jazzman / with gold teeth and swing / to break dawn].[29] For his part, Afonso Henriques Neto (123–26) constructs a six-part "jazz session," which explores the erotic via sound, performance, and audience involvement, using the metal of instruments played to reflect and project onto ethereal and speculative planes. Another intention is to assert further interrelations, of arts and peoples; for instance, the first bars of "O prodígio das tintas" (The prodigy of inks/paints) link well-known Spanish American verse and USAmerican musical eccentricity: "Sopra-nos o vento a música de seu fulgor: / um elo de ecos, um verso de Gonzalo Rojas, / a espinha do universo no piano / de Thelonious Monk em Memories of you" [The wind blows us the music of his splendor: / a link of echoes, a verse by GR, / the spine of the universe in the piano / of TM in . . .].[30] This is, appropriately, one of the selections of *Rattapallax*, one of the transamerican specimens seen in chapter 2. The figure of Monk will be taken up at some length below.

These jazz-world models of expressive behavior provide buoyant springboards. Elsewhere in Brazil, the musicians are admired, and internalized, for being elegant, majestic, touching, or inspiring. In "Jazzmen," Marcelo Sandmann (45–47) appreciates a trio of principals—Chet Baker, John Coltrane, Miles Davis—citing the most noted album of each.

I

Blue note, veludo gris:
Chet Baker sings again.
O grão da voz no chafariz,
mas em surdina.
(O amor a dor só para mim!)
Chet Baker sings.
Amén!

[Blue note, gray velvet / . . . / The grain of the voice in the fountain, /
but in a whisper. / (Love pain only for me!) / . . .]

II

Hard-bebop-free.
Salto livre no buraco negro.
Voragem, vertigem.
A love supreme:
John Coltrane
como se beijasse brasa.
(My favorite thing!)

[. . . / Free leap into the black hole. / Vortex, vertigo. / . . . / as if he
were kissing embers. / . . .]

III

Kind of blue.
"Menos é mais."
Toda a raiva o sopro lírico contido,
seta que chega em cheio.
(Meu coração sangra aqui!)
Sem mostrar a alvura de um dente,
Miles Davis smiles.

[. . . / "Less is more" / All the rage the contained lyrical blowing, / ar-
row arriving in full. / (My heart bleeds here!) / Without showing the
whiteness of a tooth, / . . .]

The world of jazz is a column in the work of Frederico Barbosa, who uses stage names and song titles to baptize poetic compositions, alliteratively admiring, for example, the artistry of a famed vocalist in "Blue Moon":[31]

BILLIE

sua voz susurra suave e viva
sob o som blue das incertas
sílabas suas soltas certas

na noite doce e lenta,
envolve-me
beija-me quente sua visão

[her voice whispers soft and lively / to the blue sound of her uncertain / syllables let loose certain // in the sweet and slow night / her vision envelops me / kisses me hot]

Then in "Star Dust" there is another musicalization where interplay envelops ideas of structure, intertextuality, and the canon. The parenthetical series (*lendo-lento-lembro*) [reading-slow-I recall] links human object of observation, communication, and speaker in a sectional composition:

(Lester Young
lendo Star Dust)

toda pele
quando ela toca
troca

arde
vira verde
trans-
parece

(Lester Young
lento Star Dust)

nada nunca ninguém
quando ela toca ou fala
toca tão completamente
quanto completa foi tocada

(lembro Star Dust
Lester Young)

[(LY / reading . . .) // all skin / when she plays / trades // burns / turns
green / appears // (LY / slow . . .) // nothing never no one / when she
plays or speaks / she plays as completely / as she was played complete
// (I recall . . .)]

These are purposeful recognitions of luminaries who brighten lyric paths
in a transamerican execution (Barbosa did visit the USA in the late 1980s).
An entire section of the poet's second book, *Nada feito nada*, is titled "Rep-
ertório"; it comprises eleven titles taken from the world of music, notably
a stock of standard jazz and show tunes—"Night in Tunisia," "Solitude,"
"Stella by Starlight"—with some name-dropping, such as Cannonball Adderly, that might limit reception by Brazilian readership but makes the intent of outreach unmistakable. A discerning local critic still believes that
it is a "poetry to the sound of a distant jazz, almost inaudible, that is, the
materialization of a sonorous residue, of the memory of deliciously dis-
cordant sounds" and concludes that "a discovery occurs of what rigorous
improvisation music may have; where the maximum objectivity seemed to
be the ideal, a private subjectivity ends up taking over."[32] This disposition
is shaped by acts of absorption and sharing.

The artistry of jazz and the transgressive bent of many of its makers are
the best-tuned channels through which Brazilian poets receive—transmis-
sions, messages, suggestions. Nowhere is this USAmerican popular music
of African American origin even remotely associated with alienation or
cultural victimization at home. On the contrary, jazz embodies qualities
that need greater nurturing in the age of consumer-driven cultural globalization. One of the five views of this conglomeration of processes is seen by
Martin Hopenhayn as an "apocalyptic" crushing of the sublime; he rightly
perceives core differences between end-of-the-century diversions and midcentury pillars: "like television zapping, the city combines speed and de-
composition. The video game, zapping, the shopping centre and feverish
consumption have obliterated silence and the fleeting pause, those subtle
features that gave so much intensity to modern art: to the music of Miles
Davis or John Cage" (148). The value implied here suggests why jazz, more
than just a sign of postwar spread of USAmerican cultural products, can
actually be figured as a restorative in the face of lamented cultural homogenization.

Two of the most inspiring figures of jazz for poets are the ever-evolving trumpeter Miles Davis (d. 1991) and the revolutionary pianist Thelonious Monk (d. 1982). Long-distance post-mortem contemplations were composed by one Franklin Alves Dassiê, clearly taken with the interface of sound and color in "Miles Davis, Lado B" and "Monk Solo." He plays with the colors blue and red in the complementary pair of jazz poems. In the former, he makes verse, odd textuality, (il)legibility, and nonconformity flow together in the ironic "flip side" of an artist who was tremendously successful yet misunderstood, underappreciated:

um tipo de azul, vermelho
esta música, verso cego

Miles Davis e seu livro nenhum,
que ninguém escuta

Nada adiantará, é hora:
gravata lírica, traça
arguta, mesa anatômica
alguém perde o fôlego

tocando a música de erros
necessários

[a type of blue, vermilion / this music, blind verse // MD and his none book / that no one listens to // It'll do no good, it's time / *lyrical necktie*, ingenious / moth, anatomical table / someone loses his breath // playing the necessary / music of errors]

Monk was a legendary eccentric who was isolated by his own strange difference, and subject to a sort of aesthetic solidarity of appreciation across the hemisphere:

Este olhar na janela
um tipo de vermelho
orquestrando com outros azuis,
a sobrar,
solo
Palavra-tecla, Monk
afinando seus nervos

retesados, a
linha
e riscos.

[This gaze in the window / a type of vermilion / orchestrating with
other blues, / to be left over, / *solo* / (Piano) key-word, Monk / tuning
his hardened / nerves, the / line / and scorings (scratches).]

From a more objective vantage, the acutely genre-aware Leite ponders
the same legendary eccentric of improvisational instrumental music, in
"Thelonious Monk":[33]

Os toques breves
De precisão—recônditos
E abstratos
De uma mente absconsa
Explodem em timbres
Seções cônicas melódicas
Geometria (desarmônica)
De alma reclusa

[The brief touches / of precision—recondite / and abstract / of an ab-
sconse mind / explode in timbres / melodic conic sections / geometry
(inharmonious) / of a recluse soul]

These tense, compressed lines about an artist function both as interlocu-
tion and as an implicit poetics, in the lineage of Cabral and of concrete
poetry, as well as of Pound, Williams, Creeley. Fellow constructivist poet
Júlio Castañón Guimarães builds his own macrosymbols of antinormative
fracture and contention upon the oddball keyboardist—"Mero léxico para
o piano de Thelonious Monk" (Mere lexicon for the piano of TM): "farpas
farpas / farpas metálicas // ângulos arestas / quinas esquinas // lâminas e
cortes / aparas e fios // gumes pausas / o ermo o ermo // contrapulso / bate
a luz // súbito súbito / o silêncio súbito // e estilhaço / se fratura // prisma e
cortes / contraluz vário // pulso e estaca / fere e prisma // mas risca / e rasca
e bate // quando a pino / fagulha e esconde // se quebra / se farpas // luz e
pontua" [barbs barbs / metallic barbs // angles edges / extremes corners //
blades and cuts / trims and floss // blades pauses / secluded one // counter
pulse / light strikes // sudden sudden / sudden silence // shard / fractures //

prism and cuts / varied counterlight // pulse and stake / wounds and prism
// yet strikes through / and scratches and strikes // when straight up / sparks
and hides // breaks / if barbs // light and points].[34] This parade of words
is like a simple or "mere" vocabular reflection of the unusual timings and
skewed configurations of sound characteristic of the feted composer.

From her subjective perspective, Claudia Roquette-Pinto explores, in
the condensed verses of "Jazz," mental and physical stimuli in elevated
sounds, which are not clear, organized, or rational and which provoke a
self-searching question to conclude:[35]

> a noite tece ao redor.
> há uma lua uma abó
> bada um rosto de lilian gish
> que alguém deixou de propósito.
> atrás da mureta a
> aspereza azul levita
> e torna a afundar
> abrindo prata e ror nessa hipnose.
> correm notas pela escada
> pérolas as teclas
> os degraus.
> eis: e depois
> um sax desperta flores nos quadris.
>
> de que lugar em mim verto esse caos?

[night weaves around. / there is a moon a cup- / ola a face of LG /
that someone left on purpose. / behind the retaining wall / the blue
harshness levitates / and sinks again / opening silver and lotsa stuff
in this hypnosis. / notes run up the stairs / pearls the keys / the steps.
/ behold: and later / a sax awakens flowers in my hips // from what
place in me do I spill this chaos?]

After this series of examples in which the saxophone, piano, and trum-
pet shape responses, wondering, and spatial desire, the potential of revived
jazz voices, even to incite inquiry about poetic speech and imagery, may be
realized in "Chet Baker Sings Again," also from Guimarães (59):

> uma voz às vezes
> às avessas uma voz

de si própria
se oculta

esgarça imagens

se esgarça
em silêncios
para erguer-se
um mínimo e tanto
acima de um e outro
silêncio

[a voice at times / inside out a voice / hides from / itself // it tears images // it frays itself / in silences / to stand up / the minimum or so /
above one and another / silence]

The name of the celebrated trumpeter-vocalist has a distinct significance
for musically knowledgeable Brazilians, because he was one of the exponents of "cool" or West Coast jazz who impressed the foundational figure
João Gilberto and others in the formative years of the Bossa Nova style
in the 1950s. The incomparable singer-guitarist from Bahia teamed with
saxophonist Stan Getz in the early 1960s, as the latter was one of the select
few players who best understood the restrained excitement of the new style
and most successfully accompanied and adapted it in North America. Thus
the arrangement of a Brazilian poem of affection, "Chet for Getz," in which
Camilo Lara (19) joins a pair of USAmerican figures with resonance.

cada nota penetra
o espaço do vôo
rebate e desata o silêncio
da voz em pouso suspenso
do sopro jazz lodo do dia

está posto o tema
desvôo da nau em destino
porto da voz medindo a linha
sopro jazz tecendo o linho

[each note penetrates / the space of flight / beats down and unties the
silence / of the voice in suspended rest / of the breath of jazz mud of

the day // the theme is set / un-flight of the ship in destiny / port of
the voice measuring the line / blowing jazz weaving linen]

Various nouns of movement (flight, ship, port, line) collude here to make
a vague spatial association with a former colony in South America, while
voice and instruments are welcomed into the sphere. Jazz in this case, as in
so many above, is a means of fresh breathing, detour (from routine), break-
through, revelation, with both makers and listeners benefiting. In this pair
of short poems, Chet Baker's sparse and muffled voice, which influenced
and was influenced by Bossa Nova, is perceived to share room with a cohort of poets who value concision, controlled touch, and careful selection
of notes, read João Gilberto, as appreciated by Augusto de Campos in his
singular inter-genre studies. For example, in "Informação e redundância
na música popular," the poet-critic theorizes relations between bebop and
Bossa Nova, both mold-breaking innovations. Thus are constituted excellent examples of intercontinental attitudinal convergence across formal
divisions.[36]

The allure of USAmerican popular music and its referential domains
extends beyond jazz and verbal discourse, as seen, for example, in the artful dexterity of Arnaldo Antunes. In the generation of poets who begin
to make their names in the 1990s in Brazil, new types of rock music are
more likely magnets for attention. The poetry of song in the Anglo-American reign of the 1960s–1970s was rather modest in comparison to Brazil's,
where it comprised a major trend into the 1980s. The impact of the poets of
the hybrid post-Bossa trend known by the acronym MPB for Música Popular Brasileira, from Chico Buarque to the Tropicalists, and the generational
significance of countless national musical connections with literature, are
widely recognized. If Bob Dylan stood practically alone as a "literary-qual-
ity" exponent of sixties musical lyricism in English, the music and musician
of blues and rock did offer multiple inspirations for subsequent Brazilian
poets, as additional prods to the imagination. From the point of view of a
comparative historian, Pike concluded that rock truly influenced cultural
production and public opinion in Latin America, while reducing primitivist stereotyping in the United States.[37] Sensitivity to the poetic potential of
jazz and other forms is melodically encouraged by the declarations of poet-
composer Caetano Veloso in "Errática": "Busco o estilo exato, / A tática
eficaz / Do rock ao jazz / Do lied ao samba" [I seek the exact style, / the
efficacious tactic / from rock to jazz / from Lied to samba].[38]

Jorge Mautner, whose proud "Dionysus in Brazil" is a surprising first poem in Brasil and Smith's *Brazilian Poetry (1950–1980)* (9), has intermingled poetry and popular music in creative essays to explain cultural vitality in a North and South American "renaissance" (see chapter 6). This writer-musician with a hemispheric bias mixed literary and musical figures in such forward-looking expressions as "Castro Alves & Walt Whitman, Allen Ginsberg & Bob Dylan & Jorge Ben & Gil são o otimismo panamericano" [. . . are the Panamerican optimism].[39] For his part, sui generis artist of the word Glauco Mattoso has consistently mixed English and elements of Anglo-American popular music into his parodies, mock poems, song lyrics, and copious sonnets. "Spik (sic) Tupinik" mixes linguistic references of the 1950s (decade of emergence of rock 'n' roll, Sputnik, James Dean) with examples of fusion (of the imported and some national musical genres):

Rebel without a cause, vômito do mito
da nova nova nova nova geração,
cuspo no prato e janto com palmito
o baioque (o forrock, o rockixe), o rockão.
Receito a seita de quem samba e roquenrola:

[. . . vomit of myth / of the new new new new generation / I spit on the plate and dine on hearts of palm / baion-ock (forró+rock, rock+maxixe), big rock / I subscribe the sect of those who samba and rock 'n' roll]

A meticulous specialist asserts that under scrutiny this piece, one of the writer's earliest successes, can be seen as "a hybridized 'pop-' or 'rock-sonnet,' with requisite repetition and musicality maintained throughout the poem."[40] Therein, other implied or articulated ingredients—speak, beatnik, cornflake, milkshake—are varied and cement the USAmerican motivation, but the musical impact is strongest. The 1950s ring of the extremely playful text is countered with a sarcastic "nova nova nova nova" to poke fun at impatient chroniclers of literature and to reorient temporally the reading. The first version of the poem occurred during the heyday of "marginal poetry," of which one of the most representative poems is "My Generation" by Chacal (42), which is based on citations of the counterculture of Anglo-American rock:

aquela guitarrinha ranheta
debochada desbocada

my generation
satisfaction

aquela mina felina
cuba sarro cocaína
do you wanna dance
don't let me down

aquele clima da pesada
cheiro de porrada no ar
street fighting man
jumping jack flash

[that brash little guitar / debauched foul-mouthed / . . . / . . . // that
feline dame / cuba [libre] get it on cocaine / . . . / . . . // that heavy
climate / smell of shit-kickin' in the air / . . . / . . .]

This modest quasi-adolescent text exemplifies a prototype of youth poetry
in the 1970s: it is short, epigrammatical, ironic, colloquial, and based on real
life, not on literary knowledge (of the reader or writer). The final quatrain
integrates in the climate of conflict musical and behavioral references while
the last word echoes a common technique, the flash, or quick perception.
Paulo Leminski (d. 1989), widely regarded as the most important Brazilian
poet born in the 1940s, at the same time that he parodies the dependency
on experience in this type of poetry, also avails himself of English in a
phrase of a commercial hit:[41]

it's only life
but I like it
let's go
baby
let's go
this is life
it is not
rock and roll

For his part, Ricardo Corona—in a nominal amalgam used as an epigrammatic opening of a CD of spoken verse and poetry set to music—merges
Stein-Einstein-Eisenstein-Stones to connect innovative literature, revolutionary scientific theory, historic film, and pop music.[42] He also acknowl-

edged, (co)translated, and interpreted Jim Morrison as *o poeta do rock 'n' roll*. A scintillating section of Paulo Henriques Britto's *Macau*, with the title "Nove variações sobre um tema de Jim Morrison" (Nine variations on a theme of JM), is inspired in a verse by the influential vocalist of The Doors.[43] In more than one interview, nineties poet Ademir Assunção confirmed principles of fusion. He indicated that his multitoned volume *Zona branca* (which also has one section called "jazz kamaiurá") was inspired by the rock opera *Joe's Garage* by Frank Zappa. It is revealing to hear a key phrase about the origins of Assunção's poetry from an exchange with fellow poets: "But the person who really led me to write poetry was Jimi Hendrix. When I heard that guitar buzzing, I thought: 'Shoot, I want to write with that same electricity.'"[44] The instrumental feats of a groundbreaking USAmerican blues-rock artist provoking the writerly consciousness of a poet-to-be in southern Brazil is as relevant to transamerican poetics as any print source. As with literary figures, rock references, allusions, and quotations can punctuate any stage of the discourse of lyric. For instance, Floriano Martins places an epigraph taken from Tom Waits's "The Black Rider" and later blends it into the text—"I'll shoot the moon right out of the sky for you baby"—to color with a real citation the ground of a symbolist love encounter.[45] The gruff voice "Waits" is the object of a whole poem and "a soma da beleza de todas as eras" [the sum of beauty of all eras] in the set of "New York Poems" (29–38) by Beatriz Azevedo that revisits a metropolitan thread seen in chapter 2.

The blues informed both jazz and rock 'n' roll, and the essential USAmerican genre, certainly well known in Brazil, has appeared in contemporary poetry in countless titles and poems. To illustrate the capacity of the form to inspire in the late-1990s scene of the city of Belo Horizonte, there were the title of a local chapbook *Belo blue* (Beautiful blue(s)) and an ironic line of reaction, a retort to the news of the death of poetry: "um *blues* reanima o inusitado desapontamento" [a blues revives the unheard-of disappointment].[46] Poet-anthropologist Edimilson Pereira suggests the communitarian quality of his poetry with the title *Zeosório blues*. Salgado Maranhão binds the blue of song (emotivity) with the white of the page (space for thought) in a metapoem tellingly titled "Penúltimo blues": "grafar no azul em branco / inaugural / a voz / —matéria mater— / do vôo" [to graph on the blue on white / inaugural / the voice / matter mater / of the flight].[47] Singers who can be associated with a gamut of musical styles in the USA represent wide poetic capacity as well. In "Solilóquio de Nina Simone,"

Donizete Galvão imagined a hyperaware singer and factors of ethnic heritage, assuming the voice of the vocalist who sang "Backlash Blues," written by her friend Langston Hughes.[48]

Habitou-me um deus espesso.
Sangue da cor de fígado.
Veneno talhado, macerado e amargo.
Fez morada em cada célula.
Nos alvéolos, nas entranhas, sob as unhas.
Expande-me a veia do pescoço.
Sangra por minhas gengivas.
Lateja-me nas têmporas e nos pulsos.
Planta arrancada da terra africana,
finca suas raízes fundas de baobá
e traz-me gosto de lama à boca.
Sabor atávico a relembrar o homem
do brejo em que ele se originou.

[A thick god inhabited me. / Liver-colored blood. / Sculpted, mortified and bitter poison. / He took up residence in each cell. / In the alveoli, guts, under the fingernails. / (He) makes the veins of my neck stick out. / Bleeds from my gums. / Pounds in my temples and pulse. / Plant torn from African land, / grows deep baobab roots / and brings the taste of mud to my mouth. / Atavistic flavor to remember the man / of the marshes from where he originated]

Within a multidimensional geohistorical view, across genres and territories, a sensitive blues-rock homage is "Tributo a Alberta Hunter," with these transcultural passages:[49]

conheceu a injustiça,
o lodo, a lágrima,
como todos de nossa raça.
e no entanto você era o canto
a essência do triunfo.
milênios de beleza
encontram em sua voz
o axé dos orixás.
a vitalidade da fé
Africalegremente oculta

no élan dos ritos,
nas figas de marfim,
nas pérolas, nos búzios
e nos blues.

. . . .

 conheceu os porões da América,
a meca industrial,
o coração atômico do ocidente

[(you) knew injustice, / mud, tears, / like all of our race. / and yet you
were the song / the essence of triumph. / millennia of beauty / they
find in your voice / the life-spirit of the orishas. / the vitality of faith
/ Africa-happily (you) hide / in the elan of rites, / in the amulets of
ivory, / in pearls, shells / and the blues. / . . . / (you) knew the cellars of
America, / the industrial mecca / the atomic heart of the West]

Admiration of individual achievement is overtly tied to a collective awareness, African origins, related New World culture, and "injustice," which
can be spelled out as the harsh historical realities of captivity, forced labor,
and postslavery suffering in the industrial giant of America (= USA). This
is a reflection in poetry of the palpable influence of Afro-American movements of the sixties in Brazil. The black-consciousness movement—"Black
is beautiful," Black Power—inspired Brazilian youth culture and politics
from the 1970s into the 1980s.[50] Elsewhere, the same author interrelates
Brazilian and North American experience through music and words in a
32-line poem. The very naming of "Deslimites 10 (táxi blues)" is a gesture of
breaking down barriers.[51] The main title roughly translates as "dis-limits" or
"un-boundaries" and the subtitle incorporates directly the popular musical
designation. The deterritorialization of the expressive practice has a vocabular counterpart in the pairing of *urubus*, vultures, with *blues* to produce
urublues, a sort of hybrid Afro-indigenous lament in a poem that speaks
against the historical oppression of forcibly removed peoples. As Valente
(146) aptly perceived in comparatist perspective:

Questioning the definition of identity of Brazil in particular and of
the New World in general as a synthesis of various ethnicities, exemplified by the "fable of the three races" in Brazil and by the myth of the
"melting pot" in the United States, "Deslimites 10" is a critical meditation on the situation of marginalized groups and the role that poetry

fulfills as an element both of preservation and of transformation of its history. Similar to what William Faulkner, referring to the fortitude of the descendants of slaves in the US South, characterized as "endurance," the poem opens bringing into focus the notable capacity for survival of those groups—blacks, indigenous, backlanders—and contradicting the supposed passivity that is often attributed to them.

An Afro-diasporic voice thus expresses hemispheric African-American solidarity, constituting a specific case of the positionality that Buarque de Hollanda sees as defining the nineties. One of the more striking selections in her anthology is by Paulo Lins, author of *Cidade de Deus* (1997; *City of God*, 2006), the powerful reality-based fiction of a violent Rio housing project. Expressive poetics is the main thrust of "Seu nome é meu" (Your name is mine), inspired by Tropicalist poet-lyricist Torquato Neto, whom the speaker presumably addresses.[52] In the midst of this shared existential meditation, however, the personal gets placed geohistorically and the lyric self takes on expanded public significance: "Hoje não existe Península Ibérica, nem África, nem a ânsia de mundo novo. . . . Eu, que tantas outras vezes, morri / de tiro / facadas / porrada / e América / de novo pronto para morrer / do novo" [Today the Iberian Peninsula does not exist, nor Africa, nor the anxiety of a new world. . . . I, who so many other times, died / of shots / knifings / beatings / and America / again ready to die / from the new].[53] The playing down of origins—Portuguese mother country, the colonized other (dark) continent, and the assertion of identity through hemispheric differentiation—is consistent with a favoring of self-examination yet still serves to recall those enormous issues. The causes of repetitive symbolic and real deaths are urban violence, nothing unusual or unexpected, and, in a continuous reading, America, an ambiguous addition that might be read as historical conflict within the Americas, a common affliction, and/or as US intervention, which would underline a line of counterdiscourse more in line with the lament of Alberta Hunter. The speaker's preparedness for renewed death is tied to some novelty, a new end-of-the-millennium conjuncture? In a discontinuous reading of the ellipsis, impending death can be attributed to America, the first one conceivably being the conquest of indigenous peoples, the new one being, say, environmental disaster driven by industrialization and imperial designs. In short, exploring commonalities—like *cordiality* in its root Latinate sense—can lead to matters of the heart that spark joy and pain alike.

Within the hemispheric ethos in play here, most musically-inspired lyricism is celebratory. The unique poems of Maranhão and Lins, while eulogizing voices above all, also insinuate malaise in a neoliberal, globalizing present. Other strategies to express perplexities and questioning stances in this regard embrace ironic minimalism, fragmentations, disassemblies, and hybrid discursive combinations. Via Jameson, Raymond Williams, and Roberto Schwarz, the Brazilian observer Cevasco perceives in immediate poetry of the nation "a new structure of feeling forming as a resistance to the ideology of globalization." Her examples are drawn from Francisco Alvim's *Elefante*. "Read together," she believes, "the poems map Brazilian collective experience ranging from remains of slavery to contemporary politics in the capital, Brasília. . . . they structure the current version of the country's integration in the world order."[54] This collection of speech-based locutions is not explicit in any such disposal—the 132 short and miniature poems are often epigrammatic in the manner of the *poema-piada*, or joke-poem, and sometimes bewildering in the manner of Duchamp's displayed urinal—but the analyst concludes that Alvim's barbs "show how the particular malfunctioning of the great themes of the ideology of globalization—pluralism, variety, integration—in the Brazilian situation sheds light on their pretences to general validity." If this extrapolation and willful interpretation could benefit from evidence of more varied provenance, the very focus on lyric in a complicated peripheral nation stands as a singular maneuver of cultural critique.

In extranational contexts, another productive disposition is to embrace the gaze of visitor, tourist, outside viewer. With respect to the allure of USAmerican media culture, a rich object of observation is the Disney empire. *How to Read Donald Duck* is a widely recognized predecessor to critical accounts of cultural globalism in the 1990s and beyond.[55] Some of the social-scientific understanding in such studies may suffer poetic infiltrations. These may develop specular insights of the society of spectacularity. Bonvicino, for instance, relates "Um dia em Magic Kingdom" (One day in . . .) and the (in)sight of litter receptacles: "Em homenagem a Mickey Mouse, / objetos depois do êxtase / num exílio organizado" (*Outros poemas*, 44) [In homage to MM / objects after the ecstasy / in an organized exile]. The combination of elements lends an expansive quality to the experience: an entertainment-industry character of maximum weight, the symbolic strength of public waste (from enraptured consumption to deposited trash), a stereotype of North Americans (keeping order) alongside a manifestation of the draw of this setting for foreign clientele (massive Brazilian attendance at Orlando theme parks). This episode, alongside texts in the same poet's US release *Sky-Eclipse*, are parts of a transamerican travel paradigm. Elsewhere, Amoreira builds a long poem around navigations up and down his country's coast, intertwined metaphorical explorations, and a delirium of individual/collective self-situating, coming to play on the folk expression "Deus é brasileiro"—God is Brazilian—and the national taking to Disney cartoons and travel to Orlando with a question of divinity: "Deus é Disney?"[56] O'Dougherty has demonstrated how Disney, especially the theme park in Orlando, is tied in Brazil to cultural capital, modernity, and a transnational social circuit. The trip to Disney World is like a teenage rite of passage, "a quasi requisite for social validation" and central to parents' class identity (98). The pilgrimage to the special site is a "quest for distinction through association with 'modernity' globally conferred and locally defined" (127). This aspect of being is lived in Bonvicino's poem and floats forcefully in Amoreira's.

The second epigraph at the outset of this chapter is an ultramodern haiku that has a cosmopolitan air (travel, film, fashion, urban pleasures) with a touch of earlier mass culture, as the nickname for New York and the images evoke a comic-book, television, and film superhero, a personage who may also thus symbolize loss of "authentic" tradition and the spread of mass-media diversions. That reference surges to orient Joaquim Paiva in *Aos pés de Batman* (At the feet of Batman), an ingredient-heavy prose poetry that efficaciously agglutinates several issues of modernity, nationality, and Americanness seen in the deliberations of this study. A complex consciousness engulfs mentions of antiquity, folk tradition, transgressive popular music, nature, information technology.

> joguei flores ao mar brancas de
> espuma odeio os inimigos da antiga
> Babilônia amei o heavy metal nadei por
> mares de peixe espada rezo para que o
> MacIntosh Plus desprograme os meus
> jogos inconexos   (18)

[I threw into the sea flowers white with / foam I hate the enemies of ancient / Babylon I loved heavy metal I swam through / seas of swordfish I pray for / Mac Plus to deprogram my / disconnected games]

um peixe espada uma paleta de
pintor uma pipa el abanico estamos indo
do Velho ao Novo Continente piso por
um fio a vida me vale de lâmina não fora
o vale de lágrimas uma arraia um bico
de gaivota vou jogar-me aos pés de
Batman   (21)

[a swordfish a painter's / palette a kite "the fan" (Sp.) we're going /
from the Old to the New Continent by a thread / I step on life it's
worth a blade if it weren't for / the vale of tears a stingray a beak / of
seagull I am going to throw myself at the feet of / Batman]

The whole odd sequence is replete with citations and allusions, from the
Bible to symbolism and the avant-garde, but the controlling image is from
USAmerican mass culture. These traits are typically "postmodern," in an
age when marketing supersedes classical culture. Yet the Old World / New
World dichotomy still haunts a delirious odyssey through nature, treach-
erous waters, and "advanced" civilization. An attitude that underpins a
transamerican poetics emerges unimpeded.

If invoking European intellectual tradition in current contexts of Brazilian lyric is as honest and necessary as ever, the relative interest in USAmerican referents and pertinent functions in discourse appear, with greater
frequency, to be more natural, as argued throughout here. The lead piece
of Lopes's intention-laden *Polivox* is an extended (116 lines) and multivalent
composition.[57] There are epigraphs from German, French, and USAmerican authors about linguistic dispersions and disruption of systemic continuity. The poem itself, "c:/polivox.doc" (10–15), draws on a surfeit of registers: IT—information technology, including products and the Internet; the
first word is "On-line"—arts, advertising, news, and proverbial wisdom,
paraphrasing or actually quoting from a variety of sources, from mythology
and philosophy (including Wittgenstein) to literature and underground
film. Multiplicity is affirmed in a self-defining phrase: "A dança do duende
entre a floresta dos signos" [The dance of the sprite among the forest of
signs]. This is symptomatic of turn-of-the-millennium lyric attuned to
transtemporal, planetary planes of discourse of lyric or subject to absorption by lyric. It can be seen as a literary version of the socioanthropological
variety of expressive Latin American popular culture posited as "multitem-

poral heterogeneity" (García Canclini, 3). Visual culture (film and beyond) directs a commodified, mystified society, and, in conclusion: "Não há como escapar" [There is no escape]. How not to admit the implications of massive media presence and the imbrication of languages and nations? There is no suggestion of celebration here, nor of confrontation; but rather questioning, pondering. The international frame of reference, finally, is structured by a certain USAmerican prominence—especially mediated culture: Pound, "Sonho Americano" (American dream), Madame Yahoo, Dell, *matinês americanas*—that means, in the long run, transamerican awareness.

This long series of examples in contemporary Brazilian lyric—with prismatic utilizations of graphic arts, films, actors, songs, popular musical genres, eminent names, affinities, and New World constructions—is tied together by various factors. There is a surface presence of non-Brazilian input and an accompanying attitudinal stance, which may sometimes be critical but is always hemispherically toned or tinged, looking to the "other giant" of the Americas, the USA. Over the decades since 1980, things North American have been textualized with measures of acceptance of an otherness often viewed with suspicion in previous generations. Poets of different ages and locations share familiarity with USAmerican cultural production and a propensity to work contents of mass culture into their own texts. One can hardly expect them to do so in consistent or uniform manners, as some prize neo-avant-garde aesthetics most highly, others emerge from the days of social protest and/or counterculture, and still others grew up in circumstances in which the culture industry could be taken much more for granted.

In the late twentieth century and early twenty-first, such poetic outreach is just one way to help conceive the variety of lyric experience. National questions still matter above all in the domain of lyric in Brazil, as most everywhere, but the transamerican, mediated and meditated upon, as exemplified here, is a significant thread too, a meaningful component of the whole. Many voices show how, cannibalizing matter from myriad sources and adapting (imposed) items of foreign provenance to their own designs, poetries can actually be agents of anti-acculturation, how "the low tech of literature acts as one of the sole imaginative bulwarks against the encroaching, anti-human global homogeneity of mass culture,"[58] and how, from all points of view, lyric continues to adapt to mutating circumstances.

4

◇

Three Centuries, Three Americas

Epical Fellowships and Hemispheric Imperatives

America is therefore the land of the future, where, in the ages that lie before us,
the burden of the world's history shall reveal itself.

A prolific Brazilian jazz pianist living in New York in the late twentieth
century writes that her latest release aims to attain broad musical coverage,
"to capture the musical essence of each America and combine their various
rhythms and sounds to beat as one heart."[1] Given the vast array of popular
musical forms in South, North, and Central America (including the Caribbean), the stated artistic intentions are more than ambitious if taken literally, so they are better heard as metaphors for a project that might bring
together, in space and affect, a spectrum of tonalities, varied repertories,
musicians from different backgrounds, and diverse audiences. The kind of
epic (grand, bold) spirit that animates this album—these original compositions, covers, and songs—has motivated poets, bards, singers of tales in
several epochs and sites of the Americas. After the classical epic model had
ceased to be viable, new modes of epic, epical, or epiclike poetry developed
with which to come to terms with evolving realities in the hemisphere, a
literary phenomenon that stretches from the mid-nineteenth century to
the dawn of the twenty-first—in universally respected and lesser-known
voices alike.

Beyond the strictly geographical meaning of the three Americas, the
tripartite configuration can also be understood according to dominant
cultural and linguistic factors (the Ibero-American, the Anglo-American,
the Franco-American) or via origins, race, and ethnicity (Indo-American,
Euro-American, Afro-American) in an organizing frame that changes from
nation to nation, region to region, area to area.[2] All three of these ways to

draw the three Americas have manifested in long works of verse, notably in a trio of unconventional Brazilian works which supersede national focus, moving toward assertion of hemispheric perspectives, both Latin American and all-inclusive, and which emerge respectively during the late Romantic age, in the avant-garde decade of the twentieth century, and at the turn of the twenty-first, the start of the third millennium.

To respond more fully to any work of pan-, trans-, or inter-American poetry that makes epic gestures, it is useful to review, however briefly, manifestations of the genre and subsequent variations in the New World. Conventionally, what defines epic poetry, sung or written, is the verse narration of the deeds of a hero who stands for a society or a nation, whether in classical antiquity or a period of Western literary history up to Romanticism. While heroic adventures may have fabulous or even superhuman elements, depiction of historical human achievement remains essential. After the rise of the novel, the independence of New World nations, and the transition from neoclassicism to artistic modernity, inherited models of the epic of old begin to collapse and give way to different concepts of the long poem. The most powerful example in the Americas, of course, is the lyric-epic of Walt Whitman in *Leaves of Grass*, a multiform and constantly growing collection composed of many connected lyrical instances, and an unfolding story of democratic life.[3] Whitman reworks the episodic fabric of the traditional epic and treats the objective plane with subjective emphasis, seeking a founding work for the USA. Whitman is the point of departure for any discussion of epical lyric / lyrical epic with Americanist tenor, most notably the grandest Latin American example, *Canto general* (1950) by Pablo Neruda.[4] Elsewhere, neo-epic may be exemplified with Édouard Glissant, *Les Indes* (1956; *The Indies*, 1992), a six-canto poem concerning the history of Martinique that begins with the travels of Christopher Columbus and the colonialist decimation of natives.[5]

Whether in the case of modern endeavors or deep history, it is useful to underline a situated assessment of the literary mode by Earl Fitz: "as a literary genre, the epic was particularly well suited to the portrayal of the conquest and colonization of the New World. Both the bloody and violent clash of cultures that the conquest occasioned and the subsequent rise of the American nations lent themselves to retelling via the epic form. But just as the struggle for control of the Americas involved different types and degrees of conflict, so too did the numerous American epics come to differ in subject matter, mode of treatment, and style" (*Rediscovering*, 48). This observation will apply quite well to the three Brazilian examples taken up below. In Latin America, during the buildup to the political independence attained in the early nineteenth century, there were numerous efforts to create epic poetry, with some outstanding results. Once new nations were formed and elements for a cohesive consciousness were sought, as an important analyst wrote, "a good deal of energy was devoted, not least by poets, to proving how little Spain and Portugal mattered culturally. It is here that we first find that concern . . . with all that the European conquest suppressed and destroyed in America."[6] A central feature of Brazilian and Spanish American thought and art from about 1820 forward is Indianism, an exploration of indigenous phenomena from the Aztec in Mexico to the Tupi in Brazil.[7] This nativism, with its share of presence in epic verse, paved the way for subsequent poetic interest in local non-European populations, the mixed gaucho or African-descendant communities. Indeed, the principal possible "origins" for Ibero-American poetry reside both in a common Latinity and in "violated local or 'mother' cultures" (Brotherston, 3), which still rings true a century or more later in neo-epic works.

Both for its implementation of classical Renaissance rules and its historical narrative, the greatest example of epic in Spanish America, or the Americas at large, is *La araucana* (1569–89; *The Araucaniad*, with English versions in the 1600s) by Alonso de Ercilla y Zúñiga. This national poem of Chile is an epic of conquest.[8] In the seventeenth century, there were several titles of religious and heroic epopeia, none really notable. Since the nineteenth century "Latin American poets have recognized the challenge of writing on a continental scale, of creating a 'poem of America,'" an endeavor fraught with difficulties in reconciling moral compass, geographical identity, personal resolution, and even the very possibility of epic, "given the nature of American experience"[9]—in the sense of makeup and character, of course, not flora, fauna, and environment, which are mainstays of the New World literary imagination. Several titles of post-1800 Spanish-language works tellingly incorporate the name "America" or its adjective. Decades after the baptism of local constitutions, the occasion of the quatercentenary of Columbus's arrival elicited a number of literary responses in Hispanic America. Events and politics of the late 1890s—the overbearing USAmerican stance at the Pan-American Conference in 1889–90, the US-Spain war of 1898—naturally motivated Latin Americans to articulate renewed definitions of self in the hemisphere. Rodó's famous essay *Ariel* (1900), which painted the USA as helplessly materialistic and Latin America as more spiritual, affected intellectual exchange and poetry of all kinds. A manifestation of an ideal humanism concerned with the soul would be José Santos Chocano's *Alma América* (1906), which has epic characteristics. The aesthetic prestige and collective function that the genre maintained can be gleaned from the following example of a prestigious writer promoting the local masterwork of gaucho literature. Acclaimed poet Leopoldo Lugones, in a 1916 essay on folk verse, "raised *Martín Fierro* to the rank of epic. . . . he made it *the* epic of Argentina, giving it vital national significance":

> To produce an epic poem is for any nation the greatest proof of its vitality, because such a creation expresses the heroic life of its people. This life is the epitome of supreme human achievement and represents the greatest heights that the race can attain: the affirmation of its identity with the rest of the world.[10]

Even greater than a national affirmation would be a regional, fraternal, communal poeticization of the Latin American experience, from pre-Columbian Mexican splendor and the heights of Macchu Pichu to the shores and woes of Brazil, occupying the eastern half of South America. That was the aim of Neruda's *Canto general*, which remains a monumental and inexorable point of reference for poetry, epic, and transnational cultural relations in Latin America, as seen in the execution and criticism of the three expansive and ecumenical works focused on in this chapter, which share background and precedents in national letters. Other salient examples of evolved epopeia in Spanish America include Octavio Paz, *Piedra de sol* (1957; *Sun Stone*, 1963), which is written, according to Roberto González Echevarría, in "epic mode," extending as far back as Aztec mythology and cast in a "dizzying numerological mold that reaches back to Dante and medieval conceptions of the organic nature of the cosmos" (55–56). Christina Ramalho, in her unique study of Brazilian neo-epic by women, *Elas escrevem o épico* (79–91), presents an important Spanish American example, *Poema de Chile* (1967) by Nobel Prize–winning author Gabriela Mistral (d. 1957). For his part, specialist Leopoldo M. Bernucci, in a study of what he terms "modern Latin American epic," highlights the wide sweep and textual reconfiguration of history in a 1964 Peruvian work, Antonio Cisneros's *Comentarios reales*, and in a powerful text written in 1959 by the poet of the Sandinista resistance and revolt in Nicaragua, Ernesto Cardenal.[11] The parameter of "poetic justice" applied here will be quite apt in the case of the Brazilian bard Accioly, seen below.

In Portuguese America, colonial production of epic verse was written, unavoidably, in the shadow of Camões's *Os Lusíadas* (1578), the incisive narration of the Lusitanian nation and exploration that sits alongside the *Commedia* and *Paradise Lost* in the pantheon of European epic poems of classical formation.[12] The earliest imitation of the Camonian model in the colony dates from 1601, and most examples in the following two centuries were hardly inspired in a literary sense. An alliance of poets educated in the Old World gave voice to new feelings of domestic belonging in the New World in the province of Minas Gerais, expressing a protonational spirit in consistent epic poems. *Caramuru* by José de Santa Rita Durão (1722–1784) comprises ten cantos on the Portuguese arrival in Bahia. *O Uraguai* (1769) by José Basílio da Gama (1741–1795) narrates the Luso-Hispanic war against the Jesuit missions of southern Brazil. This epic of crossroads demonstrates, as Bernucci affirms, some sympathy with the native cause, while in contrast Durão uses indigenous people to glorify Portuguese colonialism.[13] Independence in Brazil spawned "a school of 'Americanists' . . . influenced in turn by Herder's enthusiasm for a literature of the people deriving from the unlettered and more 'primitive' elements of the nation ('Die Wilden')."[14] Thus continue to emerge in the Romantic period glorious military accounts mixed with attention to the (imagined) history of indigenous tribes in epic verse. One Brazilian work even extols European expansionism in the figure of Columbus.[15] In his search for American forms of identity, Brazil's main early Romantic poet Gonçalves Dias included a section called "Poemas americanos" in his first collection in 1848 and left an incomplete epic based on a tribal story.[16] Even Machado de Assis—the greatest prose-fiction writer in Latin America before Borges, and known for his universalist textual cosmopolitanism from 1880 forward—wanted to pay homage to Gonçalves Dias and his Indianist interest, publishing in 1875 a collection christened *Americanas*, a title that showed not so much a hemispheric mindfulness as simply location on this side of the Atlantic Ocean.[17] It is in this prerepublican period that the exceptional poetic composition by Sousândrade, *O guesa*, appears, upsetting received notions of being "American" and making epic in Brazil.

During the reign of Parnassianism and symbolism in the country, which coincided with the infancy of the Republic from 1889 on, lyrical elegance (rather Eurocentric, frankly) was valued above all. Celebration of everything that was national returned with vigor with *modernismo* in the 1920s and 1930s. Several works of this vanguard period have been associated with epic impulses. Oswald de Andrade's *Poesia Pau-Brasil* has been touted as "a residual epic which, by mingling excerpts from historical chronicles and flashes of historical and geographical perception, redraws Brazilian history as an anti-epic, less by what is said than by what is insinuated between the lines."[18] Contemporaneous works of note include the myth- and folklore-inspired sagas *Martim Cererê* (1928) by Cassiano Ricardo and *Cobra Norato* (1931) by Raul Bopp.[19] After the apogee of iconoclastic Brazilian modernism, other long poems with epic traits are Jorge de Lima's *Invenção de Orfeu* (1952), which is a complex private periplus of creation that even parodies *Os Lusíadas*, and the heroic collections of Cecília Meireles, *Romanceiro da Inconfidência* (1953) and *Crônica trovada da cidade de Sam Sebastiam do Rio de Janeiro* (1965), a treatment of the colonial conspiracy for independence and a chronicle of the city of Rio in which she "intends to articulate traditional epic materials in a new spirit."[20] From the point of view of transamerican poetics, however, the most significant *modernista* work with epic qualities was by poet-diplomat Ronald de Carvalho (1893–1935). *Toda a América* (1926; All the Americas) sits chronologically at the center of early Brazilian modernism, midway between 1922 with the inaugural Modern Art Week and 1930, the conventional end date of the "heroic phase." The expansive collection just precedes the movement's two most memorable works, Mário de Andrade's rhapsodic novel *Macunaíma* and "The Cannibalist Manifesto" by Oswald de Andrade (both 1928). Those two works have their own idiosyncratic connections to an extranational American aesthetic awareness, but the biggest sweep certainly comes in Carvalho's offering.

If the preceding series of examples illustrate modes of modern and/or modernist epic that succeed the historical epic (as celebration of great deeds for a nation), long poems that begin to appear in the 1970s might be thought of as postmodern epics. Of this type, Brazilian works that have made the transition to English translation are Ferreira Gullar's *Poema sujo* (1975), Affonso Romano de Sant'Anna's *A grande fala do índio guarani perdido na história e outras derrotas* (1978), and Adriano Espínola's *Táxi, ou Poema de amor passageiro*. Such examples of postmodern lyric- or neo-epic are comparable to what has been called expansive poetry in North America, extended works having broad perspectives, significant collective content, and strong narrative threads. All of the foregoing—historical epic, highpoints of Spanish American–Brazilian–USAmerican letters, histories of conquest and resistance—is incorporated, in one fashion or another, into the voluminous *Latinomérica* (2001) by Marcus Accioly. He occupies himself with literary inheritance largely in the context of colonialism and neocolonialism, holding steadfastly to an ideal of committed writing, to the idea that poetry should address legacies and structures of oppression. Despite a conceivably overeager political bent, Accioly's neomillennial work is a rich fount of poetical material to contemplate the trajectory of epic, Latin American poetry, and the hemispheric imagination, which had been poeticized uniquely more than a century before.

The three works chosen for analysis in this chapter are particularly fitting for several reasons. They carry the voices of citizens of the hemisphere, and the avowed transamerican spirit they share is foremost with respect to the central concern of this book. In terms of content, the three neo-epics provide a historical breadth from the pre-Columbian era to postmodern days, and as works published in different epochs, they effect a temporal spread from the time of the centenary of USAmerican independence and republican spirit in Brazil to the interwar period of cultural effervescence, and forward to the turn of the millennium and the celebration of the five-hundredth anniversary of the invention (discovery) of Brazil. Individually, each work has particular significance. Sousândrade's grand poem bridges the late nineteenth century and the twentieth in terms of invention—stylistic innovation—as it demonstrates traits that would be considered modernist or avant-garde. Ronald de Carvalho's sequence is the most Americanist work of Brazilian modernism, and a model for all times as regards inter-American grasp. Accioly's opus may have had less critical reception, but it offers an excellent opportunity to relive literary history and the history of Brazil as a nation within a hemispheric configuration; it is replete with material for continental discussion and debate.

Errant in the Hemisphere: *O guesa* and Transamerican Imperatives

A unique and unsettling work of the late nineteenth century, *O guesa* by Joaquim de Sousa Andrade or Sousândrade (1833–1902) is a long poem in thirteen cantos (four of which were left incomplete) based on both mythical sources and real-world histories. The periplus traverses nearly all parts of South America, Mesoamerica, and the Antilles, with its most striking moments in the United States, above all New York City and the stock exchange. Reflecting both an intensely New World ethic and a deep involvement with the grand tradition of Western (European) civilization, *O guesa* is quite a remarkable work for the extent to which it differs from the dominant literary styles of the epoch, especially as practiced in Latin America, as well as for the outright novelties it incorporates on an international level. First published in a short version in 1876 in New York as *O guesa errante* (The errant guesa), it appeared in London during the 1880s in an expanded edition filling more than 350 pages.[21] Given both the foreign publication sites and the eccentricities of the work, it did not circulate a great deal in Brazil in its own time, nor for more than a half a century after the author's death.

Within the norms of Brazilian Romanticism—nationally focused nation-building neo-epic, celebratory Indianism, sentimentalism, exaggerated subjectivity—it was very difficult to place *O guesa* and Sousândrade's equally idiosyncratic volumes of lyrical verse. Thus, they were the object of extremely little critical attention until the mid-1960s, when the concrete poets of São Paulo took it upon themselves to correct what they called a "blackout of history," to rescue and promote the effectively lost treasures, recovering the "clandestine earthquake" that the forgotten figure of the Romantic eccentric could be understood to represent. The discovery of the inventive Sousândrade was quite convenient for the Noigandres poets as they undertook their advocacy for the recognition of *invenção* in national letters.[22] *Revisão de Sousândrade* provided a detailed critical appraisal of the author's repertory, in both national and international frames—with the benefit of the perspectives of symbolism, modernism, and beyond—as well as an anthology of selections from the epic and the titles of his unusual lyrical verse. The only part of *O guesa* that was reproduced whole was an exceptional extended episode in canto X that the concrete critics dubbed "O Inferno de Wall Street." To this day that odd and powerful passage stands as the most celebrated piece by Sousândrade, and most readers know only the selection of *O guesa* done by the Campos brothers, not the lengthy work as a whole.[23]

The title character derives from a myth of Muisca Indians of present-day Colombia. Guesa (meaning without-home, wanderer) was a child taken from his parents at birth, educated by priests (*xeques*) at temple, and taught to follow the peregrinations of the Sun-God, all in order to be sacrificed at the age of fifteen. Consistent with his fundamentally cosmopolitan outlook and social agenda, Sousândrade, in a foreword to the first edition of the work, answered those who complained that his narrative poem did not really follow the legend, which was known through the ethnography of the German pioneer Humboldt and a French compendium.[24] The poet affirmed that the only difference between the lore and the literature of his creation was that, while the ancient highway was only a few miles in length on a plateau, the modern highway "went around the world," but "without the truth of the matter suffering," and further that "the poem in the end will be accompanied by its historical and geographical map."[25] This defense is indicative of the author's wish to associate the victim of ritual sacrifice in indigenous lore with representative peoples of the nineteenth century, including tribal descendants. Above all, the literary hero is directly identified with the poet himself, who lived in trying transnational circumstances and could be seen, by extension, also to be a victim of "civilized" sacrificial ritual, staged at the New York Stock Exchange in *O guesa*.

While Sousândrade further claimed that his work was not lyric, dramatic, or epic but simply "narrative," it is clear that the mixed tale is a sort of epopeia, albeit with myriad generic, stylistic, and diegetic peculiarities.[26] Glorification of "heroic" and "national" deeds are prime characteristics of epic, and Sousândrade certainly wanted to glorify his polyfacetic protagonist, different places, and diverse constituencies. His broad aims encompassed his home state of Maranhão (whose capital city here is the Ithaca-like home or center of the world), Brazil (the people and country, not the state of Empire, which the poet opposed and targeted in the poem), the ancient Incan empire, and the Americas as a whole. *O guesa* is wholly New World, as brief jumps to Africa and southern Europe are simply to explore what truly takes root after cross-Atlantic migration. The narration commences up in the Andes, and it is significant that the journey should begin on high, as physical location embodies admiration, exaltation, and a lofty position in a moral sense. Canto I opens:

> Eia, imaginação divina!
> Os Andes
> Vulcânicos elevam cumes calvos,
> Circundados de gelos, mudos, alvos,
> Nuvens flutuando—que espetac'los grandes (199)

> [Oh divine imagination! / The Andes / Volcanic elevate bald peaks, / Surrounded by ice, mute, white, / Clouds floating—what grand spectacles!]

This altitude sets up a descent to the tropical lowlands and, later, a hemispheric ascent to North America. The rest of the first part includes harsh reminders of the Spanish conquest and heading on to the vast Amazon region. Canto II moves to and through Amazonia, with its endless natural marvels, including recollections of grand times past but also painful degradation of rituals. In the third canto the bard sings of the magnificent jungle, laments the slavery of Indians and Africans, and depicts a river ride that leads to the mouth of the world's largest fluvial way. The guesa reaches (the poet's) home in canto IV, which concerns first love and exile, among other matters. The verses of canto V move around the state of Maranhão, traversing plantations, tropical forests, and a vast space of memory of youth, while the present of Rio de Janeiro and the imperial court, corrupting foreigners and all, are the subjects of canto VI. One of the incomplete cantos is VII, which comprises an exploration of roots in African nations, Iberia, and the Mediterranean. The hero shipwrecks upon the shore of the poet's homeland in canto VIII, and in canto IX the pilgrimage continues to the Antilles, also a site of condemnable slavery, and to Central America and Mexico, preparing an approach to the United States. Canto X, the central section in several respects, visits different states, focusing especially on New York, Manhattan, and, in a rhetorical exhibition, Wall Street.[27] Following the contrast of utopian and distasteful elements in that chapter, the narrative moves to the Pacific ocean and Panama in canto XI, intoning a hymn to the Americas and remembering Bolívar and other liberators in Colombia and Venezuela. Further contemplation of the Incan civilization sets up canto XII, which travels down the west coast of South America, returns to the Andes, visits Chile, and sails around the Horn to Argentina. The final canto, also left incomplete, is a sort of epilogue that involves another return to Maranhão and the death of the poet-protagonist, who remains somehow suspended in time. The temporal dimension of the poem is, in the words of a present-day poet concerned with Latin American legacies, "synchronic, mixing a mythical past, the early colonial era and the century of the machine in a kind of non-time. . . . The synthesis of simultaneous and analogical events comprises a break with the idea of linear historical time in the narrative sequence, signaling a poetic time (or un-time) that does not recognize spatiotemporal limitations."[28]

In elaborating this imposing poem, Sousândrade had to juggle aesthetic and geohistorical allegiances. This balancing act integrates momentous Old World bards and masterworks consequentially, but ultimately they are subordinated to New World human and natural horizons, from valiant indigenous tribes conquered by rapacious Iberians to democratic USAmerican

political models and Transcendentalist writers.[29] The European drive is illustrated in the supposed motivation of the poet for changing his pen name
to Sousândrade, to wit, because the merged name produced an attractive
Hellenic sonority and because it had the same number of letters (eleven) as
Shakespeare. In *O guesa*, especially the Wall Street episode, canonical intertextuality and invocations of names are legion. There are continuous quotations, allusions, and minor/major elements taken or adapted from classical
mythology and epic, the Bible, Dante, Camões, Milton, Lamartine, Edward
Lear with his limerick form, and Byron, with *Childe Harold's Pilgrimage* as a
sort of immediate inspiration. Yet despite many characteristics shared with
Paradise Lost, for instance, Sousândrade is fundamentally "concerned with
the political and ideological acceptance of South American peoples" and,
more diversely than Dante in his *Commedia*, the Brazilian author constructs
a "tripartite narration, comprised of an omniscient narrator, enunciations
of the poet-protagonist, and unspecified voices of the people, a form of
dramatis personae."[30] Those many voices include subalterns and subdued
communities of the colonial past. The social vision that Sousândrade builds
via his hero also draws on ancient and current sources. He implies a model
for an ideal human organization associated in a utopian manner with the
communitarian society of the Incas alongside Greek concepts from Plato's
Republic and even freely interpreted roots of Christianity. The democratic
United States, eventually, offers much to be admired, even if forms of oppression, corruption, and colonialism merit satire and lyrical derision.

The Sousândrade of *O guesa* reveals a fundamental Americanism in
paratexts and verses alike. In his preface, having cited Homer and acknowledged other literary columns, he underscores his own hemisphere and the
inevitable newness of expression on this side of the Atlantic:

> It is not through the *old world* behind that we shall get to the golden
> age, which is still ahead. The biblical and the Ossianic, the Doric and
> the Ionic, the German and the Luso-Hispanic, some are repugnant
> and others, if they are not, modify themselves to the nature of the
> Americas. In this nature are the very founts, grand and beautiful like
> their rivers and mountains; she in her image modeled the language
> of her Natives—and it is there that we shall imbibe the form of the
> original literary character, whatever different language we may speak.
> The Guesa, having the inverse form and the natural heart of the sav-
> age with no academy, accepts it thus—at least as the spirit of liberty,

and because he loves ye, and because he has a social *end* and because
"I shall sing a new song that rings in my breast: never was there a song
so lovely or good that resembles any other song." (195)

The cantos of *O guesa* are oriented by a mindset that honors select artistry of European heritage while affirming superior character and potential
in the New World. The overarching hemispheric sentiment and sympathetic respect for peoples dominated by European conquistadors are evident in canto XI. In a symptomatic passage, the poet-hero is speaking to a
limeña—a woman from Lima, Peru—and, in typical Romantic fashion, he
invokes native flora, fauna, and language. Beneath the sense of beauty is the
doleful consciousness of the evil conquest of the Spanish and the fall of the
great Inca empire. Yet the sense of cultural betterment in the New World
still remains:

Porque tudo suaviza-se na América,
  Do idioma os tons, os mimos das crioulas,
  Onde as morenas tardes hão d'angélica
  E à dolorosa queda ainda consolas,
Floripôndio inclinado no horizonte,
  E de fragância enchendo a natureza!
  Vos diviniza o amor, vos beija a fronte,
  Na doce terra divagando o Guesa. (262)

[For all is softened in the Americas, / The tones of the language, the
Creoles' caresses, / Where the brunette afternoons have angelica /
and thou still consolest the painful fall, // Floripondio inclining on
the horizon, / And filling nature with fragrance! / Love divinizes thee,
kisses thy forehead, / In the sweet land Guesa wandering.]

A profound concern for the land and peoples of the Americas is carried
by the hero to the colossus of the North. In canto X there is a clear statement of esteem for the land of Washington and Lincoln, who are mentioned, as well as a manifestation of awareness of the importance of the
United States on the world stage: "—Oh! creio e te amo / Jovem América
ainda a delirares, / E mais de ti, portanto, é que reclamo. / De ti depende o
mundo do futuro" (576) [Oh, I believe and I love thee / Young America still
delirious, / And so of thee I demand more. / On thee depends the future
of the world]. As suggested above, Sousândrade saw an ideal, utopian po-

tential for development and democracy in the United States. He absorbed the influence of the "poet of democracy" Walt Whitman and the idea that the "United States themselves are the greatest poem" (preface to *Leaves of Grass*, 1855). As Lobo notes (*Crítica*, 153), the Brazilian poet, who wanted to escape the Empire of Dom Pedro II and took his daughter to study in Manhattan, portrays New York as the port of entry to the good fortune of democracy open to all immigrants, also in canto X:

> Vinde a Nova Iorque, onde há lugar p'ra todos,
>   Pátria, se não esquecimento, —crença,
>   Descanso, e o perdoar da dor imensa,
>   E o renascer à luta dos denodos
> A República é a Pátria, é a harmonia:
>   Vós, que da religião ou da realeza
>   Senti-vos à pressão da barbaria,
>   Vinde! a filha de Deus não vos despreza.

[Come to New York, where there is room for all, / Fatherland, if not forgetting, —belief, / Rest, and the pardon of the immense pain, / And the rebirth to the struggle of the valiant // The Republic is the Fatherland, is the harmony: / Ye, of whom the religion and royalty / I felt of ye the pressure of the barbarity, / Come! the daughter of God does not disregard ye.]

Such passages establishing the poet's fundamental veneration make the parts critical of particular phenomena in North America all the more powerful. On its own "The Inferno of Wall Street" might lead one to conclude that Sousândrade nourished xenophobia or anti-Americanism. But the 176 strophes must be read in their overall context, which involves considerable measures of hybridity. In the first strophe, one grasps the geographical sweep of the poem as a whole, sees the "villians" of the myth (the *xeques*, priests who sacrifice the young chosen one), begins to appreciate how the poet perceives the ugly side of burgeoning US capitalism, and witnesses a textual confrontation of Western heritage with Indo-American figures.

> (O Guesa, tendo atravessado as Antilhas, crê-se livre dos Xeques e
>   penetra em New-York-Stock-Exchange; a Voz dos desertos:)

>   —Orfeu, Dante, Æneas, ao inferno
>   Desceram; o Inca há de subir . . .
>   = *Ogni sp'ranza lasciate,*

Che entrate . . .
—Swedenborg, há mundo porvir? (343)

(GUESA having crossed the ANTILLES, believes himself rid of the
XEQUES and enters the NEW-YORK-STOCK-EXCHANGE;
the VOICE, from the wilderness:)

—Orpheus, Dante, Æneas, to hell
Descended; the Inca must ascend . . .
= *Ogni sp'ranza lasciate,*
Che entrate . . .
—Swedenborg, do future worlds impend?] (585)

In subsequent stanzas, various news events—notably the meeting of
President U. S. Grant and Emperor Dom Pedro II, who came for the 1876
centenary celebration in Philadelphia—provide platforms to satirize imperial folly and also to expose some of the imperfections of the Republic of the
North. If in principle the land of Lincoln is seen as a site of nonmonarchical
opportunity, Sousândrade was a sharp critic of the darker side of expanding USAmerican capitalism. He keenly perceived the often corrupt and
rapacious nature of big business in the days of robber barons, unregulated
expansion, and influence peddling. Sousândrade's excited scenes interlace
mythical figures, corporate players, politics, and often hypocritical religion,
as in the second strophe:

(Xeques surgindo risonhos e disfarçados em Railroad-*managers*,
Stockjobbers, Pimpbrokers, etc., etc., apregoando:)

—Harlem! Erie! Central! Pennsylvania!
= Milhão! cem milhões!! mil milhões!!!
—Young é Grant! Jackson,
Atkinson!
Vanderbilts, Jay Goulds, anões! (343)

(XEQUES appearing, laughing and disguised as Railroad-*managers*,
Stockjobbers, Pimpbrokers, etc., etc., ballyhooing:)

—Harlem! Erie! Central! Pennsylvania!
= Million! hundred million!! ten digits!!!
—Young is Grant! Jackson,
Atkinson!
Vanderbilts, Jay Goulds are midgets!] (585)

In the first flourish of stanzas, the imbrication of moral, behavioral, financial, and political factors continues uninterrupted across scandals in different professions. In strophe 7:

(*Mob* violentada:)

—Mistress Tilton, Sir Grant, Sir Tweed,
Adultério, realeza, ladrão,
Em masc'ras nós (rostos
Compostos)
Que dancem à eterna *Lynch Law!* (344)

(Violated *mob*:)

—Mistress Tilton, Sir Grant, Sir Tweed,
Adultery, royalty, outlaw,
Knot masked (grim faces)
Disgraces,
Let them dance th'eternal *Lynch law!*] (587)

Dozens of passages below, in strophe 71, the historical arc that reaches back in time to ancient and primitive civilizations connects environs of the emerging financial capital of the world to the court of the Empire of Brazil:

(*Freeloves* meditando nas *free-burglars* belas artes:)

—Roma, começou pelo roubo;
New York, rouba a nunca acabar,
O Rio, *antropófago*;
= *Ofiófago*
Newark . . . tudo pernas pra o ar . . . (360)

(*Freeloves* meditating on the *free-burglars* fine arts:)

—Rome, robbed right from the beginning;
Robbery's rampant in New York town,
Rio, *anthropophagous*;
= *Ophiophagous*
Newark . . . wholly turned upside down . . .] (602)

This delightfully dialogical strophe synthesizes different examples of larcenous imperial enterprise, social disorder, and concomitant manifestations of decadence (such as sexual mores or opium use). The irony of the pandemonium here depends both on placement—as this strophe follows a sequence involving Emperor Dom Pedro II with President Grant—and juxtaposition, as the most "savage" of acts in the Christian world, cannibalism (so prominently discussed in the early chronicles of Brazil), is alluded to in a relativistic fashion that implicates the comparable practices of Wall Street. With this reference to anthropophagy, one may perhaps comprehend how a mid-twentieth-century critic saw fit to draw a comparison between Sousândrade and the modernist provocateur Oswald de Andrade.[31]

Toward the end of the infernal interlude, in strophe 155, the poetic voice likens himself to the explorer whose name became synonymous with the epoch of the New World, deterritorializing in Creole fashion an early animal-rights outlook and counterpoising the most profound rhetorical inheritance in the West, the Bible, against a native product and consumer item, coffee, that would become an icon of Brazil in Old World consciousness. The invocation of European reason versus technology may even be a suggestion of victimization, the targeting of locals, of subaltern natives as nuisances or pests, animal specimens trapped in cutting Euro-experiments that actually or ultimately mean irrationality.

(O GUESA sorteado em CITY-HALL; CANDIDE-VOLTAIRE:)

> —Jurado de todas Américas,
> Qual Columbus sou cidadão.
> = Bíblio . . . com Jacó e o café
>   Dos 'Cânticos'; . . fé; . .
>   Opor à ratoeira a razão; . .
>   E julgar à vivissecção! (381)

[(The GUESA's ticket wins at CITY-HALL; CANDIDE-VOLTAIRE) / —A jury of all the Americas, / Like Columbus I'm a citizen. / = Bibli'al . . . with Jacob and coffee / Of the "Songs"; . . faith; . . / Oppose reason to rat-traps; . . / And judge vivisection!]

Thematic approaches to *O guesa*, especially "The Inferno of Wall Street," inevitably collide with the work's multiplicity of intricate, strange, even bizarre formal aspects. The numerous neologisms, baroque figures, syntactical twists, apocopations, and "synthetic ideogrammatic" imagery can be daunting. In addition, as some of the above examples illustrate, there is a considerable quantity of obscure era-specific allusions to events and persons. The poet's having drawn freely and significantly on a singular journalistic source—*O Novo Mundo*, an editorially unabashed Brazilian newspaper published in New York in the 1870s—can be considered the most fruitful explanatory basis for a genetic critique.[32] "The Inferno of Wall Street" can be a hermetic collage, difficult to penetrate, on its own and as a section of the encompassing megapoem. While the New York dystopia may indeed prove to be discouragingly difficult, it is possible to read the work "running one's eyes over the text, moved by the tremulous exuberance of the sequence of fragments with which the writer takes apart the growing myths of big capital in order to reveal its tensions."[33] Questioned about his painstaking research of the poet's opus, Augusto de Campos affirms the need to dissect and document in order to be able to account for the very weirdness of the verses:

> Sousândrade's text is unique in the world. It deserves detailed scrutiny. Nobody made as he did in his time a poem focusing on the flowering of savage capitalism, with the New York of the "robber barons" as his stage, walking through the shouts of the Stock Market, and ending up in the infernal circle of financial speculators. To compact and transmit in poetic language the shocking conflict of his vision of the Republic of the North, at the same time source of liberty and progress and headquarters of excessive profit, Sousândrade had to create a new, difficult, almost unintelligible language. A kinetic prefuturism, that suggested the arms of cinematic montage and plastic collage. (Campos and Campos, 576)

From the point of view of transamerican poetics, it is vital to highlight the Hispanic links in Sousândrade. The first serious historian of Brazilian literature, Sílvio Romero, did not rank him highly, but he made a point of stating that he was "the only one of our poets to concern himself with an American matter outside of Brazil, a matter taken from the Spanish republics" (79). This fact did not escape the celebrated Peruvian writer Ricardo Palma, who selected *O guesa* as one of the three works that best achieved an ideal Americanism: "*La araucana* by Ercilla, *O guesa errante* by Souza Andrade, and *Tabaré*, are the poems that, in my view, satisfy most completely the ideal of literary Americanism."[34] Sousândrade's epic whole (with hero, myth, geography, and history) cites native chiefs and Columbus alike, and spans the hemisphere from Niagara and Mexico to Patagonia and Tierra del Fuego, in a profound geocultural linkage that brings to mind other poetic accomplishments. Claudio Daniel in "A poética sincrônica" finds that the end of "The Inferno of Wall Street" anticipates the dissolution of language in *Altazor*, by the Chilean poet Huidobro. Haroldo de Campos is impressed by the linguistic implications of *O guesa*, whose scope can only be seen to be matched, nearly a century later, by the grand Latin American epic *Canto general* by Pablo Neruda. Sousândrade and the great Chilean Nobel laureate both chastised the cruelty of the conquest and celebrated revolutionary leaders such as Bolívar, O'Higgins, Páez, and Lincoln. The two bards "converge and concur in the epicedial celebration of Incan tragedy. The Brazilian's republican socialist-Christian view as well as the Chilean's Marxist-nationalistic utopia with libertarian ends bring to the fore the social rescue of the conquered peoples." (Campos and Campos, 548–49).

Spanish was one of some twelve tongues that Sousândrade employed in a polylingual epic that connected classical literature (Greek, Latin), indigenous knowledge (Tupi, Quechua), and other colonial languages (English, French). The linguistic gregariousness mirrors an encompassing ethic and pan-national aesthetic that found itself integrally in Brazilian Portuguese. Sousândrade's idiom became a wandering structure that absorbed sounds, names, words, and ideas as it moved through the Americas, in previous centuries in poetic realms, and in the nineteenth century in actual history. In contemporary Brazilian lyric, there has been a trail of linguistic impact of the sui generis epic poet from Maranhão. The concrete poets are known to have exposed renowned singer-songwriter Caetano Veloso to several previous poets of invention, including Sousândrade. A sharp-edged example in song of that contact was his avant-gardesque setting of a single verse with several melodic variations in "Gilberto misterioso," which recognized the mellifluous spawning of the cofounder of *tropicalismo*, Gilberto Gil: "Gil-engendra em gil-rouxinol." This wonderfully musical verse, in sound and (figural) sense, is challenging to translate; Brown rendered it, needing a masculine end-rhyme, as "Gil engenders gil-nightingale's call." One of Caetano's and Gil's most perspicacious critics said that the experimental LP where the minimalist song appeared, *Araça azul* (1973), was on the whole an implicit, and sometimes explicit, tribute to Oswald de Andrade, Sousândrade, and the concrete poets. The greatest homage to the author of *O guesa* was not in the setting itself but rather in the album's general climate of formal daring, with apparently chaotic fragmentation and critical juxtapositions understood to have begun with the mad genius of Maranhão.[35] Veloso again showed deference to Sousândrade, and Gil, in the song "Ele me deu um beijo na boca" (He kissed me on the mouth), with a direct quotation of the poet: "toca de raposa bêbada" [den of a drunken vixen].[36] Mentions by pop intellectual and superstar Veloso have certainly aided the growth of interest in Sousândrade over the decades.

The rich contribution that the author of *O guesa* has made to poetic consciousness in Brazil is best captured in book poetry in a fractured poem of the early twenty-first century by Adriano Espínola, author of the lyric-epic with a stop in New York noted in chapter 2.[37] The Cummingsesque poem of homage hinges on convenient coincidences of morphemes (por, port-, guesa):

Sousândrade

yea!
na
lín
gua

por
tu
guesa
a

por
tou
er

rante
um
guesa

[Yea!-in-the-Por-tu-guese-lan-guage-there-port-ed-an-err-ant-*guesa*]

The original periodical publication of this poem had a dedication to contemporary poet Salgado Maranhão, a further geographical connection to the Romantic poet. Other details reveal measures of transamericanity and intertextuality. The initial "Yea!" is taken from the end of strophe 109 of the "Inferno de Wall Street" ("Por *guildens* sessenta . . . *Yea! Yea!*"), as Indians sell haunted Manhattan to the Dutch. There is a double linguistic irony as Sousândrade recalls the ill-fated historical exchange and Espínola opens a poem about the Portuguese language with an English word, which inevitably suggests internationalization. The word *errante*, in addition to the sense of "wandering" associated with bards, is an obvious citation of *O guesa errante*, as well as a subtle self-allusion with maritime linguistic content.[38] The external structure of the poem—fourteen lines, divided into two sets of four and two of three—hints clearly at the sonnet, that classical form with such resonance.

As much as he contributed to Portuguese and to textual invention in Brazilian literature per se, a wider lens is called for to see Sousândrade in proper perspective. Since his rediscovery, Brazilian criticism has focused sharply on the poet's unique place in world literature. Luiz Costa Lima cannot separate the formal novelty and content, saying that Sousândrade's "anticipation exceeds national limits and makes him one of the first Western poets who intuited the significance of capitalist development in terms of human values. . . . The 'Inferno of Wall Street' is one of the first or perhaps the first aesthetic correspondent of the world of liberal capitalism."[39] For Argentine-Brazilian critic Jorge Schwartz, *O guesa* embodies "a true cosmo-pan-americanism"; he draws a succinct comparison between Sousândrade, Baudelaire, and Whitman as contemporaneous avatars of cosmopolitan poetics.[40] Indeed, the Campos brothers had likened Sousândrade to the poet of *Les Fleurs du mal* as nineteenth-century groundbreaker, and to the Ezra Pound of *The Cantos* as maker of a multifarious (plotless) epic. In the larger picture, the São Paulo critics noted that the voice of Maranhão "got involved with international problematics, anticolonialist struggles, seeking to raise consciousness about Americanness in continental terms and having denunciatory premonitions about the contradictions of capitalism" (123). For Lobo, the recourse to the lessons of the United States are key; she sees Sousândrade as one who "dared to pass beyond the frontiers of colonialist literature of his epoch to seek an echo of his vision, that of a displaced emigré who took refuge not in the closed system of Europe but in a new and open society that reflected in part the same conflicts as his own" (*Tradição*, 88). From the merger of these various perspectives of late-twentieth-century critics there emerges a sense of an extraordinary individual who could only embrace collectivities on a local or national level when these were understood against their historical and artistic backdrops and married to overarching continental and hemispheric phenomena. More than any contemporary in eastern South America, Sousândrade conceived of Brazil as a continuous link to Latin American neighbors and as a potential site for republican life inspired by the best of the United States. Via comparative and comparatist parameters, *O guesa*, the textualization of a poet-hero who emerges from a singular periplus conceived in multiplicity and complicity, the hemispheric dimension is the closest to home.

A Poetics of New World Creation: *Toda a América*

The most "American" (meaning "of the Americas") or "Americanist" work of Brazilian modernism was a thematically focused volume by poet-diplomat Ronald de Carvalho (Rio de Janeiro, 1893–1935). The brilliant young intellectual began his government service in 1914 in Lisbon, where he established his modernist credentials by coediting the inaugural issue of the forward-thinking literary journal *Orpheu*, featuring Fernando Pessoa, who would become the greatest name in modern Lusophone lyric. Carvalho returned to Brazil to shed his lingering Parnassian-symbolist garments and to become an active voice in the emergent vanguard. He helped organize the Modern Art Week in 1922 and continued to participate in change-oriented activities. Subsequent travel to North America, via the Antilles, and the Andean side of South America, as well as engagement with artists and thinkers attuned to cultural redefinitions, inspired the poetry collection *Toda a América* (1926), which confirmed in verse the author's hemispheric philosophy. Carvalho had also made a name as a critic-historian of letters with the award-winning *Pequena história da literatura brasileira* (1919), the third edition of which (1925) was the first account "to reflect the Modernist idea."[41] It did so by closing with assertions of the need to get beyond the boundaries of the nation:

> The modern man of Brazil, in order to create a literature of his own, ought to avoid every kind of preconception. He has before his eyes a great virgin world filled with exciting promises. To organize that material, give it stability, reduce it to its true human expression: these should be his basic preoccupations. An art direct and pure, deeply rooted in our national structure, an art which will secure the tumult of our people in gestation, that is what the modern man of Brazil ought to seek. To that end, it is meet that he should study not only Brazilian problems but also the grand American problem. The pri-

mordial error of our elite up till now has been their insistence on applying artificially the European lesson to Brazil. We have reached the hour of the American lesson. We have at last come into our own time.

Carvalho the poet put that attitude into practice, as "he takes his place on the American plane rather than on the Brazilian plane" (W. Martins, 237). Criticism of this unusual poetic posture has involved, somewhat in passing, comparison to nationalist projects such as Oswald's *Pau-Brasil* and, consistently over the decades, compaginations with the obvious model of Walt Whitman as well as overall assessments of the relative depth of the hemispheric or continental approach, which can be called pan-, inter-, trans-, or even omni-American.

While necessarily wide in spatiotemporal proportions, *Toda a América* is not exactly epic in character, as there is no hero, sustained voyage, or narrative flow. Rather, it is a sort of lyric-epic, a geocultural sequence organized by the outlook of the speaker(s) through space and time. The book is comprised of twenty-one units: a foreword (*advertência*); a first long poem about Brazil; nine poems about the Lesser Antilles, North America, and Spanish South America; a grouping of nine epigrammatic texts on Mexico; and the titular composition "Toda a América," subdivided into five sections (I–V), which confirms, solidifies, and enriches, with frequent metapoetical urgings, fundamental strains of the preceding lyric instances. If some of these seem to remain at a surface level, or if there are evident gaps in the tricontinental textual mapping, the final quintuplet can be understood, in a sense, to compensate with its range and intensity. In addition to the steady traits and moods of the speaker(s) in the purely textual dimension, the continuity of the original (and facsimile) version is reinforced by abundant illustrations, which for the most part imitate Incan and Aztec graphics, though one recurring maternal figure has conceivably African tribal features. Following the frontispiece (figure 9) there is a graphic arrangement of the poet's motto "cria o teu ritmo livremente"—create your rhythm freely—which incorporates the driving values of freedom to create formal individuality, of liberty as an American primacy. Color, light, and grand contours dominate the fields of imagery. Most important, all that these represent is not available to conventional rational consciousness, as the foreword shouts in a wholly indicative apostrophe:

Toda a América

9. Nicola de Garo, frontispiece to *Toda a América* by Ronald de Carvalho, 1926.

Europeu!
Filho da obediência, da economia
e do bom senso,
tu não sabes o que é ser Americano! (29)

[European! / Son of obedience, of economy / and of good sense, / you
do not know what it is to be American!]

Naturally, such perceived difference abounds in the poems that follow,
which often carry intention-laden appositions of the European and American, the Old World and New World. Such counterpoising can be understood to structure the whole of the volume. This hemisphere comprises
freedom and a singular felicity related to finding: "terras livres, ares livres,
/ florestas sem lei! / Alegria de inventar, de descobrir" (30) [free lands, free
airs / forests without laws! / joy of inventing, of discovering]. Such procla-
mations become recurring motifs in physical and psychic spheres.

One contemporary of Carvalho's rightly saw a biblical parallel in the
text's transatlantic revitalizations: "*Toda a América* is the great continental
and insular poetry. There is an insistence upon the visionariness of the
American Canaan, for the fatigued old age of the Europeans."[42] The sense
of promised land indeed emerges in geographical and human landscapes
from start to finish. Calling the collection "continental" means both that it
spans North and South America and that its appeal was grand. While the
impact of the Spanish translation has been remarked, even tied to Neruda,
there have not been English or French renderings.[43] The employment of
"insular" in this comment has a literal rationale—Carvalho's poems of the
Antilles—and a particular figurative interest for the present study, where
the question of insularity and Brazil's relative connectedness in the hemisphere is explored throughout.[44] *Toda a América* is clearly a textual effort
to combat isolation and self-absorption.

While this poet of outreach never displayed the brash avant-garde spirit
of some of his colleagues-in-arms of the unfolding movement of *modernismo*, his thematic volume was compared by a leading anthologist to the
first programmatic proposal of a prime provocateur:

the Pan-American note of Ronald de Carvalho corresponds to a
transposition, on the continental plane, of the nationalist spirit of
Poesia Pau Brasil, invented by Oswald de Andrade, whose verses, unlike those of the Carioca bard, were characterized by synthesis and by

the dryness of the language. In Ronald intelligence was predominant over emotion. It was under the sign of calculation that he composed his verses. Hence the practice of a "supercivilized poetry," as Vinicius de Morais rightly recorded. (Brito, 41–42)

More than literary technique per se and possibly attendant ideological compasses, it is attention to the technical side of modern civilization, in a wider sense, that links the poetic endeavors of Carvalho and Andrade, who also should not be viewed, in any case, as being more emotional than rational. A fundamental principle in the "Manifesto of Pau-Brasil Poetry" is the interaction and valuation of natural world and industrial society: "the yearning for shamans, and military airfields . . . The forest and the school" (187). In the first section of Carvalho's concluding poem, in turn, the hemisphere is simultaneously celebrated for her "cafezais . . . seringais . . . canaviais . . . carretas de bois" (118) [fields/plantations of coffee, rubber, cane; oxcarts] and "locomotivas . . . elevadores . . . guindastes . . . comportas de aço cromado" (118–19) [locomotives, elevators, cranes, chrome steel canal locks]. References in *Toda a América* to geometrical shape suggest an awareness both of cubist perspective and of such lines in Oswald's founding document as "Synthesis . . . geometric equilibrium . . . the credulous and dualistic race and geometry" (186).

There are numerous such confluences of interest between the two wide-angled sequences, but there is a chronological doubt to consider when speculating that *Toda a América* (1926) is a transposition from Oswald's scheme. The pair were acquainted and collaborated on the Modern Art Week, but the simple fact is that much of Ronald's collection was written before *Pau-Brasil* appeared in 1924–25. The poems that constitute a sort of travel log of the poet-diplomat are dated 1923 or 1924. The more grandiose texts are not dated and thus could have been written later, having suffered the influence of *Pau-Brasil* and/or critical comments about it.[45] Whether there is a direct connection or not, there is indeed a shared interest in national achievement, both cultural heritage and in-progress innovation, and projection onto other screens, as *Pau-Brasil* is offered as poetry-for-export and the voices of *Toda a América* shout across mountains, plains, and oceans.

If Oswaldian rapport has been understandably limited, essentially every critical mention of *Toda a América* refers to Walt Whitman. Since the 1920s, the Brazilian work's critical fortune has largely wavered between admiration and reproach, at times for conceivably overbearing Americanist attitudes, and always for the implementation of Whitmanian models. A USAmerican chronicler chose to highlight a skeptical pedagogical reading by the "Saint John the Baptist of *modernismo*":

> Despite the sublimity of his artistic ambition, Ronald de Carvalho forgot . . . that the freedom, joy, and lyrical and varied substance of the Americas had already been expressed and almost exhausted by the truly continental voice of Walt Whitman. Hence the ample rhythms and the sparkling rhythms of his [Carvalho's] American poems sound to us like echoes, maybe more harmonious, but less naïve, less "innocent" than the more powerful accents, the more genial accents of *Leaves of Grass*.[46]

Indeed, when one reads "Eu ouço o canto enorme do Brasil!" (35) [I hear the enormous chant of Brazil] followed by multiple repetitions of the first-person verb conjugation in the course of the poem "Brasil," the echo of "I Hear America Singing" is loud and clear. And when Carvalho lyrically catalogues what he sees, especially human groupings like workers, the sensory scans of "Salut au Monde" and other Whitman wide casts are ineluctably invoked, despite the Brazilian's idiosyncrasies. In addition to the vast and generous character of *Toda a América*, analysts have detected therein such Whitmaneseque features as parallelisms, distribution in charts, elevated rhapsodic notes, and serial namings. The poets express a rich democratic sentiment at all social levels in free rhythms defined by ideas. In particular, "Crossing Brooklyn Ferry" merits detailed comparison to "Broadway."[47] A Brazilian specialist, Maria Clara Bonetti Paro, has done the closest comparison of the *modernista* poeticization of the hemisphere and the great American tome of the nineteenth century.[48] She verifies and confirms numerous intersections, yet the similarities (even pastiche-like instances) in certain poems do not justify an extrapolation onto *Toda a América* as a whole, which has plenty of self-styled moments. Carvalho could be seen as an individual who assumes a pan-national attitude, with a few universalist streaks, while Whitman is an intense, nationally identified self who wants to merge with a metaphysical ensemble of people, places, and things. There is every reason to agree with a fundamental differentiation articulated by Brazilian specialist Wilson Martins, who stresses the core motivations of the respective bards:

But the truth is that when Whitman sang America, he sang his own country, or rather he did something very like what the "Brazilianists" in Modernism were doing. On his part, when Ronald de Carvalho "sang America" he fled the geographical and spiritual borders of his country to create a kind of continental poetry which the North American poet had never even vaguely conceived and which, as a matter of fact, was alien to him. (237)

Ronald de Carvalho opposed the Americas, not simply Brazil, to Europe, while Whitman was at bottom concerned with the nation of manifest destiny and other nations as they were perceived from his vantage in the USA. Thus there prove to be important distinctions when comparing the two poets.

The 1920s witnessed in experimental and moderate modernist literature appreciable interplay between writerly urges toward discovery or local awareness and resistance to the demands of the European gaze motivated by exoticism. Writers in Brazil and Spanish America alike confronted difficulties with exploiting what was distinctively local (from the micro-settings of villages to the macroframes of hemisphere as an entity) without ceding ground to long-standing European desires for captivating native material. In *Latin American Vanguards: The Art of Contentious Encounter*, Vicky Unruh explores how, given the wonders of the New World, writers of the vanguard period generally portrayed the Americas as marvelously new, primordially telluric, or essentially organic (in the sense of unified). Even with reservations about European expectations, Ibero-American authors probed the potential of vernacular expression to affirm an American art and experience. Particular authors did, however, critically question such representation more aggressively and pursued more nuanced approaches. The Mário de Andrade of *Macunaíma* (1928) and the extraordinary Peruvian poet César Vallejo were among those to tackle Americanist questions head-on or to cast vernacular subjects in New World frames. Unruh (130–35) believes Ronald de Carvalho in *Toda a América* makes similar efforts to get beyond the lively assertion of locality to offer more problematized versions of America.

Before exemplifying those expansive gestures, it is instructive to see how critics of Carvalho's own epoch and subsequent decades were led to focus on native land and sometimes found his presentation to be naïve, overly taken by virgin settings, or too facile in its commitment to extranational-ism. A journalist of the mid-1930s, wondering whether *modernismo* was over, called Carvalho "the American who forgets his own self in a fascina-tion for virgin land and endless space," certainly suggesting that the telluric had come across the heaviest.[49] In an obituary, the poet was seen to have "impressed wide political sentiment on the literary cogitations of the day," and his poetry was remarked for having "the flavor of the land and taste of American blood. He understood landscapes, beings and things of the continent, sounding the heart of men and the heart of the land."[50] Lush sensorial textuality can be read as a reflection of space: "There is a virile and voluptuous sensualism emanating from his poems, revealing the wealth and lustful attraction of the virgin hemisphere."[51] *Toda a América*, in sum, has been taken as a show of a "commitment to Americanism, a naïve desire to show the superiority of the new world, and enthusiasm for the future."[52] One could affirm, with such examples, that the perception of a fanciful tinge increases with increases in chronological distance.

There are poems in the collection that in isolation lead one to think of romantic fantasy, essentialization, or touristic bias. The conclusion of one of the Mexican lyrics reads "India da Avenida Juarez, / toda florida de ritmos, / tu és o México, ou Deus não existe!" (112) [Indian girl on the avenue, / all flowered with rhythms, / you are Mexico, or God does not exist!], while the beginning of the next gushes "Guadalajara, tu és toda / uma dança!" (113) [you are all / a dance!]. Undiscriminating celebrations of color or festivity, however, do not prove to dominate in the hundred pages of poetic movement through the Americas. Carvalho is more prone to query givens and to confront platitudes in his Americanism. He seeks to affirm an American(ist) stance with a sympathetic eye and a sharp eye. Many lines trace an open-minded mapping of emergent sites, honoring both indigenous and Iberian pasts, while remaining open to diversification and plurality. "Broadway" is an axial example of an avenue of change, a site of synthesis and confluence that transcends geographical limits:

> Aquele chão carrega todas as imaginações
> do mundo!
> . . . .
> . . . é uma paisagem em marcha.
> Chão que mistura as poeiras do Universo e

onde se confundem todos os ritmos do
passo humano (62–63)

[That ground carries all the imaginations / in the world! / . . . it's a
landscape on the move. / Floor that blends all the dusts of the universe and / where mix all the rhythms of / human steps]

Imposing natural locations allow for appreciations of native beauty and
joy, as well as projections onto urban worlds and immigrant populations,
as in "Puente del Inca" (Incan bridge), which inquires: "Que cidade imensa
nascerá de todos esses / milhões de mãos que se agitam em ti?" (75) [What
immense city shall be born of all those / millions of hands stirring in thee?].
Hands of all stripes that "mix the oceans, raise beams of sixty floors, dive
into oil wells, fill and empty transatlantic holds" (76). If an Andean site
can house a mental territory that contemplates all from the pampas to the
skyscrapers, then, in a subsequent poem, a stark remote Chilean spot can
offer modernized views too: "Mas há nessa virgem solidão / uma perturba-
dora poesia geométrica / pirámides, / cones,/ cubos" (88) [But there is in
this virgin solitude / a perturbing geometrical poetry / pyramids / cones /
cubes]. Such lines relate to a final flourish built on notions of *poeisis*.

To place this work and others exhibiting a similar modus operandi in a
larger historical and ideological context, Unruh (160) considers the significance of expansiveness:

In Latin America, the impulse to encompass all was evident in manifestos' hyperbolic language and grand schemes. . . . this totalizing
drive was particularly evident in the vanguards' Americanist vein, not
only in manifestos that imagined a colossal continent of the future but
also in creative texts inclined to represent America as an all-encompassing whole. But in the construction of this portrayal, these works
employ strategies of containment that undermine the notion of New
World integrity and reveal an overflowing and disconnected American experience, simultaneously too out-of-bounds and too fragmented to be comfortably inscribed within an organic whole. . . . In
part, this revelation takes shape by exaggerating the organic model
in an America so full and complete that it exceeds its own whole-
ness. . . . The title of Ronald de Carvalho's *Toda a América* . . . presents
the most obvious example. De Carvalho's America, moreover, is a
world of "all imaginations" that merges "all cosmologies."

The title of the book does make the totalizing impulse rather indisputable, and given the legal, academic, diplomatic, and intellectual formation of the author, one would hesitate to ascribe any long-run ingenuousness to his poetic construct. Multiplicity, polyethnic input, and variety make this poetic world. Carvalho's grand sequence constitutes an excellent example of "America's flea market of images in vanguardist works," and America, in this Brazilian work, "presents an assemblage of 'indisciplines' as it brings together" and mixes pre-Columbian, classical, and biblical founts (Unruh, 164–65). What is further convincing is an evident keenness for novelty, a pervasive sense of what can be tagged constructivism, that accompanies appreciations of the autochthonous and growth.

The five variations on "Toda a América" will offer the most examples of increased consciousness. In section I: "Em ti está a multiplicidade criadora do / milagre / a energia de todas as gravitações" (118) [In thee resides the multiplicity that creates / miracles / the energy of all gravitations], followed, in II, by "O mundo nasce outra vez em ti" (125) [the world is reborn again in thee]. The finishing touch is an interlacing of the poet (that specially endowed being) and America, centuries-long site of discovery, otherwise known as invention, factitious lyricism, and creative enterprise. As the bard begins to bring his vision to a close in V, he foresees: "Oh! América, o teu poeta será / um construtor" [thy poet shall be / a builder], of ships, of dynamic machines, architectural calculations, with "a rude imaginação do inventor" (153) [the rude imagination of the inventor], and he concludes: "o teu poeta caminhará no milagre da / criação" (154) [thy poet shall walk in the miracle of / creation]. America is native but all in process, a work in progress of immigration and human ingenuity. This too is a manner of next-level aesthetic cognition that sets certain wide-lens vanguard works apart from others. If well-placed productive plurisignification is a sign of such distinction, witness "Toda a América," and the collection of the same name. The last word *criação* connotes godly bringing into existence and human, especially artistic, making. In Iberian tongues, there are added meanings that help back-sell the poetic sequence, including growing (crops), breeding (animals), and nursing (young). These polysemic, open-ended verses spell a hopeful and hyperaware end for an ecumenical journey.

Although Sousândrade did not make an Americanist splash in Brazil until after he was rediscovered in the 1960s, Ronald de Carvalho was an effectual figure in the arts and government in the 1920s and 1930s before an untimely death by accident. His cherished work *Toda a América* was read in his time and exerted some influence. For one historian, a curious bibliographical detail is proof of that work's impact. The polished modernist poet Jorge de Lima issued a volume of selected poems in 1932 in which he retitled an earlier poem, "A minha América" (1927), as "Não Toda a América." This other Americanist poem, while not very extended, does indeed have a Peruvian scene reminiscent of Carvalho's Andean stays and an enumerative section about "U.S.A." that marvels at "all the joyful and frightfully numerous rites."[53]

The legacy of both *O guesa* and *Toda a América* was remembered at the beginning of the new millennium as Brazil observed five hundred years of New World presence, historical destiny was in play, and Marcus Accioly constructed a massive neo-epic of hemispheric proportions.

Latinomérica: Solitude, Power, and Epic Realism

Latinomérica (2001) is an epic for the third millennium, an ambitious cultural and poetic atlas, and one of the most ample works of verse in the history of Latin American letters. Marcus Accioly's encyclopedic tome (620 pages) comprises twenty cantos of principal text and hefty paratexts, including twenty-five epigraphs of diverse provenance, a long table of contents (18 pages) sufficient to constitute a subordinated reading unto itself, and an attenuated appendix (45 pages) of self-explanation under a rubric, "Portulanos" (portolan charts, medieval navigation aids), that connotes the expansiveness and complexity of the poem proper. The overall title suggests the geographical and historical sweep, calling special attention to itself by virtue of the alteration of the standard (Spanish) name Latinoamérica via fusion with the name Homero, the most venerable of names in the Western epic tradition. Moreover, as the Brazilian author explains in one of the thirty sections of the leave-nothing-to-the-imagination afterword, the title and its preferred contraction allude to *Omeros*, the celebrated modern epic poem by Derek Walcott. This Nobel Prize–winning writer is a native of St. Lucia, an English-speaking entity, not part of the Spanish-, Portuguese-, or French-speaking Americas. The scope of Accioly's politically intense epic indeed exceeds Ibero-America and Latin America; his cantos address all the countries of the hemisphere, including the Lesser Antilles and the powerful United States in a surprisingly inclusive coverage that, in an implicit questioning of imperialism in a literal territorial sense, even incorporates island possessions in the Pacific. Primary concern, still, remains with colonial and neocolonial relationships in a larger context of the Western Hemisphere where USA–North America and Latin America are the big players.

Speculation about interplay among nations of the New World tempted the continental philosopher Georg Hegel, who, in the early nineteenth century, underlined the contrast between Catholic South America (with Mexico) and Protestant North America. Convinced of essential differences between old Europe and the former colonies, he drew the conclusion quoted as chapter epigraph above. Hegel is not crystal clear in the encompassing passage, but the sensation it gives is that he foresees greatness in the North, which will inevitably battle with the South. In a comment whose relevance to poetry is suggested in this chapter, Hegel notes that true epic, no longer possible in Europe, will have to emerge from (the) America(s), whose voices will be able to narrate a reverse conquest of the nations of origin. That sense of reversal and north-south conflict imbue Accioly's long poem in a way that qualifies his as another case of the "poetic justice" that Bernucci ("Justiça") has posited in modern Latin American epic—text with underlying historical ire, deep-seated dissatisfaction based on unjust developments, and an imperative of present protest about official versions of events.

Keys to understanding *Latinomérica* are the organization, layout, and unfolding of the narration. The overarching motivation (central theme, leitmotiv) of the work is the search for identity (Accioly, 561). The thousands of lines—mostly in the heroic ottava rima used by, among others, Camões in *The Lusiads*, but also occasional metric variations, in both learned and popular forms—represent a struggle to come to terms with conquest, linguistic and cultural dispersion, and centuries of oppression, tyranny, and uneven relations. Five hundred years of New World history, mostly Latin American, supplemented by pre-Columbian myth, are the object of commentary that is free to roam chronologically from the 1500s to the 1800s and the late 1900s. The middle of the twenty cantos, which all told number 422 titled poems, is set up according to the model of a boxing match: the thirty main countries of the hemisphere are presented in two sets of fifteen rounds. Overall, one way to see the external structure is a tripartite grouping: cantos I–VIII would be invocations, preliminaries, and preparations (judges, vestments, codes), cantos IX–XIII the combat (IX as fifteen rounds in South America, X as interlude, XI as fourteen rounds of Central America, Mexico, and the Caribbean, XII as "shadow boxing" in the Lesser Antilles and artistic USA, XIII as round 30 in the political and economic USA), and cantos XIV–XX would be evaluations and contemplations. Single interrelated poems mark the opening and closing of the work.

A specialist in epic discourse in Brazil systematizes *Latinomérica* with a six-part scheme. The first division, cantos I–III, is formed of a metapoetic overture, with very self-aware characterizations, presentations of language issues, and the legacies of epic. A second segment would be before the bout, defining the strategies of attack and defense, in cantos IV–VIII. The third and by far the largest part is the match proper in cantos IX–XIII (with 225 poems), with rounds in the ring, breaks, and restarts. The fourth set, cantos XIV–XVI, is after the fight, and the fifth concerns the identity of the poet and the poem, in cantos XVII and XVIII. The sixth element is a metapoetic closing, cantos XIX and XX.[54] The first and last cantos, again, are individual poems; they develop a vital apposition of solitude and power.

Earl Fitz has noted that "as a literary motif American solitude possesses distinctively cultural, historical, and psychological dimensions which . . . animate some of the New World's most powerful works of literature . . . bringing into contrast not only the New World/Old World dichotomy but a new and critically self-reflective intra-American perspective as well."[55] One of the most prominent works in this regard, Gabriel García Márquez's *One Hundred Years of Solitude* (1967), also stands, especially for English-language readership, as a prime example of the market-label and fictional tendency of magic realism, which has been used to the point of exhaustion. Both solitude and magic realism relate significantly to the framing of *Latinomérica*. The opening salvo, "Carta aos cegos do poder" [Letter to the blind in power], is subtitled, setting up the pretext of pugilistic encounter, "O poder da solidão X a solidão do poder" [The power of solitude vs. the solitude of power], which will be reversed for the final lyric. This epistolary form brings to mind the letters of discovery of Iberian explorers (Columbus, Caminha for Cabral), instituting the paradigm of conquest, which is complemented subsequently with references to villainous historical strongmen (Somoza, Pinochet) and salient examples of the "novel of dictatorship," a recognized manifestation of Latin American fiction (Augusto Roa Bastos's *Yo el supremo*, Alejo Carpentier's *El recurso del método*, and others mentioned in the appendix), usually involving the solitude of the tyrant.

With *Latinomérica*, Accioly in effect puts into operation many points of a proposal for poetry that he had written in the 1970s during the period of military dictatorship in Brazil and neighboring countries, as well the international heyday of magic realism. As he points out in the appendix to his grand epic project, the poet previously authored the creative think-piece *Poética: Pré-manifesto ou anteprojeto do realismo épico (época- épica)* [Poetics: Premanifesto or draft of epic realism (epoch-epic)]. The document, while advocating for aesthetically challenging and socially conscious discourse, is composed somewhat like a constitution, with main titles, sections, articles, paragraphs. Topics and binaries pondered include nature/ machine, time/space, tradition/imagination, artistic movements, and real/ marvelous. To get beyond the lyrical mode per se means an engagement with historical dimensions, and a crucial conclusion is that "magic realism," though a fictional category, will spawn a poetic "epic realism" in the Americas and other continents. The somewhat amorphous awareness of European and American literatures in this manifesto carries over into *Latinomérica*, where names and titles of all ages are purposefully distributed.

Here, as in Sousândrade's *O guesa*, a strong Americanist attitude never implies underutilization of the Western literary heritage stretching back to Greece; there is a productive contrast and interplay of Old World heritage in letters and New World repertories. Accioly begins with mixtures of tribal drums and muses, plus simultaneous pagan and Christian invocations. As indicated by the use of Walcott's *Omeros*, intertextuality in *Latinomérica* is paramount. Largely through condensed homages or citation of authors and titles, this erudite compendium encompasses everything from indigenous creation myths and the several works of epic poetry in colonial Latin America to renowned contemporary musicians and singer-songwriters of Brazil (Luiz Gonzaga, Tom Jobim, Chico Buarque, Geraldo Vandré) and Spanish America (Astor Piazzolla, Violeta Parra, Victor Jara). The concatenation of this series of performers implies an ideal integration into one great song of the Americas. Most abundant are canonical names of poetry and fiction of all the Americas (including *Toda a América* and "O Inferno de Wall Street"). The strongest link, not surprisingly, is with the *Canto general* of Neruda, who sought to sing the entirety of Latin American reality and to poeticize a socialistic worldview.

Issues of language are central to Accioly's grand creation. An entire early canto (III) is dedicated to the topic, and followed by a canto about writers and literature. Related thematizations are omnipresent. The loss (or extreme marginalization) of native languages, in confrontation with Spanish and Portuguese, is lamented serially, and the singularity of American varieties of colonial languages is a natural focus. In one interlude the bard turns linguistic separation upon himself:

(América Central) ao teu ouvido
falo o meu idioma português-
espanhol (*portunhol*) mal-entendido
(no Sul como no Centro) e cada vez
que me encontro em mim mesmo mais perdido
de menos te encontrar (indago) "fez-
me Deus para eu cantar o continente
ou descobrir a sua língua ausente?" (305)

[Central America in thy ear / I speak my Portuguese-Spanish language / (Portuganish) badly understood / (in the South and in the Center) and each time / that I find myself more lost in myself / for encountering thee less (I ask) "did / God make me to sing the continent / or to discover her absent tongue?"]

The domination of English and entertainment media in the age of the global village, tinged by a momentous curse in *The Tempest*, is another ottava-rima punch in round 30:

teu idioma agride nossos tímpanos
com uma guitarra-elétrica e a música
(que nada tem da quena sobre os píncaros
nem da zampoña na planície rústica)
tenta colgar o fôlego dos índios
que sopram do toré (agreste tuba)
uma víbora-viva (áspero som)
com a praga (a maldição de Caliban) (444)

[thy idiom agresses our eardrums / with an electric guitar and the music / (which has nothing of the Incan flute on high / nor of the pan-pipes on the rustic plateau) / tries to hang the breath of the Indians / who blow from their rural tuba / a live viper (harsh sound) / with the plague (the malediction of Caliban)]

Literary allusion and linguistic construct in numerous instances conspire toward charged plurisignification in Accioly's confrontations. The last reverberations of the first bell of round 18, *O grito das araras* (The cries of the parrots) mixes, in a more popular meter, an aural affirmation of workers' right to strike with a foundational anagram of Brazilian and New World literature:

além do grito da greve
graves araras falantes
gritam mais alto teu nome
(vermelho aos verdorizontes
azuis) *"Iracema"* (*"América"*)
ó anagrama (ó pocema)
os lábios de mel dAmérica
nos bicos deste poema (335)

[beyond the cry of strike / grave talking parrots / shout thy name louder / (vermilion in the blue verdure-horizons) / *Iracema-America* / oh anagram (oh war chant) / the honey lips of America / in the plumes of this poem]

The reference here is to *Iracema*, one of the classics of nineteenth-century Brazilian fiction, a novella in which the European hero fathers a child with a native beauty whose name, presumably meaning lips of honey, is a symbolically rich anagram of America.[56] The rhyming Tupi-derived word *pocema* works so well here because it means not only war chant but native song and hubbub of voices, just as in the final line *bicos* signifies both beaks (birds' bills) and pens (writing utensils).

Also notable here are the examples of contraction, *verdorizontes* (verdure-horizons), which is suggestive of mixing and the grandeur of nature in the New World, and *dAmérica*, one of some two dozen spots in *Latinomérica* where possessive pronouns, prepositions, or nouns (ending in -a) are contracted to form one lexical unit. The frequency of contractions subliminally reinforces an essential notion of New World cultural formation, including language: miscegenation, otherwise and variously understood as syncretism, hybridity, synthesis, amalgamation.[57] These instances often occur in passages related to repression, tied to the overt and insistent binary of victimizers and victimized in the course of the epic. A word like *aguiamericana* (Americaneagle) is, in concert with the anti-imperialist ethos, set against the grand condor. Ethnic blendings are inexorable, *IndiAmérica* and *AfricAmérica*, which is so fundamental that it names a section unto itself. The twenty-four lines of round 28, titled *PatriAmérica* (Fatherland+), exemplify the strategy of employing contraction, with *América* and/or other

words, as a vehicle of specific ideology, in this case unity. The key item of
the Pan-American poem is *latinunidade,* which is supported by such others
as *globOceano* and topped off with "de um só povo e uma só Ilha / dentro
do MarOceano" (395) [of one people and one Isle / in the ocean-sea]. Thus
presents itself the most obvious image of a desired organicity and togetherness in an apostrophe to the three Americas under one imagined flag.

This unitary configuration is ideal. The general idea of union relates to
an overarching structure and guilelessly elaborated metaphor of *Latinomérica*: the interrelation of father, mother, and son—conqueror, continent,
offspring—which is developed in the full course of the work but treated
fully in canto XVII, *Corpo-a-corpo* (Body to body). Foundational violence
and potential for trauma in the family are patent in the title of the most
explicit poem in this regard, titled "A relação brutal" (The brutal relation):

> ó minha mãe (América-Latina)
> paixão maldita (incestuosa) tu
> que me deitavas no teu colo e em cima
> do teu ventre eu cresci (menino nu
> que ao útero voltou pela vagina
> de onde saiu) em ti o meu estu-
> pro foi mais natural que o de Pizarro
> e o de Cortés (sou filho do teu barro)
> . . . .
> porém (antes de mim) tiveste um coito
> com meu pai (foi Colombo ou foi Cabral?)
> um almirante ou um fidalgo afoito
> teve contigo a relação brutal
> de quem conquista pela força o corpo
> e goza o gozo virgem (bestial
> como quem usa a espada em vez do membro)
> ah preciso esquecer do que me lembro (507)

[oh my mother (Latin America) / accursed (incestuous) passion you
/ who lay me down in your lap and on / your womb I grew up (naked
child / who returned to the uterus through the vagina / he came out
of) in you my rape / was more natural than Pizarro's / and Cortez's
(I'm the son of your mud) / . . . / yet (before me) you had coitus /
with my father (was it Columbus or Cabral?) / an admiral or a bold man-
of-means / had with you the brutal relations / of one who conquers

by force the body / and enjoys the virgin pleasure (bestial / like he
who uses the sword instead of his member) / ah I must forget what
I remember]

In the search for identity, acknowledged central concern of this epic poem,
the Latin American son (remember the child of Iracema) looks for his father (embodied in explorers, conquerors) but cannot find him, so he instead seeks to return to his mother. This return to the womb can only take
place sexually, incestfully. The son returns to his roots, his origins, which
implies a second rape of the land. Thus from the outset and subsequent
oedipal chapter the destiny of Latin America is defined by violations, and it
shall remain in peril throughout time, finding modern expression in struggles with its own dictators and, more forcefully, with the giant of the North.
The United States succeeds Spain in the colonialist project.

In a frank review of *Latinomérica*, a contemporary poet-diplomat notes
that Accioly, in his transcontinental textual edifice, did not conceive of a
"geographical poem" but rather a "long political poem whose construction enforces one fundamental principle: art as attack and commitment,
or as an instrument of denunciation or persistent combat." Updating the
theme of violence, the hyperbolic and Manichean result is "the most anti–
United States poem in Brazilian literature."[58] Herein, two ironies of form
and content emerge to be weighed. If the poem seeks to question the colonial mentality or to take an anti-imperialist stance, is the metrical scheme
of Camões, the grand voice of the Portuguese empire, the most appropriate? Accioly discusses the choice in his appendix (570–72), offering as his
primary defense the fact that in *Omeros* Walcott revived Dante's epic meter,
terceto, in a postmodern fashion that sanctions (re)use of elements from
any period. Similarly, how to write against the empire using a structure
based on the rules of the US-based International Boxing Association?
Again, Accioly adds his perspective in the afterword (588–90), justifying
this arrangement, most notably, with Roland Barthes' brief commentaries
in *Mythologies* about the boxing match and with the Joyce Carol Oates piece
"On Boxing," in which artists are compared to professional prizefighters. A
compatriot of the poet of the Brazilian Northeast questions whether poetry
and pugilism actually mix and whether his metrical preference would be
paradoxical since he seeks above all cultural independence.[59]

Published in 2001, *Latinomérica* was being composed as the Americas
approached the quincentenary of Columbus's landing in the New World.

The last full canto was completed after that observance and as Brazil, once dubbed the "land of the future," anticipated its own five-hundredth birthday, as the speaker-poet makes clear, not in the prose of the appendix, but in the verse of the penultimate poem:

> eu termino meu livro quando a América
> (sem que os fios se contem dos seus dias)
> quinhentos anos faz de descoberta
> (ou de inventada pelas utopias)
> eu entrego ao leitor *Latinomérica*
> quando (ó ano dois mil) já anuncias
> (ao terceiro milênio) o quinto século
> de um país sempre e nunca descoberto
> . . . .
> . . . ano de mil / novecentos e (já) novecentos e seis (531)

[I finish my book when America / (without the threads of her days being counted) / five hundred years since discovery / (or invention by utopias) / I deliver *Latinomérica* to readers / when (oh year 2000) you announce / (to the third millennium) the fifth century / of a country always and never discovered / . . . / . . . year of 19(already)96]

That year is midway between the quincentennial of Columbus (1992) and that of Cabral (2000), situating the author in a sort of chronological equilibrium to contemplate and to have contemplated his home nation, Latin America's largest, the region as a whole, and North America as well. The explanatory "Portulanos" ends (signed 2000) with reference to *navigare necesse est, vivere non est necesse*, an ancient phrase regarding navigation and life made famous in the Lusophone world by Fernando Pessoa and Caetano Veloso, which is played off against statements regarding poetry by Hölderlin and Cortázar. Thus are maintained both the Latin American view and connections with the canon of European literature, which is never dismissed in the affirmation of American being. *Latinomérica* is still a recent work; its critical reception is in progress; but surely Accioly's epic contains more American content than any single work in Brazilian literature since 1500.

5

◇

Banda Hispânica

Spanish American–Brazilian Links in Lyric and Landings

Soy loco por ti América
Soy loco por ti de amores
Soy loco por ti América
Soy loco por ti de amores

Since the 1990s the major development in all areas of human endeavor involving communication has most certainly been the diversification and unbridled spread of the Internet. On the World Wide Web, dissemination and exchange of information, in the widest sense of the word, have exploded in heretofore unimaginable ways at the macro level of global digital networks, the micro level of local online communities, and the intermediate level of virtual connections within large geographical divisions or between neighboring lands. Transamerican relations in the arts, as seen throughout the present writing, can unfold multidirectionally to concern all the countries of the far Western Hemisphere, be limited to a bilateral configuration in the two titans in size and population, Brazil and the USA, or focus on Latin America as Ibero-America, the lone Lusophone land vis-à-vis twenty Spanish-speaking nations.

Banda Hispânica is an Internet location that embodies cultural embraces via technological means. Brazil occupies a rather prominent place in cyberspace, and postings on poetry—national and international—are legion.[1] The most extensive and well-connected Brazilian Web site dedicated to lyric sponsors a "Hispanic band" that is subdivided into ever-in-progress sections on the various Hispanophone nations. With both recognized and emerging names, its bandwidth contains poems, interviews, studies, images, and links in both Spanish and Portuguese with the express intent of

10. Promotional poster for music publisher, circa 1986, concept by José Carlos Capinan and Virgínia Andrade, art by Washington Falcão. Used by permission of José Carlos Capinan.

improving mutual knowledge and international lyrical relations. Thus, this place is literally and symbolically a gateway to the study of poetic fraternization between Brazil and Spanish America toward the end of the twentieth century and in the beginning of the next. The platform of this electronic journal and live archive cites a politic idea advanced by José Martí, the theorist of Cuban independence, the poet residing in the USA and advocating Latin American consciousness: "knowing diverse literatures is the best way to free oneself from the tyranny of some of them."[2] A primary aim of Banda Hispânica is to help overcome the half-millennium divide between the Spanish and Portuguese Americas. The project seeks integration with Hispanics of the New World, "so close yet so inexplicably distant," and "systematic diffusion of cultural fora that do not habitually maintain dialogue."[3]

Since the 1990s, in conjunction with new bids to forge political and economic ties in Latin America, there have been admirable missions to build bridges in cultural realms, including literature—even poetry, admittedly more difficult because of linguistic factors. Such outreach comes against a historical backdrop of disengagement and some discord. Since the turn of the twentieth century, many statements have been made concerning an unfortunate lack of cultural connection between Brazil and her neighbors, but in counterbalance there have also been a series of meritorious activities related to networking and comparative deliberation, the sum of which invites consideration of reasons for historical separation and for more recent togetherness. A dialectic of separation and attraction in international affairs has memorable and provocative reflections in the domain of poetry.

Curiously, numerous mediated statements quite symptomatic of capital aspects of Spanish American–Brazilian relations have been made in the United States, the New World metropolis in effect, the Colossus of the North. The 1994 World Cup of soccer was held in the USA. The instant that Brazil's penalty-kicks victory over Italy in the final in Pasadena's Rose Bowl was realized, the Argentine broadcaster for Spanish-language USA television, Andrés Cantor, shouted: "¡Bra-si-i-i-l! ¡La copa se queda en América!"—the cup will stay in the Americas. This moment of excitement and joy involved a shared pride: a win by Latin America's largest state over an Old World foe was a triumph for all sister nations in the hemisphere above and beyond any intraregional rivalry. On a different stage, in 1995 Brazil's internationally renowned singer-songwriter Caetano Veloso reached out with the recording of *Fina Estampa*, a collection of high-impact Spanish American songs, especially bolero, a quintessential genre of Hispanic musical emotivity. When he presented the show in support of the album in 1997 in multicultural Miami, Veloso was unsure whether to speak English, Spanish, or Portuguese, so he employed all three to explain his neighborly gesture, the wherefore of his Hispanic repertory.[4] Lyrically and linguistically, Veloso embodied end-of-the-century combinations relevant to transamerican poetics.

While showing a sense of Latin American unity that may extend to activities in the USA, these two examples also suggest the rationale for lamentations over the comparative disadvantage of literature in cross-border cultural rapport. Brazil may be well known in Spanish America for mass culture, most prominently sports and popular music, but it is still relatively unknown, and understudied, when it comes to letters—as a Rio de Janeiro-based researcher of Hispanic American attention to Brazilian authors, Lígia Vassallo, has asserted outright.[5] To athletics and song/dance music, Ana Pizarro, a Chilean scholar vitally interested in literary dealings between Brazil and Southern Cone neighbors, adds *telenovelas*, soap operas, as an active Brazilian presence in Spanish America, citing the cutting-edge research of a noted Caracas-based media theorist. For her, mutual cultural awareness is enhanced through comprehension of "confluences." Relations between Spanish- and Portuguese-speaking "blocks" emanate from "productive symbolic nuclei" that have been articulated through the integration of tensions in cultures subject to peripheral conditioning. The "construction of an emergent alternative space during the colonial period," national aesthetics that tend to homogenize, and "regional-cosmopolitan tensions of modernization," even if they also show divergences, do provide "a sense of unity." Academic activities have been vehicles of the new proximity and applied interests.[6]

Along these lines, another revealing stateside event involving a prominent Brazilian figure was a televised speech by former president Fernando Henrique Cardoso (b. 1931).[7] In a question-and-answer session, the new at-large professor of international relations at Brown University fielded an inquiry about the possibility of Latin American integration. Cardoso first distinguished between commercial and cultural integration, the former being somewhat easier to achieve. He illustrated the role of inherited perceived differences in expressive identity with an anecdote of discovery: He had found out that he was a "Latin American" when as a student in the 1950s he went to France, where he associated with Argentinians and other Spanish speakers. He had thought of himself first as a Brazilian and second as a Francophile. That all changed with exposure and history, as the committed social scientist Cardoso fled to Chile soon after the 1964 military coup in Brazil and became an original voice of the widely influential "dependency theory" of Latin American development.[8] In his Washington appearance, Cardoso further pondered how Latin Americans have in fact been integrated by certain commonalities. While not forgetting the obsession with "football" (soccer), he referred more conceptually to a "sense of space" (personal, group, perhaps geopolitical), as well as to a "sense of humor," a Latin American attitude quite set off from French reserve. Transatlantic contrasts extend to New World geography, to kinds of societies, to greater social mobility, and above all—and Latin America shares this with the USA—to a "different sense of hierarchy," a point that obtains even though Brazil, unlike any other country in the Americas, was fully constituted as an empire in the nineteenth century. Even with monarchy, Brazilians simply related on different levels, without the same sense of royalty as Europeans. There can be a long stretch between academic and diplomatic portrayals of socialization and discourse, yet Cardoso's sense of hierarchy certainly does pertain to language use and, in the long run, to poetry, over the centuries and at present.

The title of the first chapter in the wide-ranging collection of essays by Richard Morse, *New World Soundings: Culture and Ideology in the Americas*, is the comprehensive "Language in America." In different conditions, the processes of modification of English, French, Spanish, and Portuguese during the centuries of colonization shared important features, not the least of which are the evolution of local diction and the addition of native vocabulary, whether created in response to circumstances or borrowed from indigenous idioms or from the speech of African "forced migrants." A break with the mother tongue is a natural corollary to political independence, and subsequent tension between Old World correction and New World corruption takes form in all European languages on the other side of the Atlantic, most notably, in literature, in Romanticism and nationalistic modernisms. Morse singles out a declaration made by Jorge Luis Borges around 1940 regarding the status of Spanish in the River Plate, applicable in much wider scope: "Our discourse is Hispanic but our verse, our sense of humor, are now from here." The "*transplantation* of European cultures and institutions . . . also entailed *re-creation*" (19, 23), which reverts both to the formative period of European history and to civilizational novelties in the

Americas. Despite major geo-ethnic dissimilarities, Morse profitably associates the Anglophone Caribbean, Andean Peru, and cosmopolitan São Paulo and their philosophical and linguistic positionings vis-à-vis cultural heritage expressed through modernist literary creation. Americanness, in poems or statements of tendency, can be specific and concrete or abstract and intuited.

José Kozer, Caribbean-born poet resident in Spain at the time, spoke in an interview of this sense of distinction in the Americas: "We are thinking seriously of going to live in Miami, gateway to the Americas: with countries like Cuba, Mexico, Brazil, where language, literature, a profound disquiet, a state of alert and alarm about the current world, are all strong, alive. One *lives* rupture with modernism, an ecological, visceral, moral rupture. Everything is questioned . . . an ecumenical voracity." For him, Old World language suffers from "sclerosis." All this is affirmed in alliance with a perception of Europe as focused on its own worn-out self, a Europe that has become a museum of itself. Kozer's publications in Mexico and Brazil, as well as his dealings with the maker of Banda Hispânica, are transamerican exemplars. An exhortation for exchange in lyric has a historical point of departure: "it's time for us to extend a cordial arc, differential yet fraternal, between our literatures. It would be good for poetry in general and more concretely for that done in these two languages, with a common trunk and different branches."

Consanguinities of Spanish- and Portuguese-speaking constituencies hark back to the beginnings of poetry in the Iberian peninsula, where the tongues of Cervantes and Camões would emerge as national languages from the numerous neo-Romance varieties in the area. In the medieval period, Galician-Portuguese was the language of choice for troubadours and courtly authors in western Iberia and Castile-Leon. In the latter, it is significant that King Alfonso X "el Sabio" (the Wise, r. 1252–84), grand patron of the arts and learning, commissioned and wrote verse in the language of Galicia. While political and military rivalry marked overall relations between Lusitania and the rest of Hispania for centuries (the threat of Castilian invasion is a main constant in the history of Portugal), the memory of a common means of expression sets the field of poetry somewhat apart. Competitive spirit between Spain and Portugal transferred to the New World, as the two kingdoms led the Age of Discovery and pursued overseas domains. The Vatican-negotiated Treaty of Tordesillas (1494) created a line of division in the Atlantic on either side of which Spain and Portugal

could claim discovered lands for their crowns. The geographical demarca-
tion of that treaty is symbolic to this day of the divide between Brazil and
Spanish America, especially since the former's eventually tremendous size
was largely due to encroachment beyond the assigned meridian. Spanish
influence over Portugal and her possessions was greatest during the period
when Spaniards occupied the throne in Lisbon, 1580–1640. In the colonies,
disputes over the River Plate, the future Paraguay, and the vast Amazon
region, largely ceded to Portuguese rule in the Treaty of Madrid (1750),
left a contentious diplomatic legacy. These and other occurrences—such
as the Brazilian occupation of the future Uruguay (1806–28)—made for
substantial material for literary treatment, as seen in some examples in the
preceding chapter.

A fundamental feature of Romanticism in the Americas was the quest
for linguistic registers capable of rendering what was unknown in England,
France, Spain, or Portugal. If there were certain commonalities of colonial
experience in Brazil and Spanish America, their divergent paths toward
independence, political emancipation, and subsequent international poli-
cies factored into discord within Ibero-America. Compared to Portuguese
domination, the Spanish conquest of Mexico, Peru, and other areas was
much more violent, as were, for the most part, the wars of independence
and civil wars in Spanish American lands. In the nineteenth century, Brazil
was singular as a monarchy, first as host of the Portuguese reign (1808–22)
and then as an independent empire (1822–89), often more aligned with
the United States than with Spanish America, which splintered into different republics where local strongmen (*caudillos*) often held greatest sway.[9]
In the nineteenth century, developing national identity included, for some
in Brazil, a utopian sense of difference from the rest of Latin America, "a
valorization of unique qualities" and superiority in relation to the "other"
América.[10] At different times over the decades, fear of a Brazilian brand
of regional imperialism had developed in Spanish America.[11] As seen in
chapter 1, the forged notion of "Latin America" has never been uniform but
rather varied and fluid since its emergence in the mid-nineteenth century,
and in the 1890s, Pan-Americanism was mostly a geopolitical concept, suggestive above all of USAmerican hegemony. Toward the turn of the century,
in Rubén Darío, José Martí, and other Hispanic American writers, there
was an innovative self-interest in lyric discourse, but it would be difficult
to confirm that solidarity in the poetic imagination truly included Brazil.
Martí's essay "Nuestra América" (1891) is an oft-cited point of departure in

the mapping of challenges to USAmerican mental domination, in the effort to identify other possible senses of America. It exemplifies an "ideological discourse about America" in Spanish-speaking nations that has, according to São Paulo specialist Irlemar Chiampi, "a vehement and obsessive quality unmatched in North America or Brazil."[12]

There are a series of critical and creative instances since 1900 that scholars and poets have highlighted to demonstrate lack as well as countermeasures in general literary and specifically poetic relations between Spanish America and Brazil. José Veríssimo (1857–1916) was a beacon during the First Republic. Presenting Spanish American literature to Brazilian readership, he recognized problems with distance, poor communications, mutual ignorance, and even prejudice, yet stressed historical and cultural affinities with neighbors over purely aesthetic interests. The noblest function of a work of art, he declared, is "establishing a communion of feeling and thought that . . . creates union between men" (76). Veríssimo enacted a continental desire with cultural carryovers from political criticism and essay into poetry. He attempted to span cultural chasms with appreciations of Spanish American verse and its chief makers, having welcomed Darío, complete with apologies for "mutual ignorance," to the Brazilian Academy of Letters in 1912.

In one of the epoch-making texts of the 1920s, *La raza cósmica*, Mexican essayist José Vasconcelos made Brazil a fundamental part of his "cosmic race," and he exercised, in turn, influence on the pivotal figure who was the poet-ambassador Alfonso Reyes. The latter Mexican thinker's years as a diplomat in Rio de Janeiro were partially dedicated to literary affairs, and bond-making was one of his goals on all fronts. In *Monterrey*, the arts circular he published while in South America in the 1930s, he pondered how to make "a new expression, a new feeling and a new making, that might better correspond to the realities of life in the New World."[13] Elsewhere this belief is tied to poetry: "the curiosity of poets broke the ill-fated spell. It is the poets—that is to say, the disinterested force of the spirit—who are returning coherence and unity to *all-the-Americas*." He refers here to the sequence *Toda a América* by Ronald de Carvalho, seen in the preceding chapter.

The axial figure of Brazilian modernism was Mário de Andrade (1893–1945), chiefly for his championing of liberating technique and native substance, but also for his attention to folk/popular culture in Brazil at large beyond metropolitan Rio and São Paulo, as well as to intellectual and artistic life in neighboring lands. Archival and textual research concerning his relationship with Spanish America, mostly Argentina, has resulted in a series of valuable studies. Raúl Antelo, an Argentine scholar relocated in Brazil, has studied the leader's appreciation of South American literary fellows, as well as Argentine reception of Brazilian authors.[14] In the nineteenth century, and decades into the twentieth, literary crossovers comprised mostly travel writing and cultural essays; an anthology prepared by Antelo contains only half a dozen poems. Where poetry is concerned, an appreciable move by Mário de Andrade was his recognition of the genius of a certain Jorge Luis Borges. Emir Rodríguez Monegal supplied a sharp reading of the two figures from the points of view of comparatism and Hispanism.[15] The Yale critic was careful to register that no actual exchange took place between them but that the critical approach was warranted by their common interest in founding, especially in poetry, a contained nationalist modernism—not an overly experimental avant-garde, which both opposed, but a new art critically appreciative of literary heritage. Both were averse to "Pan-" or "Latin American" postulations that advanced sameness in unrealistic utopian fashion, to the detriment of necessary national insights. The early Borges was more given in his poetry to memory, myth, and the past than was Mário, as an assiduous scholar of their comparative profiles concludes.[16] Most significantly, the inaugural collections of the two national heroes have fruitful parallels. *Paulicéia desvairada* (1922; *Hallucinated City*, 1968) by Mário de Andrade kickstarted the combative phase of Brazilian modernism with a multifarious poetic scheme.[17] Borges's *Fervor de Buenos Aires* (1923) also relies on urban focus and enjoys historical prominence. Critical reception of the São Paulo sequence has invited comparisons with other cardinal Spanish American *vanguardia* texts.[18]

Still, Borges maintains a special place in the lyrical imagination in Brazil, having come to constitute a veritable motif in the contemporary corpus. His urban sequence directly inspires, for example, "Sobre *Fervor de Buenos Aires*" by Luciana Martins: "passeio na tarde / de um Borges / pleno de jovialidade /—rapaz itinerante / de ruas e rios, mas também / mares e mármores" (89) [an afternoon stroll / of a Borges / full of joviality /—itinerant fellow / of streets and rivers, but also / seas and marble]. And a perception in Mexico City is clarified via the great Argentine writer: "é cego como Borges / ou a Justiça" [blind like Borges or Justice].[19] He becomes a self-doubting poetic persona unto himself in "Poema escrito por Borges" (Poem written by Borges), whose quatrains conclude:

Borges é acaso de Borges.
Mas, como não acredito,
passo a perdê-lo, e perdido,
sem Borges, eu me resigno.[20]

[Borges is chance casualty of Borges. / But since I don't believe, / I lose him, and lost, / without Borges, I resign myself.]

A Spanish-language text forged via the spectacle of bullfighting, "Fiesta brava," reaches highest:

No le pasa argentinamente
que Borges tiene un agujero
blanco para los ojos ciegos
y otros modos de la ceguera:

del negro la dominación
sobre el campo dorado, tigre
en su presencia invisible,
el toro sabe que nosotros

sí, nosotros, los metafísicos.[21]

[It does not occur to him Argentinely / that Borges has a white (target) / hole for his blind eyes / and other modes of blindness: // of black the domination / over the golden field, tiger / in his invisible presence, / the bull knows that we // yes, we the metaphysicians].

Another engaging contact between Argentina and Brazil was the meeting of Oliverio Girondo and Oswald de Andrade. As Schwartz elucidates, their cosmopolitan vanguard works invent in intercomparable ways. They met in 1943 when Girondo paid a visit to Brazil. An encounter and exchange of material led the São Paulo writer to declare: "The panorama of literature in the Americas would be quite another if we were only more familiar with what we produce."[22] The so-called John the Baptist of Brazilian modernism, Manuel Bandeira, was in fact knowledgeable about Spanish American literature, which he taught at the Federal University in Rio de Janeiro. He published anthologies of Spanish American literature in Brazil, lectures about it, and a collection of Brazilian poets in Mexico. Jorge Schwartz was particularly impressed with Bandeira's reception of female poets, beginning with Sor Juana Inés de la Cruz and including poet-diplomat Gabriela Mistral, Nobel Prize winner, who spent the early 1940s in Brazil.[23] Bandeira translated texts by Borges and otherwise contributed to literary columns and a special section called "Pensamento da América" in the Rio daily *A manhã* organized by poet Cassiano Ricardo, during his service in the Getúlio Vargas government.[24] Other writers of the modernist phase made occasional mention of poets, or cultural configurations relevant to poetry, in their South American travel writing and columns. They include novelist Jorge Amado—who published a running report dubbed "Ronda das Américas" in *Dom Casmurro*, a weekly literary magazine that even had a section called "La diversidad del castellano en América"[25]—and the renowned social anthropologist Gilberto Freyre, whose writings regarding the Americas and Latin Americanity in the 1940s have been organized as a thematic volume.[26]

Two pioneer Spanish American historians of literature who worked in the United States included Brazil in their continental and regional approaches. Arturo Torres-Ríoseco, founder of Latin American literary studies at the University of California–Berkeley and author of *The Epic of Latin American Literature*, dedicates a separate chapter to Brazil. The Dominican Pedro Henríquez Ureña gave a series of groundbreaking lectures at Harvard that resulted in *Historia de la cultura en la América Hispánica*, using the old Roman concept of Hispania encompassing both Spain and Portugal, and by extension the countries of Ibero-America.

In the mid-twentieth century, the most influential poetic vanguard in the Americas was concrete poetry, mostly evolved from Brazilian *poesia concreta*.[27] The Brazilian Noigandres group excelled at composition and exposition, having made ambassadorial trips to Europe, North America, and other parts of Latin America. Promotion of the new poetics led to enduring increases in Brazilian–Spanish American vincula in poetry and criticism. Through theory, translation, and experiment per se, *concretismo* has advanced ties with Hispanic American artists and thinkers since the 1950s. The late-twentieth-century surge in communication technology especially benefited, in terms of exposure and understanding, the legacy of *poesia concreta* (even if somewhat tardily), as well as aiding subsequent similar experiments that relied on visuality, kinetic roles, or other nonconventional strategies. A wonderful example of inter-American poetic ingenuity was offered by Augusto de Campos, the artist who remained most faithful to the synthetic visuality of classic concrete poetry. The 1985 piece "amorse" (figure 11) is a signic homage to the inventor of telegraphic code and lays

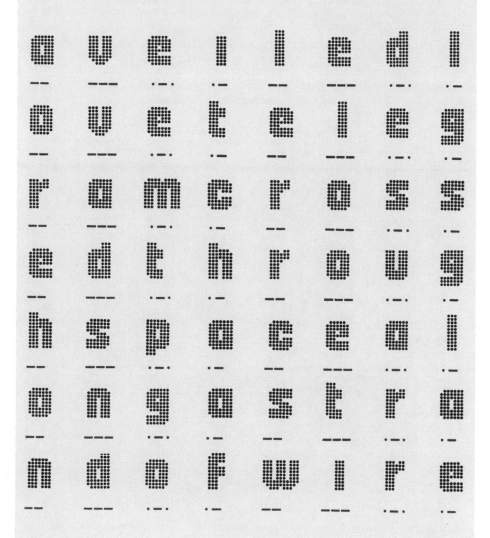

11. Augusto de Campos, "amorse," 2004, translation of 1985 visual poem in *Despoesia*, 1994. Used by permission of the poet.

bare the emotive fundaments of lyric via a line by the Spanish American *modernista* José Asunción Silva.[28]

A classic example of orthodox concrete poetry, one of whose basic methods was to identify unique isomorphic verbal constellations, was composed, as it could only be, in Spanish:[29]

hombre	**hombre**	**hombre**
hambre		**hembra**
	hambre	
hembra	**hembra**	**hambre**

Décio Pignatari later composed the eleven-frame visual poem "Vocogramas" (figure 12), which can be seen to embody central tropes of the present study.[30] The title is a neologism that merges "vocative/vocal" with words for graphic representation of signals, such as "phonogram." A sonograph machine was the productive apparatus of the foundation of the piece, making phonetic spectrograms, colored voiceprints of the physical pronunciation of the syllables of "A-ME-RI-CA-LA-TI-NA-LI-BER-TAD" which convey the theme of liberty. These "vocograms" became the sequence of figured faux cartographic fragments, green shapes over flaglike red and white stripes (reminiscent of the Russian Revolution and communism) culminating in a single image of unity on a deep blue background (suggestive of seas). Insularity is broached in the resemblance of the voicegrams to depictions of isles and other spots on (Latin American) maps, and the outcome of the artistic experiment can be regarded as a site-specific deterritorialization, a fabrication with transnational designs, artistic and practical. The poet has discovered interfaces that join speech science with art and with politics, as well as interfaces between Brazil and her neighbors. Invention is involved as the recorded vocalizations both "discover" places and implement technology in an innovative fashion. In sum, the piece comprised an outreach effort, suggesting new art and political sentiment.

Following "Vocogramas" in the section "Paracores" (Forcolors) of Pignatari's collected poetical works is "Colombo," another visual poem built on hemispheric cartography and shared legacies.[31] The material is organized in three parts on a gray background. At the top, three vultures perch on enormous cracked eggs that form the three Os of the name, in 72-point font, of the "inventor" of America, **COLOMBO**. Yellow yolk oozes from the bottom of the shells and flows down to configure an outline of the three Americas:

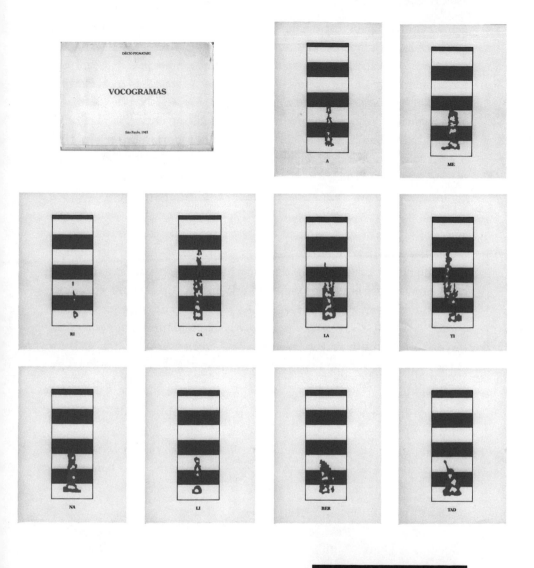

12. Décio Pignatari, *Vocogramas*, portfolio of placards by Edição Código, 1985. Used by permission of the poet.

North, Central, South. At the bottom in 24-point font appears the phrase
FECHA A PORTA DOS TEUS MALES! As a whole, the piece manages to be
humorous on several counts while keeping present some unpleasant historical memories, chiefly of slavery. These issues moved the foremost voice
of late Romantic poetry in Brazil, Antônio F. de Castro Alves (1847–1871).[32]
The concluding line to his landmark abolitionist long poem *Navio negreiro*
(1868, "The Slave Ship") was "Colombo! Fecha a porta dos teus mares!"
[Columbus, close the door of your seas], of which Pignatari alters a single
consonant to yield "males" (evils, ills, wrongs, injuries, wickedness, woes,
misfortunes), an umbrella word that can be applied to all the negative consequences of the Conquest—colonial domination, the institution of slavery,
and, in parts of Latin America, nefarious late-twentieth-century military
dictatorships. The semantics of the poem encompass what the represented
birds might imply. Vultures, as the largest land-based birds and imposing
carrion-devouring beasts, are symbols in diverse cultures around the world;
sometimes they are viewed favorably but more often negatively, associated
with rapaciousness, exploitation, taking advantage of prey. In the Americas,
there is a quite positive image of the variety known as condor, national bird
of the Andean nations and regarded as majestic in folklore and mythology.
In Brazil, the Victor Hugo–inspired social-activist poetry of Castro Alves
and followers was dubbed *poesia condoreira*, as libertarian, abolitionist, and
republican ideals were reflected in the soaring symbol of liberty and natural
wonder. The contrasting connotations of *vulture* and *condor* are evident
in a passage from Castro Alves's impassioned "Vozes d'África," historically
sensitive verses highlighted by Manuel Bandeira (83):

> What made the Poet indignant was to see that the New World "made
> for greatness, to grow, to create, to rise up," the Americas that had
> conquered liberty with formidable heroism, should stain themselves
> with the same crime as Europe:

> Hoje em meu sangue a América se nutre:
> —Condor que transformara-se em abutre,
>   Ave da escravidão
> Ela juntou-se às mais . . . irmã traidora!

> [Today in my blood the Americas nurture themselves: / Condor
> transformed into vulture, / Bird of slavery / She joined the oth-
> ers . . . treacherous sister!].

This is the type of humanistic verse that led Pablo Neruda to include a poem in homage to Castro Alves in *Canto general*. Discourses of literature and history reverberate across the page in the visualization of "Colombo." Of course the punning of Pignatari's poem fully banks on allusion to the legend of the Egg of Columbus (the seeming ease of a great accomplishment seen in hindsight and the deserved recognition of the person who actually achieved the feat), which is as current in Brazil as anywhere else. In context, this material poem (1988) functioned, with the quincentennial of Columbus's arrival in the New World growing closer, as a "verbivocovisual" link between Brazil and neighbors in the hemisphere, and as a reminder of the wide-reaching contributions and regional impact of the Noigandres group.

The influence of *poesia concreta*—evolved into the varieties of *Invenção* in the early 1960s—was initially strongest in the River Plate, but as the Mexican organizer of late-century undertakings in experimental poetry in Latin America writes, it would "shine forth as an international model."[33] An Uruguayan poet with ties in Mexico merges the influence of the movement with that of its dynamic leader:

> Haroldo de Campos is, in Latin America, the poet-thinker who managed to keep alive the spirit of the vanguards throughout the second half of the twentieth century. He founded . . . concrete poetry in Brazil in the fifties, a movement considered "the last avant-garde." That moment of his production and his thought is a key instance, a matrix, . . . an indelible mark on contemporary Brazilian poetry and on a large part of Latin American poetry. It's a crucial moment both for our poetry and for the individual conception of Haroldo's creation.[34]

Among the most celebrated recognitions of the Brazilian originators was by the eminent poet-intellectual Octavio Paz. In *Alternating Current* he wrote that, in comparison to other midcentury locations in the Americas, "an authentic and rigorous avant-garde indeed exists in Brazil: the concrete poets."[35] In the late sixties, the author of *The Bow and the Lyre* wrote that among young Spanish American poets there was no equivalent to the Invenção group. If in 1920 the vanguard was in Spanish America, in 1960 it was in Brazil.[36]

The relationship between Octavio Paz and Haroldo de Campos has been seen as the most fecund Brazilian–Spanish American encounter in the realm of poetry and essay. Their respective poetics of confluence—open to

Occident and Orient, material and spiritual inspirations, South and North America, native and innovative substance, Brazilian and Mexican contributions—inform their creative and critical writings, as well as their select translations. Maria Esther Maciel considers in depth the significant parallels and transactions between the two poet-theorists, noting the shared affinities with José Lezama Lima and his notion of voracity in Latin American culture, of its "incorporative protoplasm."[37] The favoring of synchronic over diachronic approaches to literary history in conceptualizations of the plural hybridity of Latin American expression bond Paz and Haroldo at the level of deep structure.[38] As far as avant-gardism is concerned, Horácio Costa confirms an interface between them but qualifies their respective relationships to the vanguard: for Paz it was more a literary/critical/historical topic, while for Haroldo it was a "horizon in constant affirmation," requiring the processing of "defenses and illustrations."[39]

In addition to a certain philosophical kinship, and an intense interest in the epoch-making syntactical and typographical originalities of Stéphane Mallarmé, there are numerous practical Paz-Haroldo couplings, such as meetings, correspondence, poetic exchanges, and related publications.[40] Although Paz had learned of the Noigandres group via E. E. Cummings, only after Haroldo sent material did ample reciprocation take place. In a late-sixties missive, Paz revealed that he was composing *topoemas* (plural neologism from *topos* + *poem*), a spatial, nondiscursive type of lyric inspired in concrete poetry. Haroldo was later moved to translate Paz's most unusual long poem, an experience he recalled in his own memorial verse: "tomei a mescalina de mim mesmo / e passei esta noite em claro / traduzindo BLANCO de octavio paz" [I took the mescaline of myself / and I stayed up all night / translating WHITE/TARGET by OP].[41] The bilingual version and their letters about it and about poetic affairs in general, as well as a critical appreciation of Paz, were included in an edited volume in Brazil in 1986.[42] Verses by Paz that speak to communion, placed as the epigraph to a lyrical collection in Rio de Janeiro, reveal the sense of giving that Paz instilled in poets in Brazil: "É um feixe de mãos. / Não procuram terra: procuram um corpo, / tecem um abraço" [It's a cluster of hands. / They seek not land: they seek a body, / they weave an embrace].[43]

Institutional contacts characterize the latter years of the Paz-Haroldo relationship. It was for a symposium in honor of the other's seventieth birthday that Haroldo conceptualized the "postutopian poem," a fundamental and widely influential position paper. At another commemorative event,

four years after Paz's Nobel Prize, Haroldo penned "O.P. octogenário," playing with situational ironies and ethnic commonplaces in such fragmented
verses as "a imperial máscara asteca . . . o poeta do terceiro mundo / recebe
as homenagens dos poetas do / primeiro / e sorri . . . no labirinto da solidão
/ um pássaro escarlate / jubiloso / canta / em náhuatl" [the imperial Aztec
mask . . . the third-world poet / receives the homages of the poets of the /
first / and smiles . . . in the labyrinth of solitude / a scarlet bird / jubilant
/ sings / in Nahuatl].[44] After his distinguished interlocutor passed away
in 1998, Haroldo, relatively well translated in Mexico, received the 1999
national Paz Prize there for poetry and essay. Much of the work of the two
elder statesmen remains a plenteous terrain for comparative investigation.

Parallel to the experimentally driven poetic contact between Brazil and
Spanish America in the 1960s, another area of mutual concern was socially
committed verse. Throughout Latin America, discursive engagé verse was
a constant in midcentury production, with the epic impact of Neruda's
Canto general, as seen in the previous chapter, a driving force. A neo-Pan-
American spirit, founded on anti-imperialism and solidarity, refocused
outside/against the USA, was naturally strongest following the Cuban Revolution and the turn toward socialism. Nationalist and anti-USAmerican
sentiments united writers and performers across borders. The Brazilian
manifestation of "political poetry," called Violão de Rua (Street Guitar)
emphasized popular culture, and shared attitudes with groups throughout
the region, not the least of which was hope for concurrence and change. A
utopian continuity—in play during early nationhoods, in the radical 1960s,
and later in the century—is clarified by Fernando Ainsa: "the principle of
unity has always been the same: to define what is 'American' and to project
a better future, starting with unity, political, cultural, or economic."[45] Cuba
has been a gathering place for writers of the region, whether in exile or
as visitors at cultural events, notably the awards ceremonies for the Latin
American literature prizes of the Casa de las Americas. Since 1964 Brazilians have participated both as judges and as contestants; some associated publications include those of the poets Ferreira Gullar and Thiago de
Mello, both known for sociopolitical concerns. A Brazilian observer from
the state of Minas Gerais notes that prose-fiction writers of the seventies
from her state carry over a sixties mindset: "they commune with a revolutionary utopia or show . . . that utopia which modified the way of thinking
of an entire generation."[46] This observation is equally applicable to such
other Brazilian poets as Moacyr Félix (1926–2005), who, since about 1960,

have often spoken of Spanish America via the Cuban example or of sister nations with common struggles.

The song quoted in the epigraph to this chapter—composed by 2003–2008 Minister of Culture Gilberto Gil with Spanish/Portuguese lyric by José Carlos Capinan, perhaps the most lyrically accomplished participant in the Violão de Rua phenomenon—celebrates neighbors and alludes to the revolutionary hero Che Guevara, a proscribed theme during the harshest period of authoritarian rule. Belonging to the entirely nonconventional movement of Tropicalism (averse to dogmatic or formulaic protest music), the song "Soy loco por ti América" can be heard as a sort of transamerican moment in the poetry of song that characterized the Brazilian generation that got its start in the sixties. The aspect of Latin Americanism in Tropicalism included musical elements (use of tango, bolero) that would echo decades later when Veloso recorded and performed live *Fina estampa*, which can be taken as a political work about unity in the view of Ney Matogrosso, a veteran vocalist who got started in the midst of "poetry of song" and consistently expressed a "Latinity in his blood."[47] The songs that best express his scenic humanism are "América do Sul" (South America) and "Sangue latino" (Latin blood), regional poetics of song reaffirmed into the next century.[48] After the loosening of censorship in Brazil, some Cuban song with the poetic character of *nueva trova* appeared in the repertories of artists such as Chico Buarque, for some the most prominent poet in song, and the world-renowned vocalist Milton Nascimento, who included Spanish American material in numerous projects.[49]

With extensions or remnants of the poetry of song, experimentalism and/or engagé verse as givens, trans-Ibero-American disposition in the making and dissemination of poetry in diversified modes manifests somewhat in the transitional decade of the 1980s and has been in greater evidence since around 1990. In the early eighties, with the grievous Latin American dictatorships still in place, a sense of common cause infuses lines such as these from "América e latino" by Afonso Henriques Neto: "cadáveres torturados nos labirintos barrocos . . . bem sei que latinamérica é a face evangelizada / de uma comoção sangrante" [tortured cadavers in the baroque labyrinths / I know well that latinamerica is the evangelized face / of a *sangrante* (Sp., bleeding) commotion]. In a poetic space that encompasses all the typical geographies of the continent—pampas, Andes, Amazon, Antilles, high plains—a more-than-individual speaker tries to merge words "ao vôo simples e aberto / de um pássaro américa e latino" [to the simple and open flight / of a Latin and America bird]. The nightmarish scenes of crime, betrayal, and historical shame are charged with figured language and intensity.[50]

The often manichean North-South divide that had infused much of Violão de Rua does find new expression. A poem titled "Duas Américas" (Two Americas), for example, is an extended apposition of North and Latin America, of victimizer and victimized, in which the USA cannot be seen as an emanator of art but only as imperialist entity. In a series of dystics, with late-Nerudian tones, a horizontal divide is set: "Há uma América do Norte / E outra América do mórbido . . . Há uma América do Norte / Deus salgue essa América / Outra América da morgue . . . salvem-na os que pudermos" [There is an America of the North / and another of the morbid . . . God salt this America / another of the morgue . . . may we who might be able save it]. In the same publication, the "Charles Brooks Jr. Memorial" is a paean to the first person executed by lethal injection, an irony of humane capital punishment, which as lyrical achievement reads like a civil rights poem of the 1960s or an early Bob Dylan song.[51] Another recent case of the historically sensitive poem of solidarity is this somewhat more abstracted lament of loss in Mesoamerica, "Os maias" (The Mayans) by Ricardo Rizzo. This title also alludes meaningfully to Os Maias (1888; The Maias, 1965), a Lusitanian family name and title of the most expansive novel by the master of prose fiction in Portugal, Eça de Queiroz. In the Brazilian poem, identity is defined, on the concrete side, via an infamous enterprise:

Maias porque foge
à sua gravidade
outra atribuição de nome.
E se proclama, maia,
a sede mais precária
que provou d'água
e mesmo viu a chuva
que o plantio consumiu
(United Fruit Company)
e à boca não devolve. (83)

[Mayans because / any other attribution of name / flees from its gravity. / And it proclaims itself, Mayan, / the most precarious thirst / that tasted water / and even saw rains / that planting consumed / (UFC) / and does not return to the mouth.]

Present-day descendants struggle in contrary urban settings:

Maias hoje inclusos
na face americana
das mudas constelações
e mudos de história
rebentam a cidade
boca tapada, relva
daninha na mata virgem. (84)

[Mayans today included / in the American face / of the mute constellations / and mutes of history / they bust up the city / covered mouth,
grass / weeds in the virgin brush.]

From this angle, there is greater thematic bearing in the greater Amazon
area, dominated by Brazil, where displacement of people and deforestation
have been, with some literary portrayal, real ecohumanist tragedies.

As for Latin American articulation, social agendas of wide geographical
scope qua thematic textual concern are less significant than public events
toward the turn of the millennium. If Brazilian poets have, since about
1990, largely continued to focus on national and literary heritages, they
have, as citizens and colleagues, reached beyond borders as never before.
A bilingual poem concerning "identity" by the rector of a distinguished
university in São Paulo sets the stage, as it were, for increased cultural interaction and changed consciousness, with words run together prompting
notions of unity and commonalities:[52]

IDENTIDAD

AMERICA
NUESTRAMERICANOSSA
NOSSAMERICAMUESTRA
OUTRAMERICA
YO
AMERICA
MISMAMERICAMESMA
ALTERAMERICAMATER
ALTERAMERICANOS
HOY

[Identity // America(s) / our-America(s)-our / our-America(s)-show(s) / (an)other-America(s) / I / America(s) / same-America(s)-same / alter-America(s)-mater / alter-Americans / today]

A sense of owning (alluding to José Martí's "Nuestra América") and belonging is played off against an interwoven sense of individuality within an overarching dialectic of similarity and alterity. Otherness is newness, a sensation of renewal, rebirth in a different present. The meeting of the three strokes of the letter Y in "YO"—Spanish for "I"—hint at convergence and encounter in this lyric self with collective airs, who is surrounded and defined by a geographical naming and an alternate one. In the pronominal center of the poem, the letter O can be seen as a sort of circle of inclusion. The graphic character of the piece (capital letters, vocabular fusions, overall shape) may even suggest the legacy of concrete poetry. Also helpful is the occurrence of the letters O and Y in the concluding word "HOY"—Spanish for "today"—which ties together volitional and temporal factors. The type of optimism that can be attributed to this whole poetic gesture informs multiple academic and institutional agendas near the turn of the century.

A distinguishing aspect of late-century organizational activity, as seen virtually on Banda Hispânica, has been an internationalism favoring Latin America. A symptomatic specimen would be the second iteration of a contemporary-poetry conference with conspicuous Spanish American company, including two of the most extensive essays (by Southern Cone academics) and a testimonial by Aníbal Cristobo, Argentine poet resident in Rio de Janeiro, who speculates on poetic gaps between the two major languages of Iberia.[53] His contribution to the very visible anthology by Buarque de Hollanda, *Esses poetas*, was in fact wholly bilingual. Workshops, promotions, and intertextualities welcome the most accomplished Chilean poet since Neruda, as in "Eu ouvi Gonzalo Rojas falar" (I heard GR speak): "de sua terra estreita e comprida / dos cumes, dos pedregulhos, . . . aprendiz que escolheu o espaço aberto" [of his long and narrow land / of the peaks, of the cliffs, . . . apprentice who chose the open space],[54] and in this other opening verse: "Sopra-nos o vento a música de seu fulgor: / um elo de ecos, um verso de Gonzalo Rojas" [Wind blows us the music of its glow: / a link of echoes, a line by GR], which was also seen in chapter 3 as part of a jazz thread.[55]

Determined inter-American positioning is illustrated in events organized by Horácio Costa, extended-stay professor of Brazilian literature in

Mexico City, and others. In 1990 the location that best embodies the Ibero-American soul in Brazil, the Memorial da América Latina in São Paulo, sponsored a cycle of lectures and debates on the poetic word with guests from numerous nations. Participants were widely attentive to Octavio Paz as purveyor of a "mobility of tradition" and to Haroldo Campos as the propagator of "transtemporal score."[56] But Costa's cohort remained more than receptive to other ideas of rupture over time. Maciel and Costa alike present the event as a boost to dialogue, as a point of departure and greater consciousness of critical textmaking in more open circumstances.[57] Costa also led a multinational happening in São Paulo on the vehicles of lyric—"O Veículo da Poesia"—which included North American makers as well as Latin American. Emphasis fell on production, dissemination, and purposeful excursions. In late 2007, multilateral Old and New World relations and exchange were the focus of a symposium christened "Em mar aberto: Poesia em português e nas línguas da Espanha—um diálogo histórico, uma futura aliança?" (On open sea: Poetry in Portuguese and in the languages of Spain—historical dialogue, future alliance?).[58] A like spirit motivated the symptomatically titled "Tordesilhas—Festival Ibero-Americano de Poesia Contemporânea." The happening aimed to "deconstruct" via lyric the line of Tordesilhas—the longitudinal divider set in 1494 to assign newly discovered lands to the crown of Spain or of Portugal, which has been symbolic of separation on both sides of the Atlantic—and to give expression to the search for new dialogues and agreements between poets in Spanish- and Portuguese-speaking lands.[59]

What united poets at some other early-twenty-first-century gatherings was an extranational aesthetic practice par excellence, a phenomenon that has been called the Latin American *neo-barroco*, or neobaroque.[60] This difficult, language-centered style of exuberance and effusive textual expression can claim true Ibero-American status, as two of its prime models are Lezama Lima and Haroldo de Campos, the latter primarily through his prose-poetry project *Galáxias* (1963–76).[61] Brazilian manifestations most commonly associated with this tendency, in fact, are experimental prose as opposed to poetry. This peculiarity is consistent with the frontier- and genre-busting stance taken by Haroldo de Campos in his contribution to an axial project of international Latin American literary studies.[62] The characteristics of the late-century neobaroque have been laid out by poets and academics with extensive cross-border credentials.[63] Perlongher relates contemporary decentered textualizations to the historical model: "Poética

de la desterritorialización, el barroco siempre choca y corre un límite pre-
concebido y sujetante. . . . No es una poesía del yo sino de la aniquilación
del yo" [Poetics of deterritorialization, the baroque always clashes and runs
off a preconceived and subjecting limit. . . . It's not a poetry of the self
but of the annihilation of the self], punning to devalue the personalism
of so much twentieth-century poetry in an advocacy of "lo *confusional* en
tanto opuesto a lo *confesional*" [the confusional as opposed to the confes-
sional].[64]

For his part, José Kozer notes that "the Neo Baroque does not conform
a group . . . yet these poets have a family air, a congruous homogeneity in
disparity." He imagines a "thick line" of poetry, with "the entanglement
and reverberation of multiplicity and proliferation" of such disruptive authors as Gertrude Stein. He provides "a summary of Neo Baroque poetry"
including elements as distant as medieval troubadours and as current as
environmental engineering:

> notions such as dispersion, the re-appropriation of former styles,
> styles that move in barbaric landscapes, where ruins are put together;
> a writing where the *trobar clus* and the hermetic proliferates, where
> there is great turbulence, unnatural mixtures, a joy geared to combin-
> ing languages, the dissolving of a unidirectional sense, no praising of
> the Self or the Ego or the I; polyphony, polyvalence and versatility,
> utilization of former styles in order to deconstruct them, creating a
> true explosion of different forms of writing, a soiling of materials, a
> signature towards the ugly, the sordid, the recyclable, all these char-
> acterize the Neo Baroque.

If this explanation recalls accounts of postmodernism in writing, such a
reaction is perfectly consistent with the analysis of Jill Kuhnheim, one of
whose main angles of understanding in *Textual Disruptions* is the postmodern. Her conclusions regarding the nonrepresentational extravagance
of neobaroque lyric, despite its apparent flight from conjuncture, brings
back constants of Latin American history:

> Their sensual excess offers an alternative model of distribution and
> consumption and other ways of valuing exchange. These poets par-
> ticipate in a creative and dynamic transformation that both breaks
> and maintains a cultural and historical specificity through its ties to
> the earlier baroque. The neobaroque is not simply a categorization

or a method of writing, then, but a response to colonialism and a method of reading as well. (144)

Indeed, if Lezama Lima called American baroque the "art of the counter-conquest," neobaroque assaults in Ibero-America can comprise textualities of varied functionalities.

In like fashion, an anthologist of twenty-first-century verse in Brazil, Manuel da Costa Pinto, perceives vincula with this phenomenon in the work of a poet-activist whose palette includes all manner of historical colors:

> That rewriting of history . . . links the poet with some aspects of the neobaroque. . . . that tendency . . . corresponds less to a defined style than to the affirmation of ethnolinguistic hybridism in the New World and to the idea of understanding history as a "transtemporal" succession of myths susceptible to reelaboration. Horácio Costa approaches that inclination precisely because of the unsettling of historical categories: events—undone, irreducible to concepts or grand narratives—are limited to the corporal dimension, skin as the surface of a writing. (167)

Claudio Daniel writes that the montage of clippings that characterizes much neobaroque verse breaks down time-space distinctions and reminds Brazilians of some counterpoint in the sung texts of *tropicalismo*, such as "Tropicália" and "Geleia geral."[65] After Haroldo de Campos's *Galáxias*, however, the most celebrated neobaroque work from Brazil is a plot-challenged novella by Wilson Bueno (b. 1949), *Mar paraguayo*. This is the ultimate trans-Ibero-American text, as it is composed in real and invented varieties of Portunhol, the blending of Portuguese and Spanish, mixed with Brasiguayo, a sort of border dialect of Brazil and Paraguay, and topped off with (imperfect) Guarani, the indigenous tongue of land-locked Paraguay. Editions have appeared in Cuba, Chile, Argentina, and Mexico, and, to extend "of the Americas" even further, a Canadian admirer proposed "translating" the unique quasi-nondiegetic fiction via a mix of English-inflected Quebecois French and local tribal tongues.[66] The author confirms that this is a case of "escritura paródica, polifônica, de um barroco mestiço" [parodic, polyphonic writing of a mixed-blood baroque], a cultural mix and rapprochment that "intenta espalhar a democracia e a

proliferação das linguagens" [attempts to spread democracy and the proliferation of languages].[67] The hybrid idiolect created by the writer could
be considered a fourth idiom in play, and Kozer's verdict is quite justified:
"Language is the main character of this book, perhaps its only real character; this language is a place without a place, an U-topos, the utopic instance
(for the time being nonexistent) as possibility." One of the richest motifs of
this ludic, gamesome artifice is woven around the name of a dog, Brinks,
which evokes *brincar*, Spanish for "to jump about" (as canines are wont to
do) and Portuguese for "to play" (as with a toy), as well as the USAmerican
security company. As the text progresses, the name grows in increments,
adding suffixes using the additive agglutinating syntax of Guarani; the final
iteration occupies a whole line on the page. Thus the linguistic proliferation
literally embodies the expansive geo-aesthetic gesture.

Wilson Bueno has been a regular contributor to Brazilian arts reviews
and poetry magazines that energize the transamerican temper within an
internationalist design. Since 1997 *Inimigo rumor*, based in Rio de Janeiro,
has been a salient vehicle for poetry; the journal's name, symptomatically,
is the title of the second book of poetry of José Lezama Lima. The new
editorial line includes the intention to "provoke turbulence in Brazilian
poetic production through various foreign experiences," including "new
Argentinian poetry."[68] A consistently well-stocked publication since 2001
has been *Sibila*, based in São Paulo. Its English-language Web site has included the slogan "Down with Tordesillas!" whose unifying intent is evident.[69] The curator of Banda Hispânica coedits a democratic online review where such other lyrical styles as surrealism have a voice.[70] Content
analysis of Paraná-based arts periodicals such as *Coyote* and *Medusa* show
unprecedented ecumenical editorial policy, with sustained inclusion of the
Americas, particularly Spanish America. Antelo highlights the Brazilian
version of a stellar neobaroque work.[71] An ambitious publication is seen to
be the equivalent of the free-trade zone of South America:

> *Oroboro* é tentativa de encontro, esbarros, cruzamentos . . . Mapea-
> mento de alguma substância criativa de arte que se produz hoje,
> com um alargamento de fronteiras . . . geográficas, geológicas, ilógi-
> cas . . . cruzar as margens de baixo e buscar na literatura e cultura
> recente dos países próximos, daquilo, principalmente, o que se inven-
> tou chamar Mercosul.[72]

[*Oroboro* is an attempt at encounter, bumpings, crossings . . . mapping of some creative substance of art being produced today, with a widening of frontiers . . . geographical, geological, illogical . . . to cross the margins below and to seek in the recent literature and culture of countries in proximity, that which, principally, one thought to call Mercosul.]

What this reviewer perceives in the mapping of an unremitting arts review forms part of a larger picture of cultural change in the zone that includes Argentina, Brazil, Paraguay, and Uruguay, as well as Chile and Bolivia as associates. Roxana Patiño employs the concept of deterritorialization in conjunction with the issues of multicultural diversity and postnational identities to consider a regional integration that, beyond the expected domains of economics and politics, can include literature in a communicational conjuncture dominated by the mass media of cultural industries. For Gregorio Recondo, the main issue involves generating awareness of *belonging* in the space of Mercosul, to widen the horizon of national loyalties. From the perspective of this specialist, the association will be a full-fledged reality when it "takes root" in the culture of the various national communities.[73] A new frontier philosophy is needed "to pass from a dividing line to an entryway." Thinking should oppose *economicismo* and acknowledge the omission of culture as a fundamental reason for the failure of integrationist efforts in Latin America. Without cultural integration, economic and political integration will not happen. One must stand against the invocation of pathologies (fundamentalist nationalism, patriotic hystrionics) as well as worn-out cosmopolitanism. The kind of globalization logic that dilutes national identities and seeks to stamp a seal of superficial uniformity around the globe should also be combated. Instead of such incomplete or sectarian positions, Recondo advocates "a regional consciousness of belonging," "an Ibero-American manner of being," "our characteristic way" of being universal. Such advocacy clicks loudly with the vantage of transamerican poetics and select turn-of-the-millennium arts collectives, whose words and images speak in concert.

To return to comparative literary history, it is instructive to consult José Guilherme Merquior. He concludes an honest comparison of Spanish American and Brazilian letters over the centuries by recalling the primacy of the natural divergences within Spanish America (somewhat contrived, after all, as an organic whole) and with linguistically distinct Brazil. Still, the prolific critic-diplomat recognizes that at the end of the twentieth century "the law of the world is increasing interdependency," and thus "cultural interaction within Latin America is bound to grow. Latin American unity lies in the future, and . . . it will be one more case of convergence within diversity" (382). Certainly, part of the future imagined here, to judge by critical and creative output seen above, has taken shape in the early twenty-first century. In print and online, appreciation of what Others in the hemisphere may do differently has proved to be significantly more productive than simple pursuance of self or disengagement.

Romantic peregrination, modernist urbanity, neo-avant-garde incitements, insurgent discourse, sung invocations, group action, personal procurement, invitations, texts and tallies, pages and screens, many are the ways in which the makers and purveyors of Brazilian lyric seek to overcome a historical divide with Spanish American counterparts and to change the face of interrelations. Whether in neo-epical literary constructs, invented poetic spaces, stylistic arenas, real-life continental treks, or Internet expeditions, travel is paramount, and exposure to discourses of Others is invariably productive. Holding out a reconstructive, utopian hope, essayist Fernando Ainsa, seeing bricolage and heterodoxy in action, speaks in terms of a future that one can see as ripe to move, to take poetic advantage: "el viaje, esa figura esencial del tránsito simbólico-cultural de la contemporaneidad, asegurará el registro semántico de la desterritorialización de los códigos adquiridos" (119, 231) [the voyage, that essential figure of the symbolic-cultural transit of contemporary times, will assure the semantic register of the deterritorialization of acquired codes]. Whether through movement of persons and goods between Brazil and Spanish-speaking partner countries in the hemisphere or through spontaneous growth in similar fashion in different parts of Ibero-America, cultural interchange in lyric will surely make marks in new and unforeseen ways.

6

◇

Scions of Tropicália

Of Signs, Soundings, Song, and Science

Discussions of Brazilian culture since the 1960s inevitably deal with a flourishing in the expressive arts known as Tropicália or *tropicalismo*.[1] While it was a multimedia movement, inspired in visual and dramatic venues alike, the primary manifestations of Tropicalist aesthetics were in urban popular music.[2] In addition to instituting an accommodating and internationally aware musical hybridity, the founders and leaders of this performative artistic display—Caetano Veloso and Gilberto Gil—were poet-songwriters who surged to the fore of a phenomenon that has been called "the poetry of song." The relevance of Tropicalism for an understanding of the exercise of lyric in contemporary Brazil is indisputable.[3] The presenters of the most significant anthology of Brazilian poetry in the United States since that of Elizabeth Bishop state plainly—claiming a significant difference between their country and both the United States and Hispanic America—that authors of song texts of their generation sought "a continuity with the tradition of poetry as such" and that Brazilian popular music's "status . . . is very sound, since every poet born since the 1950s not only stemmed from its roots but also, consciously or not, felt its influence. Any poet under the age of 45 who alleges otherwise is lying."[4] Given such connections between the discourses of song and poetry overall in the late twentieth century in Brazil, it is appropriate to see some of the ways the lyric dimension ties into inter-American awareness and wider artistic endeavor, and how a key musical moment manifested in the late century in ways germane to literature, reaching back to the modernism of the 1920s.

The before and after of Tropicalism, a special occurrence within popular music, are relevant to transamerican understanding in a broad sense. Poetic discourse was, again, a prominent and influential feature of the Tropicalist adventure in the late 1960s and into the next decade. There were various and diverse inspirations for Tropicalism, as performative sound production with studied verbal articulations, and sundry interpretations have followed, both on stage and in criticism. As far as innovative music and its discussion are concerned, a recording artist known as Jackson do Pandeiro (1919–1982), with his combinatory cunning and speculations about interchange, raised an issue that would become eminently Tropicalist: internationalization in popular music. The meaning of that northeastern figure was recognized by the well-traveled writer-musician Jorge Mautner (b. 1941) in his poetics and performance practice. In addition to hemispheric consciousness, works of Mautner's show essential affinities with Tropicalism and constitute vital connections with the Movimento Mangue (Mangrove Movement), an end-of-the-century cultural thriving in Recife, in the state of Pernambuco, and environs. That effervescence is comparable to the movement led by Veloso and Gil, in its general artistic nature, discourse, and poetic prospects. Such transtemporal ties allow for considerations of the breadth of Tropicalism, the wealth of its legacy, its cosmopolitan interventions, and new concepts of artistic hybridization that extend to transamerican views. The "scion" of the title of this chapter is intended to be ambivalent, ambidextrous, two-pronged, and well suited to the combinatory artistry at play here. Its meaning in human terms is "descendant, heir, follower," while in botany it refers to buds or shoots for grafting, thus touching on roots, origins, splicing, hybridity, and intentional human intervention, all relevant to Tropicalist undertakings.

One of the characteristic aspects of the discussion of cultural phenomena around the turn of the twenty-first century was a constant preoccupation with the interrelation of the local and the global, whether this last determiner is taken to connote something planetary per se or, within more defined spaces, polylocational, transcontinental, or hemispheric. Various issues discussed in arts criticism, of urban popular culture in general and of Brazilian popular music in particular, lead to the urban and urbane Tropicalist moment, with its critical revision of national culture within the atomic age, exposed to pop art while caught in the throes of an authoritarianism designed to squash social activism. The inspirations and explanations of the brief yet extremely influential and multifaceted movement can be located in diverse sources. Two of the most fertile are the gift of the above-mentioned singer-percussionist Jackson do Pandeiro and the poetics of Jorge Mautner.

The former problematized transnational musicalization in the now classic 1959 song "Chiclete com banana" (Chiclets with bananas), speculating on conditions of cultural exchange that would permit a pillar of USAmerican jazz (bebop) to meet a musical emblem of Brazil (samba), as well as on the existence of other mixes.[5] Mautner, in turn, created a sui generis art that he called Kaos, encompassing poetry, novels, and musical compositions. The most memorable of these was "Maracatu atômico" (1972), which has an extended history that links North and South American metropolises. While Mautner was not an actual participant in Tropicalism, his aesthetic behavior and manners prefigure, inspire, embody, and illustrate the trend as a mode of questioning and as an encounter of heritage and modernity. This song expresses a fundamental position of Tropicalism—the productive meeting of the traditional and the transformational—and constitutes a significant link with the principal part of the Movimento Mangue of Recife: the *mangue beat* (swamp pop-rock) of Chico Science & Nação Zumbi. Their blending and metaphorical discourses unmistakably evoke Tropicália performances and articulations of experience. In the sonorous practices of the group from Pernambuco, in their postulated ideas, and in their very nomenclature—crab, Chaos—resounds the musicalized philosophy of Mautner; and contextualizations of *mangue* appellations reveal other Tropicalist connections. Chico Science (1966–1996) in fact recorded five different versions of Mautner's most powerful song, the last session being a duet in New York, while the previous one is subtitled "Trip Hop." Evocation of this dance rhythm of international origin, as far as ecumenical and transnationalized cultural thinking are concerned, can be heard to represent a parallel to the citation of bebop by Jackson do Pandeiro. This link across decades again upholds the span of Tropicalism, its permanence, and, overall, its potentializing volition, a will ever open to syncretizing impulses, in molded sounds, words, and their presentations.

In order to gain additional perspective on the deployments of this Brazilian experience, it is useful to consider some of the definitions brought to bear in a volume that seeks to advance understanding of Latin(o) expressive culture in North America, *Tropicalizations: Transcultural Representations of Latinidad*. Aparicio and Chávez-Silverman, drawing a parallel with the foundational text of postcolonial studies that was Said's *Orientalism*, indicate that the "etymological correlative within the Latino context would be 'tropicalism,' the system of ideological fictions ... with which the dominant (Anglo and European) cultures trope Latin American and U.S.

Latino/a identities" (1). Over two centuries, writers in various genres have represented life "south of the border," most often reifying hegemonies of the North. To comprehend the "overarching discursive patterns inherent in these hegemonic *tropicalizations*," the very notion of tropicality, held to be "overdetermined for the Caribbean," requires geocultural widening to include the United States, Mexico, and Latin America, where, after all, the largest tropical areas in the hemisphere lie. Desiring to avoid any unidirectional thrust, the new "conceptual framework of *tropicalizations—its* plural form and multiple subject locations—" seeks to incorporate "the dynamics of the colony from the space and the perspective of the colonized" (2). With broader perspective and renewed vigor, the keyword "to *tropicalize* . . . means to trope, to imbue a particular space, geography, group, or nation with a set of traits, images, and values. These intersecting discourses are distributed among official texts, history, literature, and the media, thus circulating these ideological constructs throughout various levels of the receptor society. To tropicalize from a privileged, First World location is undoubtedly a hegemonic move" (8). Yet expressive culture can counter that privilege with its own versions and reversions, visions and divisions. Among the discursive genres, lyric (song, verse on the page, even material or visual poetry) can provide a stimulating part of the "perspective of the colonized," about themselves, their conditions, their peers, and the metropolis.[6] What makes inviting an interface of this approach to representation with Tropicália is the extent to which the Brazilian artists practiced such multipurpose troping, intuiting and/or purposefully applying similar properties in their contemporary coming to terms with inherited national culture, and measuring angles within Latin America. The reception of Tropicalist production in North America in the 1990s creates further attractions in multicultural environments.

The semimillennial gaze of the Tropicalists in the late 1960s and early 1970s took in an extensive field of action, acting on both horizontal and vertical planes. Slicing sharply, they penetrated paradigms of the languages of composition and performance, shaking up the very socioartistic status of the makers. Syntagmatically, they contemplated history itself. Tropicália effectuated, through popular music and the thinking associated with it, a critical revision of the development of *cultura brasileira*—nationalist culture of Brazil qua self-constituting concept—with interhemispheric relations always on the horizon. A most crucial factor was international input, filtered through Oswald de Andrade and his well-known "Manifesto of Pau-Brasil

Poetry" and "Cannibalist Manifesto," both of which are mentioned, and in some ways implemented, in Tropicalist activities. While essentially carried and played out before 1970, the visible spectrum and gamut of *tropicalismo* boasted ample citations, intertextuality, and extent of references. Its time and poetic space encompassed all, from the epoch of the invention or "discovery" of the Americas (first contact, in the prototypical Veloso song "Tropicália") and the beginnings of miscegenation, up to the dawn of the twenty-first century (with a countrified yet vanguardesque song-festival entry titled "2001" by Rita Lee and Tom Zé) and an open future (from the perspective of the sixties), which the Tropicalists would survive to see. Much of the interplay between show-business service and artistic/analytical proposals is pondered by Veloso himself in his New York–commissioned memoir, prompted by his troping of the ultimate "Latin" icon, Carmen Miranda.[7]

There was a curious coexistence in Tropicália of a mass-culture profile—with support of the cultural industry, journalistic hoopla, encouragement of fashion—and a discourse dubbed "of literary quality" by critics, or at the level of "erudite art." Although this endeavor, an anomaly of appearance and survival in the world of entertainment, constantly relativized its own self-promotion, it never failed to have the immediate quality of pop nor to qualify for the media, radio, TV, and the press. Aspiring to make a product with artistic aura that could contribute to theoretical formulations about song and to a more ambitious discourse of national tenor, and at the same time incorporate market savvy and a ready-to-use appeal appreciable by common consumers, Tropicália assumed a more learned pose that had the potential, at any given minute, to become pretentious or counterproductive. This could not fail to be problematic for the consumption and dissemination of Tropicalist material, with its built-in contradictions.

In any case, awareness of the inevitable and desirable nature of pop, of its utility and/or compatibility with "the necessity of art," to use Ernst Fischer's still valid title, distinguishes Gil, Veloso, and cohort in the sphere of popular music of that time. That well-informed position allies with the manipulation of technology (literal, and as theme) and of foreign information in the transformations effected by the Tropicalists. Contemplating such activity in a writing considered to be an axial item in mid-seventies "underground" literature,[8] the hopeful author of "Maracatu atômico" situated his generation, geoculturally and hemispherically, and recalled a notable forerunner:

We should have no fear of affirming, with all vigor, the culture of the Americas, which goes triumphantly everywhere in the world: affirmation of vitalism, sound, rock, jazz, blues, sambas, maracatus, in sum, the grand and superhealthy American negritude. . . . America arrives: jazz, black culture, rock, Beat Generation, hippies, and today all the culture that I would designate with the provisional name of hippy-Afro-renaissance-American of Indo-America, of the America of miscegenation, of black America, of the America of rhythm and pop.

Jackson do Pandeiro is among the first composers to have pop awareness in Brazil. Still, Caetano and Gil represent leaps and substantial sophistications in that movement. From Romanticism, electronics, and information science, via TV, they took us to an expressionistic renaissance that travels at the speed of electrons and is the crux of this proud culture of the Americas.

This general regional placement and specific linking of Jackson do Pandeiro with Tropicalism via pop as a cognitive concept are from *Fragmentos de sabonete: Notas sobre o renascimento americano do norte e do sul* (Bits of soap: Notes on the North and South American renaissance) (48). The very concept of the title prefigures cultural affinities decades later. In an illustrated interview published in *Transition*, Veloso himself recognized kinship with the venerable composer-performer from the Northeast of Brazil. Addressing the use of a certain verve of USAmerican music and Tropicalist mixing, Veloso said outright: "the American spirit in Jackson is quite pronounced. . . . 'Chiclete com banana' is a manifesto of this new style,"[9] meaning here his own group's late-sixties novelties. The alchemy of this tune commences with the bringing together of samba and elements of the popular music of the Northeast, a hybridizing interregional gesture in an enormous and multifarious country that shows the world diverse faces. The Tropicalist affiliation with "Chiclete com banana" was cemented by Gilberto Gil's own recording of it on a 1972 LP.

The text of "Chiclete com banana" contains attitudes that amplify in stances subsequently assumed by Veloso. The heart of the matter in what Jackson sings is an appeal for reciprocity: "I'll only put bebop in my samba when Uncle Sam" does this and that. Here, self-esteem and pride may imply a lack of perception on the part of the United States of a distinctive and productive Other: that would be Brazil itself, a cultural producer responsible for musical creations that have traveled as far as the White House and left their mark.[10] Other implications include general cultural imperialism and the hegemonic power of USAmerican industries that often results in one-way flows of information. In his own statements, Veloso never assumes a defensive attitude but rather an assertive one, accepting and using technology to his own advantage.

After the dissolution of the gang of Veloso and Gil qua movement, the nonconformist essayist Jorge Mautner kept an eye on them in their exile, noting excitedly that they were "doing something new, sailing on unknown seas full of novelties and brilliant syntheses like stars. The ever-stronger encounter of the music and culture of Brazil with the rest of Latin America and the USA."[11] Mautner in *Fragmentos de sabonete* would put forward a "pop" argument, decades in advance of cultural-globalization theory, recognizing the "breaking of various taboos and totems" in an appraisal of Tropicalism that underscores breaking down hierarchies:

> The most important heritage . . . was cultural decentralization, today the trademark of our culture. That decentralization of motifs, styles, harmonies, dissonances, cultures, was already the essence of Tropicalism. . . . decentralization, simultaneity of phenomena . . . increasing internationalization but at the same time ever deepening use of local roots . . . thus thinks the computer, the scientist of the twenty-first century, and thus thinks the artist. . . . The grandeur of Tropicalism was its promise of cultural decentralization = democratization, irreversible arrival of technology in harmony sometimes in conflict (never hostile) with nature, multiplicity of forms and contents, co-existent and harmonious admission of opposing tendencies = the simultaneous was thus introduced at the level of art–mass information. (52–53, 65)

The reference to the next century helps define an approach to the author himself, writing and recording in the last three decades of the twentieth century and beyond, and to the interests of the Movimento Mangue in tribal (of the subcultural variety) and digital signs.

Mautner's declaration is better understood in light of the panculturalism that oriented his cycle of novels (1962–82).[12] The initial trilogy espouses his "mythology of Kaos," which assimilates elements of paganism, Greek thought (Dionysian strains), Christianity, Nietzsche and other German philosophers, and existentialism. The abstract in the fiction is balanced by an enthusiasm for the potential of modern technology. As vehicles of these multivalent values, poetry and music populate the fiction, contemplation of which seemingly prompts the author to relive Jackson do Pandeiro. Says the outreach-conscious Mautner: "in my cerebral circuits I mixed rock 'n' roll and samba over a bridge filled with carnival, African percussion, negritude, and the Americas."[13] As for mixing metaphors and Americas, as noted in chapter 3, the opening poem of the Brasil and Smith anthology *Brazilian Poetry (1950–1980)*, serving in effect as an epigraph, is "Dionysus in Brazil," which celebrates difference, uniqueness, cultural formation, and vitality. The author is the same Jorge Mautner who served as secretary to US poet laureate Robert Lowell.[14] In Rio de Janeiro in the early 1970s, the behaviorally unpredictable Brazilian artist, writing in the alternative press, "translated" characteristics of the antiacademic Beat Generation.[15] Mautner's own Dionysian poems and song lyrics tend to sport bizarre juxtapositions and fusions of different perspectives. His musical discourse is conceived as part of a comprehensive project of "the same content, the beat-hip-pagan-tragic-delirious vision of the world."[16] Here he adds scientific tropes on the figuration of his aesthetic: "*Kaos* with a *k* is the opposite of *chaos* with a *ch* . . . it's the artistic vis-à-vis of relativistic physics-chemistry-math. *Maracatu atômico*."[17] The song title, then, is proffered as a trope for an encompassing project of artistic inquiry that leans heavily on sound.

Veloso's memoir tells of meeting a shy and then ebullient Mautner in London around 1970 and indicates that the "irrationalist" young artist "of the delirious transliberalism—with *batuque*" became crucial: "he was, in many respects, a precursor of *tropicalismo* (we called him, with a certain irony and affection, our master). . . . He is recognized today as a great presence in Brazilian culture, and remains for me an important point of reference, his critiques and prophecies continuing to enlighten me."[18] It is consistent with such admiration that Veloso, the long established superstar, should have recorded an album with Mautner, an "acquired taste" with a limited market, under the title *Eu não peço desculpa*, including, naturally, the latter's best known lyric.[19]

"Maracatu atômico" (Nelson Jacobina–Jorge Mautner), while composed and recorded after the heroic phase of Tropicália, is certainly an exemplary instance of Tropicalist modes. Studio arrangers attempt to imitate that overlay in instrumentation and rhythm. The sound structure of the pop song presupposes an updating of the percussion-heavy sound of the *maracatu*, which is an African-derived carnival procession in the state of Pernambuco and its respective music, which certainly was not riding any wave in the 1970s. The song became known in Brazil by way of a single by Gilberto Gil, who came to regard the song as a sort of epochal manifesto like Veloso's late-sixties "Tropicália."[20] Perhaps the best recording of Mautner's song was done in Los Angeles in 1978 when Gil made the album *Nightingale* to try to penetrate the US market, a fact that fits the internationalist substance.[21]

The lyric of "Maracatu atômico" reflects a counterposing and fusing of technology and nature, of ultramodernity and tradition.

> Atrás do arranha-céu, tem o céu, tem o céu
> E depois tem outro céu sem estrelas
> Em cima do guarda-chuva tem a chuva, tem a chuva
> Que tem gotas tão lindas que até dá vontade de comê-las
>
> No meio da couve-flor tem a flor, tem a flor
> Que além de ser uma flor tem sabor
> Dentro do porta-luva tem a luva, tem a luva
> Que alguém de unhas negras e tão afiadas se esqueceu de pôr
>
> No fundo do para-raio tem o raio, tem o raio
> Que caiu da nuvem negra do temporal
> Todo quadro-negro é todo negro, é todo negro
> E eu escrevo seu nome nele só pra demonstrar o meu apego
>
> O bico do beija-flor beija a flor, beija a flor
> E toda a fauna-flora grita de amor
> Quem segura o porta-estandarte tem arte, tem arte
> E aqui passa com raça eletrônico maracatu atômico

[Behind the skyscraper there's the sky / and then there's another starless sky / Above the umbrella there's the rain / with such pretty drops that it makes you want to eat them / In the middle of the cauliflower there's the flower / that beyond being a flower has flavor / In the glove compartment there's the glove / that someone with such sharpened black fingernails forgot to put on / At the bottom of the lightning rod there's lightning / that fell from the black cloud of the storm / Every blackboard is all black / and I write / its name just to show how close I am / The beak of the hummingbird kisses flowers / and all the fauna-flora shouts with love / He who holds the banner bearer is artful / and here comes, with electronic breeding, / the atomic maracatu]

Constructed with compound words, Mautner's text in its very form incorporates the unifying concept. The specific linguistic artifice is to extract from them a second item in order to extrapolate, speculate, and take it to another plane. It is a dialectical process that results in a series of third terms, the definitive and defining one of which is the last verse and title. The parallels elaborated in the lines all underline an "other" dimension, an expansion in space, or a deepening of a nodal point, which will imply overcoming, transcendence. Various details resonate in some particular way with Tropicália and Kaos. Placing "arranha-céu" before "céu," for example, counterpoises an urban, architectonic sign (skyscraper) and a classic natural romantic symbol (sky, heaven), while "guarda-chuva" (umbrella, rain-guard) suggests protection (from the "gotas," drops, that come from outside) countered by the "vontade de comê-las" (desire to devour them) which may allude to sexual hunger or, for attentive ears, to Oswald's cannibalistic aesthetics adopted by Veloso and friends. In the same way, the assertion of oppositions like "the forest and the school . . . the yearning for shamans and the military airfields" that the Tropicalists took from the "Manifesto of Pau-Brasil Poetry" to the realm of song echoes in almost all the images of Mautner's song text. The stress of "negro" naturally suits the *maracatu* as an Afro-Brazilian form, but "raça" (race) here has several connotations—guts, nerve, courage, vigor, determination—as part of a manifestation of a new sensibility that seeks to make accomplices of natural energies and molecular science alike.

Mautner's song disseminated by Gil eventually led to a vibrant case of new music in the 1990s. Having been a crystallizing composition expressing the confluence of the philosophy of Mautner and Tropicalist aesthetics, "Maracatu atômico" called for reflection and reinterpretation in the last decade of the twentieth century in specific local and global contexts. The *mangue beat*, or swamp rock, of the northern city of Recife and the project of Chico Science & Nação Zumbi (CSNZ) merit special attention in the study of youth culture, both Brazilian and transnational. In addition to numerous journalists and academics in Brazil, North American musicologists have probed *mangue* music from several vantages.[22] One of several angles from which to appreciate this novelty, one way to help comprehend this happening in Recife, is its parallels with Tropicalism. The movements share a sense of collective endeavor, provocative tactics, synthetic practices, and ideational approaches in the pop arena, which is not normally known for abstraction. The iconography of *mangue beat* and its metaphors of cultural enterprise are expressed in documents published as CD inserts and in Internet postings. Two potent images are basic: a "crab with brains," symbolizing a native subaltern intelligence, and a parabolic antenna or satellite dish, stuck in the mud, suggesting a technologically informed yet deterritorialized sensibility ("imagem-símbolo" says the manifesto) that aims to capture globalized information, and a badly resolved tension between the social reality of *mangue-favela* in metropolitan Recife and the world. The leader, with the memorable stage name Chico Science, pondered similarities with Tropicália, which shares, "an attitude, of launching your own satellite, searching for roots, holding the arms of culture when it's sinking."[23] Another explanation of the music of the new movement—"anthropophagical fusion of the misery of the *mangue* to the sophistication of parabolic antennas"—recalls, with no reference to sound per se, a Modernist source very dear to Tropicalism.

One of the principal lessons of the Tropicalists—"having no fear of being culturally strong (Caetano) in the act of incorporating modern international musical culture"—is quite apt for CSNZ.[24] Chico Science constructed magnetic music by superimposing or fusing global music information—US and European, hip-hop, rap, metal, punk, techno, varied dance music—with local forms, principally *maracatu* and *embolada*, a kind of supersyncopated tongue-twister, but also samba and its northern cousins. His group's electric-guitar energy leads many to view them as rock. But while mainstream Brazilian rock of the 1980s almost always followed metropolitan models, *mangue beat* privileged regional difference, a strategy first essayed by Tropicalists.[25] Gilberto Gil characterized the success of *mangue beat* in these words: "they do the same sonorous lucubration as Tropicalism thirty years before: they created a modern music from tradition without decharacterizing it."[26] Surely part of the appeal of Chico Science and Tropicalist antecedents can be attributed to the *calculated* decharacterization of certain aspects of select folk processions. Nevertheless, maintenance of essential musiquemes by young players and mutual support between them and bona fide traditionalist groups contribute, as Crook stresses, to the success both of new pop styles and of established *maracatus*.

As for discography, there are significant points of contact between CSNZ's recordings and those of Gil's team. Just as the main organ of the late sixties collective, *Tropicália ou panis et circensis*, was a true concept-album and manifesto of a poetics, two CDs of the main *mangue* band—*Da lama ao caos* and *Afrociberdélia*—have their own manifesto-like writings. The collections are structured around a discourse that has clear bonds with previous countercultures, beyond any musical context per se. The second CD opens a dialogue with Tropicalism; Gil himself is a guest artist. *Afrociberdélia* has a tripartite orientation: ethnic base, cybernetics, and the psychedelic. The young musicians sample and retool a prototype Tropicalist song that itself has those three referents: "Batmacumba" (Gil-Veloso), which combines Afro-Brazilian foundations, elements of experimental language, and what the Russian Formalists called *ostranenie*—defamiliarization, estrangement, or "making it strange." The element of "chaos" comes from punk rock and becomes the name of the local label. This work exemplifies Oswaldian deglutition of items from the cultural industry to make an intentional fusion with a native base. In the same way "Etnia" by CSNZ probes racial mixture and musical crossings, one of the points that Chico Science voices.[27] The phrase "bumba meu rádio" echoes the song-manifesto "Geléia geral" (Gilberto Gil–Torquato Neto, 1967), whose refrain "é bumba-iê-iê-boi" crystallized the pondered interjection of urban-popular-pop matter into rural-popular-folkloric material. Galinsky (33) highlights the fact that Chico Science could locate himself naturally in a vague nexus of local and global languages without real allegiance to any of them, and that is a "product of a tradition that begins with Tropicália."

In the modernist poetics of Oswald de Andrade, the juxtaposition of the old (primitive, native, savage, underdeveloped) and the new (modern, cosmopolitan, industrialized, developed) was often designed to make fun of provincial culture or to criticize unenlightened notions of Brazilian society. Such artistic acts were more frequent in Tropicalism, product of a decade characterized by repeated contraventions and controversies, than in *mangue beat*, which leaned less on humor and tended toward elaboration of sociocultural discourse preoccupied with racial issues and youth culture. By the 1990s, it is no surprise, movements could face with much greater naturalness a seemingly less mediated use of the foreign (rock, hip-hop) and its direct appropriation, like the eighties-nineties generation as a whole, according to the analysis of a Brazilian musicologist drawn to "new images and new alliances" (Magaldi). As for Oswaldian metaphorical anthropophagy, CSNZ did not invoke it overtly as Caetano had done, but their ideas are quite evidently associated with some of his. The recourse of taking local advantage of a European symbol and procedure was concretized in the CSNZ application of a marketing strategy forged by Malcolm McLaren. This manager of the punk group Sex Pistols called his production method "cash from chaos." The idea was to use rock (and counter-compartments) to reveal government and corporate injustices and to manipulate, at the same time, the systems created by them to earn considerable amounts of money. Some of the songs of CSNZ appear to want to express this stance.[28] The wardrobe of the English band included an armband saying simply "chaos," which could encompass, according to the author of *Rockin' Out: Popular Music in the USA* (1997), "the intention not to be explicitly political but to be an explosion of highly charged and contradictory signs."[29] There is local identification in the use of the name CHAOS for the label of CSNZ and in the making of a "chaotic" logo to exhibit next to the antenna and the crab on recording packaging. Chico Science was also interested in scientific theories about the consequences of randomness and unpredictability.[30] Music, he said, "is something that is recycled; from the old you make the new and from the new the old, as in chaos theory."[31] He metaphorizes chaos to musical and discursive ends, as had, as if prefiguring him, the writer-musician Jorge Mautner creating his Kaos and his most complete pop expression, inexorably Tropicalist, "Maracatu atômico." Chico Science recorded four versions of this song in Brazil, one without subtitle, another subtitled "Atomic Version," a third called "Ragga Mix," and a fourth "Trip Hop." One more version was made in New York, a binational duet with DJ Soul Slinger, on *Red Hot Rio*, following shows in Central Park and elsewhere with Gil and others.[32] This international dance rhythm may be invoked for transnationalized cultural thought, and form a parallel to the citation of bebop by Jackson do Pandeiro.

The final recording/performance of Chico Science could even be taken as an example of Oswald's "poetry for exportation," another literary idea of the vanguard 1920s that materialized musically in bossa nova in the 1960s and in the final decade of the century in a Tropicalist resurgence in the United States, a revival, as the *New York Times* called it. This remarkable surge in interest in 1990s North America in the music of *tropicalismo* presents, on the part of a pop sensation like Beck and within anonymous collectivities, high levels of recognition and cult followings for singer-songwriter Tom Zé, the innovative rock trio Os Mutantes, Gil, Veloso, and others.[33] Although they debated international cultural flows, embodied them in provocative artistry, and changed the course of popular music in Brazil, the voices of *tropicalismo* did not enjoy in their own time any such notice outside the country. The flourish of prestige in the nineties, and into the next century, while not equal to the overall reception of bossa nova abroad, did entail an aesthetic intensity associated with the practice of poetry and, in spirit, achievements akin to the "poetry for exportation" that Oswald imagined. Chico Science was his own phenomenon, with a full-length NPR interview and meaningful promotion. Like Jackson do Pandeiro before him, he also had a stage name crossing English and Portuguese in a suggestive hitching of something techno, mediatic, First World, and something organic, popular, Third World, if you will. To be significant, the two performers need not depend on the linguistic gesture nor, ultimately, comparison with Tropicália. But events a decade before and more than two decades after Tropicalism do illuminate motives, motifs, and mutinies of the Tropicalist conspiracy in contexts that now involve ample international domains.

A celebrated writer from Bahia called Tropicália "*topos* de conciliação dos contrários, da inconciliação dos mesmos" [topos of conciliation of contraries, of the in-conciliation of the same].[34] With this antithetical statement as a point of departure, keeping in mind the semimillennial Tropicalist spirit, it is profitable to consider some of the poetic resonance of the double names of the two artists of the Northeast considered here, as they counterpoise significantly terms of national and foreign origin. The first part of the nom de plume Jackson do Pandeiro derives from Jack Perry, an actor in Westerns the artist saw as a youth. The adoption of English may suggest the tendency in peripheral countries to seek legitimacy or prestige through linguistic association with the center, as well as the inescapable hemispheric impact of USAmerican communication media. The name combination, still, reveals a characteristic local creativity, for the joining with *pandeiro* (tambourine) is a Brazilian convocation, and the artist with the compound name composes with combinations and recombinations in mind. Some posthumous homages confirm the significance of his most celebrated song and his name.[35]

The name Chico Science, in turn, is also formed of a familiar Portuguese segment, a very common nickname, next to an English word from a technical domain, a consequential configuration consistent with the semantics of "Maracatu atômico." He could have adopted the Portuguese *ciência* to convey the interest in theories, such as chaos, or the notion of a crazy scientist doing experiments and mixtures in the laboratory, yet the poet-vocalist opted for English, whether for the peripheral reasons suggested above or to enforce a figurative interrelation of the scientific and the musical like

the one imagined by Jorge Mautner, as well as, in Oswaldian and Tropicalist fashion, an effective contrast in anticipation of the transnational act he
would become. Thus two ecumenical threads of Tropicalism interweave—
making local and global interventions while projecting back on remote
roots as well as on a present future of technicized fruits—and mutually
illuminate each other.

7

◇

(In-)Conclusion

Intersection Interaction Interlocution

After a journey through diverse territories and decades of Brazilian lyric in the series of chapters above, questions naturally arise from the examination of repertories that so exceed the traditional bounds of poetry, questions that interrogate the premises of interface, of peoples and styles, of invention-discovery and invention-creation, and of insularity and its geocultural conceptual cousin deterritorialization. In the wake of his exported tropicalization, for instance, one might ask if Chico Science, an innovative and internationally sought-after singer whose life was cut tragically short, actually made an impact beyond the domain of popular music. Was he heard in the esoteric realm of poets and poetry? The best testimony is a test case, a textual experiment:[1]

mangue
)cabeça
de
science
se
expande(
imensidão

[mangrove /)head / of / science / expands / itself(/ immensity]

The young poet Francisco Kaq seeks in fractured verse reminiscent of the late Haroldo de Campos to accomplish what the object of attention in the poem had done in paradigm-busting end-of-the-century popular music: a lyric disassociation with the past and sure association with the present+future in which the biogeographically defined native locale is projected, broadly and universally cast, onto a cerebral dimension of performance. The "island" of the indigent urban mangrove habitat in northern Brazil is transcended; pop and inquiry form a new interface. The inter-American quality of such musico-literary encounters is appreciable in another passage of this *Eu versus*, with its compact title that can suggest a contrary writerly self (= I versus/verses) and even the Colossus of the North (EU = Estados Unidos, United States), land of origin of the feted and electrifying rock artist of a poem dubbed "Hendrix": "asa / desquieta / de hendrix / roça // o blues / inflama-se / elétrons / seguem-no" [wing / disquieted / of Hendrix / rubs // the blues / inflaming itself / electrons / follow him]. The second part of the unfolding minimalist poem goes back to the late Romantic Sousândrade, whose transamerican epic was unraveled in chapter 4, and forward, again to the Afro-American cybernetics felt in chapter 6:

exu no
eixo
do mundo
hino

desatina:
sousêndrix

farrapos
estelares

afrociber
délica
emerge
do inferno

harpa
farpada

∗

você já
experimantou?

[Eshu in the / axis / of the world / hymn // goes crazy: / *Sousêndrix* // stellar / tatters // Afro-cyber / -delic / emerges / from the inferno // "barbed / harp" // ∗ // have you / tried it (experimanted)?]

This is an interarts-friendly poem about the meeting of minds and epochs. Eshu in West African–derived spirit-possession religions of the New World is the trickster at the crossroads, sometimes portrayed (not so appropriately) as devilish. The delirious act here is to mix the names of the peregrinating poet Sousândrade—author of "The Inferno of Wall Street" and *Harpas selvagens* (Savage harps)—and the internationally revered master of invention on the electric guitar, Afro-American Jimi Hendrix (d. 1970). One of his most notable moments was a distortion-driven instrumental version of the "Star-Spangled Banner," whose text was translated by Emperor Dom Pedro of Brazil, a fact to which Sousândrade alluded in his most celebrated long passage. *Harpa farpada*, poetic image of the electric guitar, was borrowed from music critic José Miguel Wisnik in a "Hendrixian context."[2] The poematic portmanteau gesture connects with the final line, where changing a single vowel of the normal *experimentou?* (tried it?) implicates a Joycean word blending that carries over into the very aesthetics in play. There is further allusion to the epoch-making LP by the Jimi Hendrix Experience, *Are You Experienced?* (1967). The forged name Sousêndrix sounds somewhat like Science, and the component of ethnic cybernetics also suggests Chico Science. Thus the underlined *barbed harp*, also implying a title or other reason for italicization, may encompass the antinormative verse of the nineteenth-century bard, lines of the translated hymn of the USA, the sharp-edged popular music of the star Hendrix, musico-literary criticism, and the fusion of *mangue beat*.

The currency of such hybridity is central in a technologically tinged twenty-first-century lyric of two dozen lines titled "Brazilian Frame" that serves to summarize much of the foregoing. This other young voice, Paula Valéria Andrade, ponders mixtures and melting pots, ending with jabs that refer back to the mythology of the epoch of discovery (invention), the formation of images in the Western imaginary (islands, utopia), and the age of planetary mass media (interfaces): "Brasil atual / Paradoxo do paraíso / Pós *pop* natural / de uma *jungle* industrial" [Present-day Brazil / Paradox of paradise / Natural postpop / of an industrial jungle].[3] These are simple rhymes with complex echoes: the pondering of the nation after five hundred years of European presence, the blessed mysterious insular motif, the lingering effects of the northern gaze, the local tendency to incorporate and knack for adaptation, the coexistence of truly tropical environs and cosmopolitan urbs, both with English keywords. This framing rings of and recalls contemporary poems seen above by Carlos Vogt ("Ilha Brasil"),

Waly Salomão ("Ideograma Brasil"), and others, notably the multimediatic Arnaldo Antunes. A semantically coupled pair of entries in his new-millennium album of "words in disorder" traces an arc from the ancient motif of paradise (utopia) to a timeless anticipation.[4] Like the "Céu-Hell" seen in chapter 2, these two items are constructed in a huge 72-point outline font and occupy full pages. The first displays in a three-line configuration:

AUTO
PIACONTI
NUA

This division yields varied combinations of semantic elements: act, medieval drama, self, car / sink, giant clamshell, feminine pious, Italian (ac) counts / feminine nude. Redividing the letters, one sees the contained message "A UTOPIA CONTINUA" [the utopia continues, or, the continual utopia], which can comprise a reiteration of the ambiguous values associated with the noun (isolation versus ideal location), as seen in the introduction. Toward the end of this album, Antunes offers a simple and straightforward "A AVENTURA CONTINUA" [the adventure goes on], which evokes show-business imperatives and sequels, remote colonial experience (early Brazilian explorers as adventurers), and the very adventure (quest, feat, risk) of art. The two poetic slogan-statements remain as if coauthored across time and space.

As a poetic motif, we have seen, insularity can connect to history, both national Brazilian and that shared with sister nations of the hemisphere. In real-world terms, despite all the ease of travel and of technology transfer in the current conjuncture, signs of the isolation Brazil was accustomed to over the centuries endure. The issue of language remains difficult; the currency of Portuguese as an instrument of commerce in the New World still does not correspond to Brazil's size, population, or economy. However, with the use of English, Spanish, and communication media, along with concerted efforts by dedicated people, insularity of the cultural variety has assuredly been reduced. The insular does not cease to be imbricated with the utopian, as Antunes performatively demonstrates. He and others have poeticized, often in questioning fashion, the neoliberal e-enabled consumer world that connects countries and aesthetic discourses, perhaps suggesting a metaphorical solution to the dystopic elements of isolation, relative underdevelopment, and underrepresentation on stages outside the hemisphere. If artistic experience of the "utopian" in the 1960s implied association with grand projects of social transformation, in the 1990s and beyond newer senses obtain; hemispheric fraternity, solidarity, or identity underpin meetings and writings with diverse ends.

There is a different confluence of many threads followed here in "A tempestade" ("The Tempest") by Rodrigo Garcia Lopes, which, taking its title and motif from a work whose New World element has naturally intrigued critics, looks back over the centuries and across the hemisphere to incite multidisciplinary questions.[5]

Canibal, palavra latina,
à maneira de canis, animal
de fidelidade canina.

Nas Bermudas, sublime ironia,
será um vento do cão
e vai se chamar *hurracán*.

E quando o mar de lá
de repente apontar terra à vista
então será Caliban.

Cannibal, a Latin word,
meaning, as *canis* does, an animal
with the loyalty of a dog.

In the Bermudas, sublime irony,
it will be a devilish wind
and it shall be called *hurracán*

And when the boatswain
suddenly points to a new land
Then it will be Caliban.

Very briefly, it would be imperative to note how the anagrammatic first and last words, *canibal* and Caliban, frame the three strophes in a mesh of history, linguistics, literature, and more, that is transatlantic, transamerican, and ultimately transcendent. The word *canibal* was purportedly coined by Columbus to designate the island "savages" he found in the New World, based on indigenous words for "strong men" and on affinity with the Latin word for "dog." In a Brazilian poem, it is also inevitably reminiscent of Oswald de Andrade's *antropofagia*, cultural cannibalism. The irony of the canine connection is the contrast of dogs' proverbial dedication and the use of *can/cão* to mean the devil, which can imply a betrayal of fate. The natives of the Caribbean, and by extension of New World lands in general, will also raise and live issues of servitude and loyalty and, like Shakespeare's character, wish to use the master's language to curse him. Based on a vocabular curiosity, the poem itself is a self-declared vessel of irony, a reminder of invention and insularity, an expression of New World wonder, and an interface of native tongues, Spanish, English, and Portuguese.

One of the pillars of transamerican poetics is the act of looking to other horizons and languages in search of commonalities and space for fruitful discussion. As seen in chapters 2 and 3, Brazilian poets embraced USAmerican counterparts as never before as the twentieth century wound down, and one of the points in common was critique of the establishment (especially USAmerican power structures), which, since the years of imbalanced Pan-Americanism, could be found in Spanish American poetry to varying degrees. In "Aguafuerte porteña" (Buenos Aires etching), Ricardo Corona brings together several lines of thought to assert a kind of representative Americanness. The title is borrowed from the name of a column of vignettes of Buenos Aires authored by the off-center novelist Roberto Arlt in the 1930s. The new poem, in turn, is dedicated to social critic filmmaker Michael Moore and radical political analyst Noam Chomsky, both of whom are noted for exposing corporate and government misdeeds in/by

America (meaning USA, in the singular English usage of the North). The Brazilian poet, through absence, laments assaults on democratic models.[6]

> América,
> ao norte e sob um sol falso,
> teus filhos se afastam
> > do aroma dos prados.
> Os mesmos filhos
> que atuaram contra a desobediência civil
> > de Thoreau
> > e fazem da democracia
> > > um inimigo invisível.

[America, / up north under a false sun, / your sons step away / from the aroma of the meadows. // The same sons / who acted against the civil disobedience / of Thoreau / and make democracy / an invisible enemy.]

The identifiable "they" on parade in the body of the poem are hypocrites, leaders of the military-industrial complex, multinational economic exploiters, and other undesirables who perform a disservice with respect to a revered voice who was welcomed by others in the hemisphere for over a hundred years:

> Não, América,
> não são os que Walt Whitman separou
> > feito as folhas da relva
> > e os fez americanos.
> Os americanos estão dentro da América
> —ao sul, ao norte e ao centro—
> feito o anagrama
> > "Iracema."

[No, America, / they are not those whom WW separated / like the leaves of grass / and made Americans. // The Americans are inside America / —to the south, to the north and at the center— / like the anagram / Iracema.]

This opinionated declaration exemplifies once again the respect that the author of *Leaves of Grass* maintains, shows the crucial difference between literary and official figures in the estimation of sensitive writers abroad, and restates in verse the nominal arrogation discussed in the introduction, whose implications have overarched the series of chapters that comes to a close here. The final reference about America is thoroughly Brazilian. Iracema is an indigenous-sounding name invented by Romantic novelist José de Alencar (1829–1877) to christen the native heroine of an eponymous novel (1865).[7] It is in fact an anagram of America, and the character's sacrifice as the mother of a mixed-blood child fathered by a European man is a foundational symbol of Brazil, and of other nations of the Americas. And it is a fully literary reference, at a time when readership per se is necessarily brought into question.

The aggregate of these concluding examples and the cumulative weight of other such instances throughout the book conspire to demonstrate a "complex connectivity" associated with (sub)globalized culture and driven by a hemispheric will, with some motivations dating back centuries. Old World senses of *invention* as discovery related to first encounters centuries ago are recalled and transformed, as *invention* comes to mean finding uncharted places, fresh rapport, variegated links within the evolved New World. Brazilian artists, young and some not so young, have configured some reactive and, even more, proactive postures, opening eyes and ears to international influences that resonate in the final decades of the twentieth century and the first years of the twenty-first in digital-age, deterritorialized and reterritorialized forms of expression. In Brazil, consciousness of the Other in the hemisphere has continued to prompt new concepts and shapes in lyric that, overtly or covertly, resist isolation in unforeseen ways. These contemporary creative reactions are their own form of reconfiguration of cultural space in the Americas. This making and remaking should be thought of as work going on and ongoing. Inter-American literature remains an "emergent field" (Lowe and Fitz, 1), especially where poetry is concerned. This concluding segment is named "(In-)Conclusion" not just as a parting reminder of the governing "In-" paradigm—interfaces, insularity, invention, Brazilian lyric in/and the Americas—but also to imply openness, to insinuate a nondefinitive status. As Bernstein puts it in "Our Americas" (91):

> The project of America—of the Americas—is a process not yet complete, a process that shall never be finished. . . .
> Our Americas is still in progress: as a talk, an experiment, an essay. Then again perhaps our Americas is a formal procedure, an hypothe-

sis or conditional, requiring aesthetic intervention, seat-of-the-pants ingenuity, and other-worldly reinvention.

And this is why, it could just be, that we see the possibilities of our Americas most acutely in poetry: our poetics viewed under the sign of our exchange.

This book has not been an account of the contemporary poetry scene in Brazil as a whole, nor of a genre of national literature in a particular period, of the body of work of a generation or two, but rather of a certain slice of all those—in sum, an appreciation of particular text-makers and sets of texts that sing and speak to shared interests in hemispheric awareness, the means of expression of Others nearby, the views of neighbors. Late-century and turn-of-the-millennium Brazilian lyric has been seen through a prism of transamerican poetics, colorfully and in different shapes, rarely meaning or involving uniformity, homogeneity, or unification, but sometimes solidarity against unbecoming realities, and frequently indeed common senses of New World being and ways of imagining things. A disposition toward outreach and fellowship is evident at so many turns. Transamerican imperatives are most evident in events that can declare and broadcast their intentions, whether all-inclusive in the hemisphere or Ibero-American in focus, or even with transatlantic Iberian connections. In diverse repertories of poetry, from midcentury concrete inventions to the multifarious verse of magazines and specialized presses of the 1990s and beyond, openness and will to engage—with New World others, texts and text-makers, elders and youthful peers alike—does not necessarily correlate with poets' socially defined situations, and that is in itself a statement about the variegated face of expressive culture in the new millennium.

Returning to the questions posed at the outset, it may be answered that, yes, one can be at once more oneself and more a national being through poetic appeals to the selves and signs of potent Others and their locations in the same hemisphere. Poets demonstrably feel that they expand the reach of their craft and their understanding of new times by riding nonprint vehicles, by composing in other languages that populate the hemisphere, and by redefining local and national spaces in relation to alternate regional territories. To substantiate mass media and electronic technology as cornerstones of contemporary existence worldwide and within the hemisphere is not at all antithetical to lyric; to the contrary, it is an enabling source of revitalization. Perceptions of change and of place—such as a Web-connected, sound-ready spot in a home in a Brazilian city, in a South American land, once island, in a new New World domain—are indeed topics for present-day lyric. Words, lines, poems, sequences, books, albums, sites, volumes, and collections, all can open fresh perspectives on the experiences of virtual and real environments and human landscapes.

Notes

Unless otherwise indicated, translations are my own.

Chapter 1. Insular Outreach, Moveable Outlook

1. See the special issue of the journal of the largest professional organization in literature: "Globalizing Literary Studies," *PMLA* 116, no. 1 (2001), with, vis-à-vis connections to Brazil, a color cover photo of people-filled downtown steps in São Paulo and an introduction by Giles Gunn that mentions, from Brazilian literature, the epic poem *The Uruguay*, foundational Romantic novelist José de Alencar, the first world-class author Machado de Assis, and the much celebrated Clarice Lispector. See also the next note concerning special issues about the expansion of "American" studies beyond the confines of English and the United States in the 1990s and the decade 2000–2009.

2. Kadir, "America and Its Studies," 1. The editor is translator of João Cabral de Melo Neto and founding president of the International American Studies Association; see debates about scope and conception at www.iasaweb.org. Gunn specifically wonders about "the possibility of developing a transnational cultural criticism of the Americas." He underlines that "the referential incoherence of the word *American* as a term of hemispheric designation (a reason with special significance for students of literature and ideas) has to do with the extent to which all American cultures were initially, and continue to remain, the products of a complicated process of rhetorical invention and reinvention" (*Beyond Solidarity*, 5). See discussions below on "invention" and "America(n)." In an issue of *PMLA* with a cluster "The Neobaroque and the Americas," Ralph Bauer contributes a useful overview of what he terms hemispheric studies.

3. Fitz, " Theory and Practice," 153–65. The approach is expounded in *Rediscovering the New World*. An updated perspective, largely about narrative, is in Lowe and Fitz, *Translation and the Rise of Inter-American Literature*.

4. Greene, "Wanted," 337. The original statement of orientation was made in "New World Studies and the Limits of National Literatures."

5. Bernstein, "Poetics of the Americas," 1.

6. Studies in the late 1990s nominally about poetry or fiction were often actually preoccupied with identity. See the contents of Cvetkovich and Kellner and of King. One very focused specialist, Szeman, in his 2001 "Globalization" piece, mentions literature per se only twice—*Weltliteratur*, and Marx and Engels—but exemplifies cultural exchange

with American pop music and the pair of Brazilian songwriters Tom Zé and Caetano Veloso.

7. Palattella cites fellow critic Owen to this effect. The keen analyst Brennan specifically cites Brazil.

8. Quoted in Tomlinson, 144.

9. Franco, *Decline and Fall*, 264–75.

10. Vogt, *Ilhas Brasil*, 35.

11. Buarque de Hollanda, "Two Poetics," 245, 248, 252.

12. Assunção, Corona, and Lopes, 5.

13. Daniel, "Uma escritura na zona da sombra," 27–28.

14. Pucheu, 5. "Acredito que, desguarnecendo fronteiras e deslocando eixos que se querem fixos, a força do poético se encontra na abertura para o outro, para o fora, que teimam em, saudável e intensamente, intervir."

15. C. Azevedo, "Uma vez humano sempre acrobata." The column title is taken from a text by concrete poet and critic Rosemary Waldrop.

16. Greene, *Unrequited Conquests*, 4.

17. On Brazilian modernism, concrete poetry, and the poetic side of *tropicalismo*, see Perrone, *Seven Faces*.

18. Livón-Grosman, " Questing of the Americas," 129–30.

19. Veloso, *Tropical Truth*, 6.

20. Fortuna, interview, 131.

21. H. Costa, *Mar abierto*, 423.

22. Mac Mathúna. The most complete source on this theme is the richly illustrated Cantarino, *Uma ilha chamada Brasil: O paraíso irlandês no passado brasileiro*.

23. The early-twelfth-century Anglo-Norman tale *Voyage de Saint Brendan* would bring this Celtic thematic into European high culture. Maodez Glanndour's modern Breton poem *Imram* renders it anew; see Calin, *Minority Literatures and Modernism*. In Breton, *Breizh* is the term for Brittany, and *Breizh-uhel* for Upper Brittany; *izel* is the term for "low" or "lower."

24. South of the British Isles, between 1526 and 1721, four expeditions departed the Canary Islands in search of a "promised land" still imagined to be that fabulous insular entity named Brazil, despite the name's having been adopted for the eastern part of the continent of South America. As late as 1830, Purdy's *General Chart of the Atlantic* still shows a specific latitude-longitude of a spot named Brazil, which in 1853 a certain Mr. Finley named Brazil Rock. Only in 1865 did cartographers officially reject the hypothesis of the Island of Brazil.

25. Barroso; Greene, *Unrequited Conquests*, 87–95, with abundant illustrations.

26. Creeley, 153; original letter in the Creeley archive at Stanford University.

27. Greene, *Unrequited Conquests*, 98.

28. Lajolo, 14. Toumson, 73–76, explores the geosemantics of the trio isle-archipelago-continent as evolving concepts relevant to comprehension of the New World.

29. In his foreword to a trilingual anthology (Portuguese plus Spanish and English translations) of seventeen very young poets, Frederico Barbosa observes a mission: "The initiative to publish this selection in three languages is an effort to expand their reader-

ship beyond national frontiers. It also shows the realization of the role of poets as articulators of cultural relations among countries in the Americas" ("Vacamarela," 7).

30. Gruesz, xiii. See the concise assessment by Handley (30–33). See also Brickhouse for a reassessment of the formation of American literature via interactions between texts of the USA, Mexico, and the French Caribbean, in which one can begin to discern "unfamiliar genealogies." Especially useful are her notes to "Introduction: Transamerican Renaissance," which cover extensive amounts of recent scholarship seeking to expand horizons by addressing the "blindness and binocularity" of most approaches to early USAmerican literary history. In a current context, a glaring example of thoroughly USA-centric publication is a collection that remains within its borders even when appearing to be polynational by pluralizing the name of the continent: Reed, *From Totems to Hip-Hop: A Multicultural Anthology of Poetry Across the Americas, 1900–2002*, in which African-, Asian-, Native American, and Latino content account for diversity from Alaska to Florida.

31. Bishop and Brasil, *An Anthology of Twentieth-Century Brazilian Poetry*. Her Brazil-related repertory is masterfully rendered and analyzed by P. H. Britto in *Poemas do Brasil*.

32. Brasil and Smith, *Brazilian Poetry (1950–1980)*.

33. The original (1977) full name of the piece was "CAGE: CHANCE: CHANGE, pentahexagram for John Cage." Subsequent published versions did not include the words in capitals, perhaps because the author had used them as the title of a creative critical piece on the USAmerican artist, which was published in several places, most notably as the preface to the translation of *A Year from Monday* (1985) and as the finale of *O anticrítico* (1986), a volume of transamerican interest as it contains Augusto de Campos's versions of Cage, Gertrude Stein, Emily Dickinson, Oliverio Girondo, and Vicente Huidobro. For a suitably sponsored English-language account of the poetics of the concrete poet-critic, see Perrone, "ABC of AdeC," in a publication of the Americas Society.

34. Livón-Grosman, "A Poetics of the Americas."

35. Palmer and Bonvicino, *Cadenciando-um-ning um samba, para o outro*, with preface by Marjorie Perloff. Bonvicino included another collaboration with Bernstein, "Definitions of Brazil" in his *Página órfã*, 92–94, which uses many North Atlantic clichés about the tropical and festive South American nation. Bonvicino's poems in English are available at the "Orphan Page" link at regisbonvicino.com.br. See especially "It's Not Looking Great!"

36. Lopes, *Vozes e visões* and *Folhas de relva*.

37. H. Costa, *Mar abierto*, 421.

38. See Perrone, *"Pau-Brasil, antropofagia, tropicalismo."* We will use the artist's first name to avoid confusion with other leading Brazilian poets with the same last name, Mário de Andrade and Carlos Drummond de Andrade.

39. Greene, "Anthropophagy, Invention, and the Objectification of Brazil," 117.

40. For an in-depth discussion of the term from ancient to modern times, see Castor, *Pléiade Poetics*, esp. 86–93, 95–102. The treatment of English and French therein is quite applicable to Portuguese, which suffered historical influences from the other two tongues.

41. Pound, *ABC of Reading*, 39, 43, 75. With respect to the importance of linguistic vitality and novelty in the influential USAmerican poet, see the chapter "The Invention of Language" in Kenner, *The Pound Era*. Augusto de Campos, acting in transtemporal spirit, symptomatically gave the title *Invention* to his updated (2003) collection of translations of troubadour lyrics and high Italian Renaissance verse.

42. H. Campos, "A nova estética," 9.

43. Editorial director Décio Pignatari, quoted in C. Ávila, "*Invenção*," 97. The critic relives each issue of the review and argues for facsimile editions. He notes that the quoted editorial position anticipates ideas developed in the next decade in alternative publications, which confirms the continual relevance of the notion of "invention." On this assertion, see Perrone, "De *Noigandres*."

44. H. Campos, "Texto e história," 18. The anthology did not, in fact, appear, though the idea inspired others, as seen below.

45. H. Campos, "Serafim," 102.

46. Event cited in Glazier, 149. With respect to e-poetry and digital poetics in Brazil, see the exemplary work of André Vallias, especially the remarkable site www.erratica.com.br.

47. In 2005 Daniel posted relevant sections of his preface to an online discussion of the question "What is the sense of the concept of 'poetry of invention' today?" at www.revistazunai.com/depoimentos_debates/conceito_poesia_invencao.htm.

48. Montenegro and Wagner.

49. There are more than half a dozen translations into English, often with serious shortcomings. The first to circulate in literary criticism was Bary. A specially commissioned annotated rendering is Berg. In December 2005, São Paulo hosted the multimedia EIA! (Encontro Internacional de Antropofagia) with artists and speakers from Europe and North America; see www.antropofagia.com.br.

50. Chanady, xxv. See the various essays in Sklodowska and Heller.

51. See Fernández Retamar, "Calibán ante la antropofagia." The essayist gathered variations of the original essay in *Todo Calibán*, with a new preface for a foreign reprint.

52. See Mignolo, "Loci of Enunciation" and, for an expanded theoretical discussion, "Human Understanding." These ideas evolved into the manifesto *The Idea of Latin America*. On cartography, see his "Putting the Americas on the Map."

53. The most indispensable work on this period remains Léry, available in translation. See too André Thevet, *Les Singularités de la France antarctique, autrement nommée Amerique* (1557).

54. Ardao, *Génesis de la idea y el nombre de América Latina*, is the best source for details of the unfolding of this name on both sides of the Atlantic. Resistance and reaction to the French version of genesis of the term "Latin America" carries well into the third millennium; see, for example, Kuss.

55. Rouquié, 17. Other French sources show the geographical moves: L. M. Tisserand used "L'Amérique Latine" as a substitute for "Nouveau Monde" and "Amérique du Sud" ("Situation de la latinité," *Revue des Races Latines* [January 1861]), and the priest Emmanuel Domenech, author of *Journal d'un missionnaire au Texas et au Mexique*,

1846–1852, consolidated the concept of Latin America as "le Mexique, l'Amérique Centrale et l'Amérique du Sud."

56. Salomon, Sagasti, and Sachs-Jeantet, 52.

57. Mariátegui, "¿Existe un pensamiento hispanoamericano?"

58. Mariátegui, "El iberoamericanismo y panamericanismo."

59. A. Lima, 9–10.

60. Moniz Bandeira, "¿América Latina o Sudamérica?"

61. Coutinho. See the multinational editorial roles of Grandis and Bernd.

62. He refers, in *The Idea of Latin America*, to a proposal advanced by Pierre Nepveu. Mignolo's study problematizes ideological and epistemological threads, and implications of name-anchored positionings, ultimately relevant to all the discourse under consideration in the present study. In Brazilian criticism, the sharpest recognition of Mignolo's analysis is Evando Nascimento, "Uma leitura nos trópicos: A 'idéia' de América Latina."

63. O'Gorman's *The Invention of America* is a compilation and updating of books published in Spanish in the 1950s.

64. Gunn, *Beyond Solidarity*, 5.

65. Leminski, *Distraídos venceremos*, 87.

66. Given the age of the poem, Leminski may well have known Bloom's *A Map of Misreading*, which is a follow-up to *The Anxiety of Influence* (1973). For the controversial Yale critic, poems are always about other poems, and influence is not the actual passing of ideas or images but rather the relationship between texts. Poets inevitably "misread" their precursors to begin asserting their own originality. Leminski seems to have a broader agenda of "invention" in his lyric of negation and affirmation. Early-twenty-first-century observers of the Brazilian scene have used Bloom to humorous critical ends, noting that the well-known "anxiety of influence" had become a prideful "orgulho da influência" or "furor da influência" as celebration/imitation of admired canonical predecessors became overt and declared. See Demarchi, "Sintomas." For the purposes of the present study, a new notion is that young poets may, as never before, process influence from poets writing in American English or Spanish.

Chapter 2. Allusive, Elusive

1. Lynn, 13; also cited from *Leaves of Grass* #548 by Paro in "Whitman in Brazil." Paro looks most closely at Whitman's impact on Ronald de Carvalho, *Toda a América* (analyzed in chapter 4 here), fellow modernist poet Jorge de Lima, and Gilberto Freyre, who himself wrote on Whitman, a piece reproduced alongside Paro in Allen and Folsom. See also Raab.

2. With reference to authors, publication, and promotion, see Rostagno.

3. Rocha and Torres. Flávia Rocha launched a bilingual poetry book marked by transamerican sentiment.

4. Costa and Perrone.

5. This classic example by Décio Pignatari (*Poesia*, 129) was included in both Solt and E. Williams. The poem resides on numerous Web sites today.

6. Moacir Amâncio, personal interview, 20 July 1999. The poet published "Unique-ness" in *Dimensão* 9, no. 28 (1999), 144–79, in which he ponders teaching Portuguese to a lampshade; see Perrone, "Resource and Resonance." A shorter version opens the English-language section, "At," of the poet's collected verse in *Ata*, 431–76.

7. Buarque de Hollanda, *Esses poetas*, 10–12.

8. E-mail, 25 August 2003. The poem is in Daniel and Barbosa, 317.

9. Buarque de Hollanda, *Esses poetas*, 20.

10. Antunes's wallpaper was featured in the show "Manipulated Word / Text and Image" at the Ground Level Gallery of the South Florida Arts Center in Miami Beach, which was part of "New Vision Florida-Brazil: A Festival Exchange," Spring 1996. There are four color photos of the installation in the Artes section of the Web site arnaldo-antunes.com.br. As text, "NOW / NOWHERE / HERE" appeared in Antunes, *Palavra desordem*. The volume is all brief verbal flashes (one to several words), puns, sayings, curious phrases, epigrams, slogans, aphorisms, refrains, proverbs, and the like, some straight, many twisted. The pages are punctuated with English items, the most entertain-ing one being a counterpoising of a backwards mirrored *consenso* (consensus) and *non-sense*. All items cover a whole page or spread in enormous outline fonts, 72- to 144-point. Further examples appear in chapter 7.

11. At Dentro Brasil, exhibition at the Long Beach Museum of Art, 1995. Previously released in Brazil as part of Antunes et al., *Nome*, a thirty-item package in a tripartite print-audio-video format. The final two frames can be viewed online under Digitais in the Artes section of arnaldoantunes.com.br.

12. MexicArt Gallery, Austin, Texas, Spring 2002. Antunes, *Dois ou mais corpos*, 47, has the poem in the original black-and-white, arnaldoantunes.com.br/sec_artes_obras_view.php?id=207 in color.

13. "Romântico," in Ornellas, 41.

14. Ferry, 1–2, 3, 5.

15. Respectively, Mello, Kaq, and R. Augusto, 79.

16. Caiafa, *Fôlego*, 68–69. This poem is written in both tongues, with the first strophe in Portuguese and the second in English. The two parts are not translations of each other but share elements. The word "cool" is used in the first part.

17. These four examples are from Caiafa, *Cinco ventos*.

18. Caiafa, *Ouro*, 52.

19. Poem from Salomão, *Lábia*, 63. *Elusivo* is a new word (from English) that entered dictionaries in the 1980s. Some dictionaries still do not include the word.

20. Thiago Rodrigues, *Ar7éria* (*Arteria* 7) (2004).

21. A. E. Ribeiro, 19, original bold.

22. Vasconcellos and Vasconcellos, 59, original bold.

23. There is a black-and-white version of "Céu-Hell" as calligraphy in *Como é que chama* and a megafont version in *Palavra desordem*; cf. companion pieces in chapter 7.

24. Salgado Maranhão, "Bloody Sun," trans. Alexis Levitin, *Bomb* 102 (Winter 2008): 107–8. From Levitin's translation of the book in collaboration with Maranhão, who somewhat favored sound over meaning. E-mail from Levitin, 15 May 2009.

25. Ascher, *O sonho do razão*. 33.

26. With respect to computer-related poetry and the use of English, see the attitudinally acute fine-press book (with CD) Xavier, *Save As*, digital-age free verse referring to intersemiotics, drawing, sound files, diagrams, etc., with a title piece about life on Macintosh.

27. Ramalho, "O híbrido lirismo brasileiro dos anos 90."

28. Leonardos, 67.

29. Salomão, *Algaravias*, 29–31.

30. See commentary in Dunn, *Brutality Garden*, 109, and Perrone, *Masters*, 61, with full English translation of copyrighted song text, which can be read freely online, e.g. at www.caetanoveloso.com.br.

31. A. Pereira, "Outono cool" (Autumn cool), in *Folhas do Carmim*, 17.

32. Henriques Neto, 134; Salomão, *Algaravias*, 43–48.

33. Maranhão, *Mural de ventos*, 53. The Brazilian poet was inspired by lines 5–6 of the Stevens poem, widely available online or in collections.

34. See Lopes, *Visibilia*, table of contents. Luiza Franco Moreira introduces translations of Creeley in *Inimigo rumor* 17 (2005) and contributes a poem, "An American Life," about her own residence in the USA.

35. Torres Filho, *Poros*, 47.

36. R. Corona, *Cinemaginário*, 33.

37. F. Gomes, 87.

38. "por vezes, se assemelha a um Whitman, digamos, no sacrifício da rarefação, como se o norte-americano tivesse perdido pelas ruas dos estertores deste nosso século a sua nobreza retórica quase glandular, para em troca esbarrar na fulminância estranhadora dos afetos de agora." Noll, 5–6.

39. Santiago, *Salto*, 57–76.

40. Adriano Espínola, "Meu clássico pessoal," Prosa e Verso, *O globo online*, 28 June 2003.

41. Caiafa, *Fôlego*, 69; Caiafa, *Cinco ventos*, 59.

42. Brown, 196; the encompassing Marxist analysis considers Tropicalism as movement, Oswald, and concrete poetry. The song was recorded in 1999 by Veloso on *Livro* (Polygram 526 5842).

43. F. Gomes, 77–87.

44. Mariano, 40. As for non–New York travel lyric, see the Chicago and Midwest cluster by Astrid Cabral.

45. See Daghlian, "Poe in Brazil" and "A recepção"; Araújo; Alves, with its translations by Baudelaire, Mallarmé, Machado de Assis, Fernando Pessoa, and the editor himself. On Poe and others, see Figueira.

46. Poe Studies Association call for papers, *MLA Newsletter* 39, no. 1 (2007), 25.

47. N. Castro, 15. The author plays with issues of two-language communication and sensuality in "Made in Brazil": "Oh my God! / explodes bilíngüe / quando te percorro / com a minha língua" (35) [. . . / you explode bilingual / when I run the length of you / with my tongue].

48. J. Pereira, 22.

49. Caetano, 30.

50. M. Gomes,11.

51. Borges, 72. The book includes a CD.

52. *Código* 3 (1978), visual poem by Cleber Teixeira.

53. Renato Ghiotto placed this piece in *Código* 12 (1990) as part of a homage to Poe in a special issue on poetry and science.

54. Torres Filho, *Novolume*, 136.

55. See Monteiro, "Emily Dickinson's Brazilian Poems" and "Privileged and Presumptious Guests"; W. Costa. In 2008 Augusto de Campos completed a new volume of translations of her poems, *Não sou ninguém*, for an academic press. The scholarly journal *Fragmentos* (Daghlian et al.) dedicated an issue to Dickinson, with articles in Portuguese and English.

56. Leite, *A uma incógnita*, 52.

57. Conclusion to the fifteen lines of "But Emily Dickinson," in Meira, *Corpo solo*, 37.

58. "Patamares do Jardim das Lajes," A. Ávila, 76.

59. C. Azevedo, *Collapsus linguae*, 24.

60. In *Nome* there are two versions, one of stretched white letters on a black background and the other a video version with myriad additional elements. The original appearance was in *Tudos* (1990). A reproduced version of black letters on white appears in *Como é que chama*, 120.

61. A. Campos, *Porta-retratos*. The visual poem "Rosa para Gertrude" is enhanced in a digital version with rose-colored letters and backgrounds on the artist's Web site at www2.uol.com.br/augustodecampos/08_02.htm. Images of the two versions side by side can be viewed in "Writing as Re-Writing," by Marjorie Perloff, who interprets a series of cases.

62. R. Lopes, *Polivox*, 27.

63. F. Gomes in Félix, 255.

64. Morse, "Triangulating Two Cubists," later chapter 2 of *New World Soundings*.

65. In R. Corona, *Outras praias*, 234–37.

66. R. Lopes, *Polivox*, 132.

67. See Kutzinski, *Against the American Grain*. This book was a relatively early effort to combat the narrowness of American studies and to advocate for "New World writing," though the actual analytical range went only as far as Cuba.

68. Gregory, *Quotation and Modern American Poetry*, 73. The premise of this study—the particularly crucial role of actual citation of others' words—finds strong internationalist support in the Brazilian repertories under review here.

69. Recent volumes of English renderings are by Strand (of Drummond) and Slavitt (of Bandeira).

70. Risério, *Ensaio*, 94.

71. Greene, "Inter-American Obversals."

72. R. Corona, *Corpo sutil*, 87. The quotations are of Charles Bukowski from the poem "How to Be a Good Writer" and of Celso Borges, "Manifesto."

73. "uma forma de me libertar das camisas de força brasileiras." Waly Salomão, personal interview, 1 July 2001.

74. Examples of salutation of Whitman are not uncommon. A good example is in

Amoreira, *Maralto*, 31; in this subsection of "Poema embebido em vinho" (Poem imbibed in wine), the author's typically delirious off-center chopped discourse shouts: "Saúdo Whitman! embaraçosos / todos os passarinhos e gaviões / os que bancam santos impúdicos / não há farsa alguma / nesse trato enlevo / acordo íntimo, | alma dúbia / espírito amigo" [I salute Whitman! embarassing / all the little birds and hawks / those who bank lewd saints / there is no farce at all / in this treatment I ravish / intimate agreement | dubious soul / friendly spirit].

75. Costa and Negrão, 28, by the latter. One point of departure for the influence of Beat poetry in translation may be the Keys anthology, which includes Bly, Lowell, Snyder, Gluck, Ginsberg, Ferlighetti, Plath, Snyder, and Leroi Jones. A more recent example of diffusion is O'Shea's, with names like Gluck, Pinsky, Strand, and Lloyd Schwartz, whose answer to "What Is American About American Poetry?" at www.poetrysociety. org/schwartz.html sounds almost Brazilian. One of Schwartz's students was Rezende, whose *Leaves of Paradise* is all in English.

76. See Peixoto, *Poesia com coisas*. In English, see the summary by Perrone, "João Cabral," and the *World Literature Today* issue edited by Djelal Kadir. The most recent volume in translation is Zenith's.

77. See Secchin, 98–101.

78. www.gregkucera.com/matisse.htm. Cf. Leavell.

79. In the Bishop paradigm, two especially germane titles are Donizete Galvão, "Carta a Miss E. B." (*A carne e o tempo*, 44–46) and "Miss E. B. come o fruto proibido" (*Mundo mudo*, 66).

80. Britto, *Liturgia da matéria*, 62; Hoover, Bonvicino, and Melo, "Lies About the Truth."

Chapter 3. Inter Arts Inter Alia

The epigraphs are from Paulo Leão, "TV," in *A ordem do acaso*, 3 [Consumed idols . . . / numbing / global/ocular / sense/seigneurial / sensory . . . / consumed / gone], and from Claudia Roquette-Pinto, "All-Leather," in Buarque de Hollanda, *Esses poetas*, 120 [high moon in Gotham City / shot lost in the dark / night opening the zipper].

1. Oliveira considers the significance of pop art for poetry in general, and specifically for Brazilian poet Felipe Fortuna. She qualifies her situating of textual production in terms of an "interface between literature and the visual arts" (113) in which lyric can manifest as "iconotext."

2. Santiago (b. 1936) grew up in the inland state of Minas Gerais. The term *província ultramarina* was first used by the authoritarian regime of Portugal in 1946 to designate Goa, its "possession" in India. Designed to avoid the word *colônia*, it was also applied in the late colonial period to Brazil. Santiago plays with the status of (former) colony in his title, which reflects the new influence of the USA by using a gerund instead of an infinitive, a linguistic trait attributable to imitation of English.

3. Mota, 13. The cover of Santiago's book sports an oft-utilized photo of presidents Getúlio Vargas and Franklin Delano Roosevelt in a jeep with military brass.

4. The wealth of the title merits comment: *carapuça* also designates a knitted helmet

and, with certain verbs, means insinuation, cutting remarks. *Qual carapuça!* means "no way." The Princeton poet-critic in the quotation surely refers to poet–art critic Herbert Read.

5. Goldstein, *The American Poet at the Movies*, is the most complete account of these interrelated phenomena and examines the most significant poetry *about* film and its players. On how the medium of film abstracts into the making of modernist poetry per se, see the more recent McCabe, *Cinematic Modernism: Modernist Poetry and Film*.

6. For a brief introduction to the case of Oswald's land of origin, see "The Shape of Brazilian Film History," in Johnson and Stam, *Brazilian Cinema*, 15–51, and select articles therein.

7. Editorial, *Klaxon* (São Paulo) 1, no. 2 (15 May 1922).

8. Santiago, *The Space In-between*, 121. The original of the essay "Literature and Mass Culture" appeared in *Novos estudos Cebrap* (1993). Oswald actually wrote a pair of screenplays in 1938 and 1942, when Orson Welles was in Brazil. Thanks to Claudia Rio Doce for sharing her pertinent dissertation (UFSC) with me.

9. One of the several translations of the "Manifesto antropófago" was done by the renowned artist Hélio Oiticica and published in Basualdo, 204–7. The phrase about cinema is mysteriously missing in this working version, which was not originally designed for public distribution, and archived scans of the artist's work at www.itaucultural.org.br show that he indeed omitted it. However, in a marginal note he does explain that *girls* likely means showgirls, stage/screen artists, not just young females.

10. This phrase in the "Manifesto of Pau-Brasil Poetry" ostensibly refers to linguistic correction. The temptation to read *roteiro* in Oswald's late-1920s iteration as "screenplay," a usage not yet current in the 1940s when Oswald himself wrote a script, was yielded to by Mary Ann Caws and Claudia Caliman, who inexplicably say that an alternate name of the "Cannibal Manifesto" was "Manifesto of Brazil-wood Poetry"; see *Exquisite Corpse*, cyber issue 11 (2002), www.corpse.org/archives/issue_11/manifestos/deandrade.html.

11. J. Aguilar, 19.

12. Antunes, *Psia*. In the book-CD-video package of *Nome* (BMG 1993), the text-plus-visual-clip "Diferente" comments on the omnipresence of dozens of comic-book and film superheroes in their non- or suprahuman forms.

13. The poet acknowledges European film too, but this consciously intersemiotic medium reveals itself mostly via USAmerican directions in Corona's work.

14. Amoreira, *Maralto*, 45–49.

15. Tanussi Cardoso, in Ruiz and Motta, *Ponte de versos*, 250. This volume has numerous transamerican moments via English, Spanish, literature, film, and music. As for effective utilization of stars, one of the keenest moments of visual poetry in Brazil in the 1980s was a Duchampian defacing of a (surely copyrighted) photo of Marilyn Monroe in low-cut dress with the digital numbers 50135, which, when viewed in a mirror, can be read as SEIOS, or breasts. The simple prisoner-number tattoolike addition by Renato Ghiotto says plenty about the male gaze, especially North American, and the victimization to which sensual icons are subject. See Perrone, "Signs of Intercourse."

16. Vilar, 41. That the author likes the joke-poem is evident in her gimmick "The Pill Poem" (Ao inventor da pílula anticoncepcional) [To the inventor of the birth-control

pill], which consists of a blank page. As for Cole Porter, Augusto de Campos had celebrated his verbal wizardry for years. Mixing Broadway song and utopian wordplay, a young Régis Bonvicino planted a contractionless "you are the top" across a 72-point UTOPIA in *Sósia da cópia*. Local interest culminated in Rennó et al., *Cole Porter: Canções, Versões*, which features prose contributions by Caetano Veloso and Augusto de Campos, and the latter's scintillating version of "You're the Top." This song appears on CD in the 2000 anthology *Cole Porter & George Gershwin: Canções, Versões* (Geleia Geral-WEA 398429049-2). Veloso recorded Cole Porter tunes in 1986 on his self-titled debut USA release and in 2004 on *A Foreign Sound* (Nonesuch 79823), which is entirely English-language repertory.

17. Salomão, *Lábia*, 71. See also the discussion of *tropicalizations* in chapter 6.

18. Caiafa, *Neve rubra*, 14. While the two famous actresses were of European origin, their fame was made via Hollywood. A later untitled poem (49) beginning "A bela garbo / compreendeu a ilusão do cinema" [The lovely Garbo / understood the illusion of cinema] is a short tribute to an actress who spanned silent and spoken film with extreme dignity.

19. Bosco, 66. David Lynch has toured Brazil and has a sizeable following there.

20. Weintraub, 43.

21. Gonzalez and Treece, 334.

22. Leite, *Obra em dobras*, 93. The poet's essay on film and literature confirms his interest in this interrelation: see "As relações duvidosas: notas sobre cinema e literatura," in *Crítica de ouvido*, 143–75.

23. Süssekind, 9; all subsequent quotes, 16.

24. Feinstein and Komunyakaa, *The Jazz Poetry Anthology* and *The Second Set*, which includes a few European entries.

25. Duarte and Alves, *POEZZ: Jazz na poesia de língua portuguesa*, with ten Brazilians included.

26. Leite, *A ficção vida*, 85.

27. Saul, *Freedom Is, Freedom Ain't*, on Coltrane 244–68; see also 133–43 on the general association of jazz and poetry.

28. Aleixo, 42. The poem's final punctuation is a comma.

29. R. Lopes, *Solarium*, 51.

30. F. Martins, *Alma em chamas*, 45. See also note 55 to chapter 5.

31. Barbosa, *Rarefato*, 80; next poem, 82.

32. Ascher, "A poesia que nasce da negação e da dúvida."

33. Leite, *A uma incógnita*, 32. Further to the profusion of references to the artist, the title of a collection of binational interest has the particle "-ning," extracted from a verse by Régis Bonvicino, who explains that the word "belongs . . . to the vocabulary of Thelonious Monk"; see Palmer and Bonvicino, *Cadenciando-um-ning*, 13.

34. Guimarães, in Daniel and Barbosa, 213.

35. Claudia Roquette-Pinto, "Jazz," in Buarque de Hollanda, *Esses poetas*, 121.

36. Campos et al., *Balanço da bossa*, 179–88. Some of the author's essays on concrete poetry have been translated into English, but none of his equally important criticism of Bossa Nova, Tropicália, and experimental art music. On the relation of the two musical

currents, and the poetic attractions of jazz, see also Calado, *O jazz como espetáculo*, esp. 245–48.

37. In Pike, see esp. "Popular Music and New Life for the Cult of the Natural," 358–60.

38. Quoted from Veloso, *Letra só*, a book that comprises editorial evidence of the continuity of the intersection of song and poetry. Poet-professor Eucanaã Ferraz organized the volume thematically like *Reunião*, the self-collection of Carlos Drummond de Andrade.

39. Mautner, *Fragmentos de sabonete*, 52. Castro Alves was the main late Romantic poet in Brazil, known for abolitionist positions; see discussion in chapter 5. Jorge Ben ("Mas, que nada!") was the original stage name of Jorge Ben Jor.

40. Butterman, "BRA-SILLY-DADE." For a detailed understanding of the artist, see Butterman, *Perversions on Parade*. Mattoso's "Spik (sic) Tupinik" (1977) is reprinted in Daniel and Barbosa, 165. Maxixe was the first Brazilian genre of dance music in the nineteenth century. Forré is northeastern dance music of the later twentieth century.

41. Leminski, *Caprichos e relaxos*, 96, quoting a Rolling Stones song.

42. R. Corona, *Ladrão de fogo*.

43. Britto, *Macau*, 27–37; see Corona and Britto. Britto's recent English volume includes the Morrison poems.

44. "Mas quem me levou a escrever poesia mesmo foi Jimi Hendrix. Quando ouvi aquela guitarra zunindo, pensei: 'caramba, quero escrever com essa mesma eletricidade.'" In "Um minuto cara-pálida," interview by Josely Vianna Baptista and Francisco Faria, "Musa paradisíaca," *Gazeta do povo*, 1 July 1996. Numerous contemporary poems refer to Hendrix; see chapter 7, esp. note 2.

45. F. Martins, "As tintas negras do jardim," in *Alma em chamas*, 84–85.

46. Ferreira, *Belo blue*; A. Pereira, 26.

47. Maranhão, *Palávora*, 80.

48. Galvão, *As faces do rio*, 46. The cited song appears on *Nina Simone Sings the Blues* (RCA, 1967); the artist (1933–2003) was a noted civil rights activist.

49. Maranhão, *Punhos da serpente*, 90.

50. On this relation, see Hanchard, as well as McCann.

51. Maranhão, *Palávora*, 61–62.

52. A related item is Paulo César de Carvalho's cleverly titled "Torquato Nato" (Torquato born), in Daniel and Barbosa, 340, which brings to bear the musical triad "**cool . . . soul . . . blues**." Reviewer Salvino pertinently notes (196): "É possível pensar a poesia de Torquato Neto em conversa, por exemplo, com um certo E.E. Cummings e com a música *pop* da virada dos anos sessenta para os setenta" [It is possible to think of TN's poetry in conversation, for example, with a certain EEC and with the pop music of the turn of the seventies].

53. Ling, "Seu nome é meu," in Buarque de Hollanda, *Esses poetas*, 259–60.

54. Cevasco, 103, 105. In Brazilian poetry around the turn of the millennium, perhaps the best universally-situated example of resistance per se to the invasion of USAmerican commercial language and products is Alexei Bueno, *Os resistentes*, an alarmist twelve-

canto harangue against banalization of discourse, mercantilism, and consumer culture in general.

55. Dorfman and Mattelart, originally titled *Para leer al Pato Donald: Comunicación de masa y colonialismo* (Mexico City: Siglo XXI, 1976). As Yúdice (28–29) states, this study and Fernández Retamar's *Calibán* constitute, in Latin American contexts, "the classic texts" of "cultural imperialism. Exponents of this view endeavored to unveil the will to power that subtended the reverence for Western high art, the concealment of power differentials in celebrations of the common humanity shared by all peoples as promoted in much anthropological work, and the brainwashing of the entire globe by Hollywood."

56. Amoreira, *Escorbuto*, 45. Donald Duck's association with Brazil was established in the Good Neighbor Policy Disney animations *Saludos Amigos* (1943) and *The Three Caballeros* (1945), also featuring the wily Brazilian parrot Zé Carioca.

57. The poem was translated by Chris Daniels in *Poetry Wales* 40, no. 2 (2004): 50–52.

58. Szeman," Globalization" (2005). Note in this respect what Bernstein asserts about lyric in "Our Americas" (86): "in our activities in creating a poetics of Americas we would do well to keep in mind . . . that we are creating another vision of the world, one that in its globalism does not follow the dictates of the World Trade Organization and World Bank and in its localism does not become the site of the creation of strange fruits for export, but rather commits itself to a cannibalizing process of self-creation, as first defense against the 'Western Box.' A possibility never better set out than in Oswald de Andrade's 1928 . . . Manifesto."

Chapter 4. Three Centuries, Three Americas

The epigraph is from "Geographical Basis of History," an introductory section in Hegel's *Philosophy of History*.

1. Eliane Elias, *The Three Americas* (Blue Note CDP 7243 8 53328 2 1, 1997).

2. In what many consider to be the best comprehensive overview of the region, Darcy Ribeiro's *Las Américas y la civilización: Proceso de formación y causas del desarrollo desigual de los pueblos americanos*, the well-traveled Brazilian anthropologist (d. 1997) presents the peoples of Latin America as natives, transplants, and imported (forced migrants).

3. The most basic definition of the lyric-epic is the combination of lyric and epic elements in one work. See Miller, *Leaves of Grass: America's Lyric-Epic of Self and Democracy*.

4. On the Whitmanian model in the Chilean bard, see Nolan, *Poet-Chief*, and Allegrezza, "Politicizing the Reader," as well as Santí, "The Accidental Tourist."

5. For more examples, see Fitz, *Rediscovering the New World*, chapter 3.

6. Brotherston, *Latin American Poetry*, 2.

7. Indianist features do occur before the 1820s but do not cohere as a tendency. See, as an example of early US literary criticism, Driver. A comprehensive study is Treece, examining diverse discursive genres.

8. On Ercilla's achievement, see the pioneer critical observations in English by Torres-Ríoseco, *The Epic of Latin American Literature*, 14–22. This early work of US-based scholarship on letters in the region includes a separate Brazil chapter, rather than mixing in Brazilian parallels at each stop.

9. Brotherston, *Latin American Poetry*, 27.

10. Quoted in Franco, *The Modern Culture*, 71.

11. Bernucci, "Justiça poética." In addition to Neruda and Cecília Meireles, he analyses the Cisneros work and Cardenal's *El estrecho dudoso* (1966; *The Doubtful Strait*, 1995).

12. See Giamatti, *The Earthly Paradise*; Bowra, *From Virgil to Milton*.

13. Bernucci, "Os pecados," 113.

14. Brotherston, *Latin American Poetry*, 10.

15. *Colombo* (1863) by Manuel de Araújo Porto Alegre is discussed in Toumson, *L'Utopie perdue*, 217. A visual poem of the same name by Pignatari appears in chapter 5.

16. *Os timbiras*, subtitled "Poema americano" and dedicated to the emperor of Brazil.

17. In an earlier collection, *Crisálidas* (1863), Machado de Assis included "Epitáfio do México," one of many indications "of the repercussion and sympathy in Brazil for the vicissitudes of Mexican independence," according to Manuel Bandeira (86).

18. Bonvicino and Ascher, 26. The most complete study of this notion is A. Silva, "Vertente épica."

19. Sá, *Rain Forest Literatures*, chapter 8, considers the epical character of *Cobra Norato* in relation to native lore. On *Martim Cererê*, see Moreira, *Meninos, poetas e heróis*, chapter 1. Although others have mentioned Ricardo's best-known title as an "epic" work, Moreira does not treat it as such, as the epic is so much associated with the world of the adult warrior, whereas the rhetoric of *Martim Cererê* tends toward a child's world, even infantilizing men (personal communication, 20 October 2005).

20. From the abstract of the cogent analysis by Bernucci, "That Gentle Epic."

21. A modern facsimile edition was put out in São Luis, Maranhão, by SIOGE (Serviço de Imprensa e Obras Gráficas do Estado) in 1979. On quotations in this chapter, see note 23. A volume of Sousândrade's complete works is now available, edited by Williams and Moraes.

22. According to observers of the period, Sousândrade "fell from heaven" for the Campos brothers and associates in the 1960s as ammunition in their arguments for the primacy of textuality. As told by Haroldo de Campos, interviewed on "O Brasil passa por aqui," episode of *Roda viva*, TV Cultura, São Paulo, 28 October 1998 (DVD, 2004).

23. Campos and Campos, *Revisão de Sousândrade*. Except when quoting from a different critical source, citations here of *O guesa*, including stanzas of the nearly complete English translation by Robert Brown of "The Inferno of Wall Street," are taken from Campos and Campos. It is noteworthy that parts of Brown, considered a "find," were included in the celebrated compendium of world poetry coedited by Jerome Rothenberg (3:655–62).

24. Sousândrade based his pilgrim-hero on information in Alexander von Humboldt's *Vues des cordillères et monuments des peuples indigènes de l'Amérique* (2 vols., 1810–13), XV and XVI, taken from Humboldt's *Voyage* (1799–1804) to the equinoctial

regions of the New World with French botanist Aimé Bonpland. Humboldt's influence on the Romantics is well known, as Chateaubriand attests in the prologue to *Voyage en Amérique* (1828). Ferdinand Denis (1798–1890), a chronicler of literature who lived in Brazil (1816–20) is another witness; he also refers to the Guesa legend in the entry "Colombie" in the encyclopedia *L'Univers* (1837). Further, in *Scènes de la nature sous les tropiques et leur influence sur la poésie* (1824), Denis adopts Humboldt's thesis regarding the influence of the natural environment on progress and on artistic style (Campos and Campos, 543–44). The segment from which this information is taken appeared in partial English translation in H. Campos, "The Trans-american Pilgrimage."

25. In Campos and Campos, 196.

26. On the question of mixed genre and style, "The Inferno of Wall Street" has been called "a miniature poetical theatre, where characters and historical or mythological events are juxtaposed according to a very modern technique of montage and analogical ordering" (A. Campos, "Sousândrade").

27. For a summary and appraisal of the Wall Street segment in English, see F. Williams, "The Wall Street Inferno." Specifically on feminine figures, see as well F. Williams, "Sousândrade em Nova Iorque."

28. Daniel, "A poética sincrônica."

29. Cuccagna, *A visão do ameríndio*, explores the principal poles—American/European, colonized/colonizer, republican/monarchist—that comprise the poem's oppositions.

30. Luiza Lobo, *Tradição e ruptura*, 29, 31. For other topical comparative studies, see her *Crítica sem juízo* and *Épica e modernidade*, translation of her dissertation, "Sousandrade: A Forerunner of Modernism in an Epic Frame" (University of South Carolina, 1979), which situates the poet as an innovator in the Romantic and symbolist schools.

31. The critic was Edgard Cavalheiro, and the critical piece that curiously drew a parallel between Sousândrade and Oswald de Andrade was "O antropófago do romantismo," *Estado de São Paulo*, 10 November 1957.

32. Cisneros, "Entre o Novo Mundo." See also her new rendering of selected passages of "The Wall Street Inferno."

33. Moacir Amâncio, "Sousândrade, um poeta eternamente póstumo," *O Estado de São Paulo*, Caderno 2, 29 August 2004.

34. 1900, quoted in F. Williams,"The Wall Street Inferno," 15.

35. Risério, "O nome mais belo do medo."

36. On the 1982 LP *Cores e Nomes* (Philips 6328 381). On these two compositions in wider context, see Perrone, *Masters*, chapter 2.

37. Following poem in *Praia provisória*, 63; originally in *Poesia sempre* 18 (2004).

38. Adriano Espínola, "Língua-mar," in *Beira-sol*, 14. "Ó língua-mar, viajando em todos nós. / No teu sal singra errante a minha voz" [Oh tongue-sea, voyage in all of us. / In your salt, does sail, errant, my voice].

39. L. C. Lima, 499. In *Émile Verhaeren* (1914), Stefan Zweig argued that this Belgian poet was the first to poeticize that measure of all things by money in the 1890s, a decade after Sousândrade completed *O guesa*.

40. Schwartz, *Vanguarda e cosmopolitismo*, 7–13, 9. See also Paro, "A América de

Sousândrade e a América de Whitman," which makes an interesting comparison of native-tongue place-names: Maranhão (like a river that flows) vs. Manhattan (island set upon rock).

41. W. Martins, 238, for this and the next quotation.

42. Grieco, 294; original article likely from 1934.

43. The 1930 Spanish translation was printed in Brazil for shipment to Spain but could, of course, have been distributed anywhere. The prologue calls Carvalho "un poeta integralmente representativo" in "nuestra América" (quoted in Lopes and Jacobs, 391). Brotherston, within a chapter titled "The Great Song of America" (*Latin American Poetry*, 84), suggests that Neruda may have felt the impact of *Toda a América*.

44. Further to the discussion of insularity and invention, Carvalho opens his history of Brazilian literature with considerations of Old World lore about fabulous isles and Brazil in the age of discovery (*Pequena história*, 9–17).

45. Without citing any evidence, Lopes and Jacobs (393) seem to project the acknowledged dates of composition onto the whole of the sequence, simply stating that Carvalho wrote the book during trips in 1923–24 and published it two years later. If that is entirely true, any discussion of transposition from Oswald would be much shakier. It is even possible that Ronald had some influence on Oswald's unique poetry.

46. Nist, 80, quoting a standard influential source, Bandeira, *Apresentação*.

47. Lopes and Jacobs, 396–97.

48. Paro, "Ronald de Carvalho e Walt Whitman." For a more general appreciation, see her "Whitman in Brazil."

49. Quoted in W. Martins, 121.

50. Barros, 148–49.

51. Lopes and Jacobs, 395.

52. J. Carvalho, 223.

53. J. Lima, 22. The critical citation was by W. Martins (214).

54. A. Silva, "Semiotização épica do discurso"; see also Silva and Ramalho, *História da epopéia brasileira*. On an earlier modern epic by Marcus Accioly, *Sísifo* (1976), see Silva, *Formação épica*, 88–93.

55. Fitz, *Rediscovering the New World*, 192, 210. On New World perspectives in neo-epical works that move Accioly—by Whitman, Neruda, and Walcott—see Handley, who considers *Canto General* (173–75, 217–76 passim) and *Omeros* (368–95) in depth.

56. On epoch-marking fictional works by José de Alencar, see Sommer, *Foundational Fictions*, chapter 5. See also allusions in chapter 7.

57. The recent bibliography on hybridity is extensive. In specific relation to literature in the hemisphere, see Fitz, "From Blood to Culture."

58. Felipe Fortuna, review of *Latinomérica*, *Jornal do Brasil*, 16 March 2002.

59. Moisés Neto, review of *Latinomérica*, *Le Mangue*, June 2002.

Chapter 5. Banda Hispânica

The epigraph is the refrain [I'm crazy for you Americas, I'm crazy for you with love] from the song "Soy loco por ti América" (Gilberto Gil–José Carlos Capinan), used by permission of the lyricist. First recorded in 1968 on *Caetano Veloso* (Philips R 765 026L). The "Soy loco por ti" motif has become a veritable cultural referent in forty years of circulation. In 2008 a Bahian blog appeared with this name. When Capinan was a candidate for city council in Salvador, he substituted for "América" the name of the city on his campaign visuals. Most tellingly, first prize in the 2006 Carnival competition in Rio de Janeiro went to the samba school Unidos de Vila Isabel with the theme "Soy loco por ti América"; the victorious club had received a million-dollar contribution toward expenses from President Hugo Chávez of Venezuela.

1. Specific note of the relative prominence of poetry in Brazilian domains is made, among others, by Resende. A specialist in New World Hispanic lyric, Kuhnheim, notes the e-boom in Brazil (171); an item she underscores (187)—a useful history of experimental poetry in Latin America by Uruguayan leader Clemente Padín—is posted at a Brazilian portal.

2. Martí's original words, from an 1882 article on Oscar Wilde: "Conocer diversas literaturas es el medio mejor de liberarse de la tiranía de algunas de ellas." In *Obras completas* (Havana: Editorial Nacional, 1963–66), 15:361.

3. *Jornal de poesia* at www.jornaldepoesia.jor.br. Its general editor is Soares Feitosa, the Hispanic coordinator Floriano Martins. Among other individual sites with Ibero-American poetic intentions, see www.antoniomiranda.com.br.

4. Veloso's script, a variation on the one he used when the show played Brazil, included a humorous contrast between high-minded motives—personal taste, aesthetic appreciation, brotherly altruism—and commerce in a globalized world. A key phrase—"I sing in Spanish to feel what it's like to be in someone else's skin. Or, as my manager says, to expand market share"—appears as the epigraph to a splendid essay on the singer-songwriter, Liv Sovik's "Globalizing Caetano Veloso."

5. Vassallo, 48. To illustrate her point, one perfect example is Montaner, whose book-length analysis of Western culture and Latin Americans includes a lone reference to Brazil, as a soccer entity.

6. Pizarro cites Argentina-born Daniel Mato on transformations in *telenovelas* and transnationalization of the industry. Academic events in Europe and the Americas demonstrate the growth of inter-American preoccupation since about 1990. Note the theme of the quadrilingual 2005 meeting of ADLAF (German Association for Latin American Research): "Brazil in Latin America: interactions, perceptions, perspectives." Special-issue publications in this time frame also merit attention, for example, *Terceira margem* 1 (1993), inaugural issue of a research journal in literature at the Federal University of Rio de Janeiro with the title "América: Linguagem & Sociedade" and a truly multinational focus. On criticism in North America, see the lead piece by Ignacio Corona in a notable special issue.

7. Cardoso's talk, titled "The Need for Global Democratic Governance: A Perspective From Latin America," was the fourth annual Kissinger Lecture on Foreign Policy and International Relations at the Library of Congress, Washington, D.C., 22 February 2005. It may be viewed at www.loc.gov/loc/kluge/fellowships/lectures-cardoso.html.

8. See Cardoso and Faletto, *Dependency and Development in Latin America*, written in 1965–67.

9. Among the several sources on Brazil vis-à-vis Spanish America, see Maxwell.

10. Capelato, 290.

11. In his study of author Fernando Gabeira in continental perspective, Dário Borim has confronted usefully the issues that define the discord between Brazil and Spanish America. On efforts at social and economic integration, with multiple applications to cultural realms, see Moniz Bandeira, *Conflito e integração*.

12. Quoted in Chevigny, 34–35.

13. Quoted in Ellison, *Alfonso Reyes y el Brasil*, 83; next quote, 78. There is a more skeptical view of Reyes's contributions, given the Mexican visitor's limited command of Portuguese and scant knowledge of Brazilian letters; see Jorge Schwartz, "Down with Tordesillas!" Opening on 28 May 2008, the Instituto Cervantes in São Paulo hosted an exhibition about Reyes in Brazil and his magazine; the inaugural event featured such panelists as Antonio Candido and Celso Lafer.

14. Antelo, "Modernismo brasileiro e consciência latinoamericana," an article that initiates a thematic thread continued by Antelo in *Confluencia* and especially "*Na ilha de Marapata*": *Mário de Andrade lê os hispanoamericanos*. Letters and writings concerning all fields were studied by Artundo. A unique anthropological study of translation of Brazilian titles in Argentina is Sorá, *Traducir el Brasil*.

15. Rodríguez Monegal reprints Mario's reviews of Argentine literature of the 1920s. This short essay intends to add a Hispanist point of view to the essentially Brazilianist vantage of Antelo (who, though Argentine, was writing from Brazil) and of the pioneer papers of Grembecki and Porto, which led to a section of the latter's book: Lopez, *Mário de Andrade: Ramais e caminhos*, 225–31.

16. R. Assunção, "Mário/Borges." The citified thrust of this monograph is available in Spanish in *Variaciones Borges*, with the most complete bibliography on this comparative topic. For an extensive treatment, see *Mário de Andrade e Jorge Luis Borges: Poesia, cidade, oralidade*.

17. Among other English-language studies, see Perrone, "Presentation." The now somewhat diversified Ibero-American bibliography on this topic includes J. Pinto and, much earlier, Szklo.

18. See Alcalá; Willis.

19. H. Costa, "México, 1978," in *Quadragésimo*, 64. See the brief essay and translations by Augusto de Campos in *Quase-Borges*.

20. Fortuna, *Em seu lugar*, 233.

21. Amâncio, *Colores siguientes*, 12; the set of poems is incorporated into *Ata*, 219–56. Considerations of Brazilian-Hispanic ties with an Iberian bias must take into account Gilberto Freyre, *O brasileiro entre os outros hispanos*, in which temporal perception is a central theme.

22. Quoted in Schwartz, *Vanguarda e cosmopolitismo*, 157.

23. Schwartz, "Down with Tordesillas!" 286–87.

24. Moreira, *Meninos, poetas e heróis*, 138, and "The Poet at the Window."

25. For his part, Amado expressed, in articles in both Spanish and Portuguese, displeasure with the "difficult" experimental language of Mário de Andrade in the rhapsody-novel *Macunaíma* (1928), which has several Spanish American moments. See An-

telo, *Confluencia*; Demarchi, "Devaneios no altiplano." The reports were collected by Antelo in Amado, *A ronda das Américas*.

26. Freyre, *Americanidade e latinidade*. Interest in Freyre outside Brazil has aided in widening the horizons of the discipline. Witness this opening of an Argentine-Brazilian volume with a Latin American focus: "One often hears in Brazil that 'Brazilians live with their backs to Latin America,' as if we were only interested in links with Europe and North America. Luckily, Brazilian anthropology, with its increasingly clear Latin Americanist vocation, puts in check this type of vision" (G. L. Ribeiro, in Grimson, Ribeiro, and Semán, 1).

27. On the Brazilian / Latin American origins of concrete poety, see Colón. Spanish American critical bibliography on the Brazilian vanguard has grown immeasurably with the contributions of Gonzalo Aguilar, especially *Poesía concreta brasileña: Las vanguardias en la encrucijada modernista*.

28. The English version by Augusto de Campos and Charles A. Perrone, "a veiled love telegram crossed through space along a strand of wire," has the same number of characters (56) as the original Portuguese, "atravessou o espaço um escondido telegrama de amor num fio de arame," in *Despoesia*, 51. The artist extracted the phrase "Pasó por el espacio un escondido / Telegrama de amor, por el alambre" from the poem "Obra humana," in J. A. Silva, 51. In the English version the Morse code equivalents are not translated.

29. Pignatari, *Poesia*, 127. For a fresh reading of this suggestive configuration of *man-female-hunger*, see Perrone, "Signs of Intercourse." See G. Aguilar, *Poesía concreta brasileña*, 235–37, on this emblematic poem as part of the concrete project.

30. Pignatari created the color portfolio *Vocogramas* for submission to a literary competition sponsored by *Plural* in Mexico City. Full-color plates are also in *Poesia*, 309–22.

31. Pignatari, *Poesia*, 323; originally in the fine-press portfolio *Atlas-Almanak 88* (1988), with design by Zaba Moreau, Arnaldo Antunes, and Sérgio Papi.

32. For a comparative take, see Braga, "Castro Alves and the New England Abolitionist Poets." English versions appear in Castro Alves, *The Major Abolitionist Poems* and *Navio negreiro*, the cited edition of which has critical presentations, renderings in French and German, and, most important, a portfolio of engravings by local artist Hansen to illustrate the "way of tears."

33. César Espinosa, *Corrosive Signs*, 7. The segments in this volume variously illustrate the admiration commanded by the Noigandres group in Spanish-language circles.

34. Milán, "El odiseo brasileño," 145.

35. Paz, "Los nuevos acólitos," in *Corriente alterna*, 37.

36. Paz, "The Word as Foundation." This declaration appears in the Spanish-language piece "¿Poesía latinoamericana?" in *El signo y el garabato*, 155, but originally was made in the *Times Literary Supplement*.

37. The fundamental essay of the New World poetics of José Lezama Lima (1910–1976) was *La expresión americana* (1957 Cuba, 1969 Spain). On his Latin Americanism, see Bejel, 124–47.

38. Maciel, "Poéticas da confluência," in *Vôo transverso*, 139–40. See also "América

Latina reinventada." Her published interview with Haroldo, "Sobre Octavio Paz," was posted in English online.

39. H. Costa, "Poesia mexicana e brasileira," 153.

40. The best-informed source in this regard is Mata, "Haroldo de Campos y Octavio Paz." The author completed a master's degree in São Paulo, has an appointment at the UNAM in Mexico City, and has edited Haroldo's work there. As for post-Paz followups, see his introduction and anthology in *Sibila*.

41. H. Campos, *A educação*, 60.

42. Paz and Campos, *Transblanco*. The second edition (1994) adds an exceptional exchange, concerning Paz as a figure in the Western intellectual tradition, between Haroldo and political theorist Celso Lafer, who had recommended his countryman to the Mexican thinker at Cornell in the 1960s; this was republished by Lafer as "Conversaciones."

43. The epigraph, used by Adele Weber, is taken from Paz, "La higuera religiosa," in *Obra poética*, 398–400: "Es una maleza de manos / No buscan tierra: buscan un cuerpo, / tejen un abrazo."

44. H. Campos, *Crisantempo*, 297–98.

45. Ainsa, 187. The author is an Uruguayan official of UNESCO.

46. Coelho, "Cuba e os escritores mineiros," 117. To illustrate further the local ties with Spanish America, the Marques volume of interviews with poets of Minas Gerais and other states was produced, despite no overly compelling thematic magnet, entirely bilingually.

47. Fonteles, 164–65. The quotation is taken from an interview with the artist.

48. "América do Sul" (Paulo Machado) on *Ney Mattogrosso* (Continental 101–404–105, 1975), and "Sangue latino" (João Ricardo–Paulinho Mendonça) on *Secos e Molhados* (Continental SLP 10,112, 1973). Both these signature songs have been performed since the 1970s, and occasionally rerecorded.

49. Cuba's top poet of song, Silvio Rodríguez, is included in Cardenal, *Poesía cubana de la revolución*. Future studies in transamerican poetics, complementary to the present approach, could examine Brazil in the Spanish American poetic imaginary, including social and musical lines. In this regard, one would recall poems by the Afro-Cuban Nicolás Guillén following his visits to Rio de Janeiro and São Paulo in the late 1940s and 1950s, when he struck up a friendship with poet-diplomat Vinícius de Moraes, later to be one of the foremost figures of bossa nova. Sérgio Milliet translated some poems by Guillén for publication in the neo-Parnassian organ *Revista brasileira de poesia*; see scans of related documents in *mnemozine* 1 (2004) at www.cronopios.com.br, which has since posted new renderings. Guillén penned a song-homage to a Brazilian modernist painter, "Un son para Portinari," and a song for the then capital city, "Canción carioca," combatting touristic clichés with views of the shantytowns: "Yo te hablo de otro Río . . . de no-techo, sí-frío . . . Mas pienso en la *favela* . . . es un ojo que vela" [I speak to you of another Rio . . . of no-roof, yes-cold . . . but I think of the favela . . . it's an eye on the lookout]. The author was featured in *Suplemento literário Minas Gerais*, November 2002, 7–10. The cited poems appear in Guillén, *La paloma de vuelo popular*, 61–63.

50. Henriques Neto, 71–72. Poem originally 1981.

51. Máximo, 28–29, 95–99.

52. Vogt, *Metalurgia*, 79. The author was the chief administrative officer of Universidade Estadual de Campinas, where he headed numerous diversity-friendly outreach efforts and research projects.

53. Pedrosa, *Mais poesia hoje*, proceedings of the 1999 continuation of a 1997 event.

54. Furtado, 45.

55. F. Martins, *Alma em chamas*, 45. The poem, "O prodígio das tintas," appeared in *Rattapallax* 9 (2003): 64, and was translated as "The Miracle of Ink" by Patricia Soldati and Macgregor Card, who render these lines "The wind the music blows at us with splendor: / deal of echoes, elegy of GR."

56. H. Costa, *A palavra poética*, 24.

57. Maciel, "Cartografia do presente," 39–40; Costa in Daniel, "O tumulto," 26–33.

58. São Paulo, 27–30 November 2007, curated by Horácio Costa. An earlier series of four events (August–October 2007) sponsored by the Fundação Cultural de Curitiba, with the giveaway title "Impressões Pan-Americanas," brought together writers and publishers from around the hemisphere to discuss art and literature, especially poetry, as evidenced by the participation of Paraná magazines *Et Cetera*, *Coyote*, and *Oroboro*; see below.

59. The official site was www.festivaltordesilhas.net. A report was posted at www.revistazunai.com in February 2008. Later in 2008 a notable transnational event was I BIP: Primeira Bienal Internacional de Poesia de Brasília; the majority of guests were from Ibero-America.

60. The featured guest poets at a 2006 reading and panel at the Casas das Rosas, site of the Haroldo de Campos memorial archive in São Paulo, were Peruvian-born Argentine Reynaldo Jiménez and Uruguayan Víctor Sosa. A historicized review was posted by Daniel, "Galáxia barroca."

61. Examples of this dense text in English translation are in H. Campos, *Novas*, and at www.arts.ualberta.ca/~galaxias. One of the "others" studied by Jacobo Sefami is precisely Haroldo's neobaroque classic *Galáxias*. See the new study by Greene, "Baroque and Neobaroque," for a sharp comparative reading of the *Galáxias*.

62. H. Campos, *Ruptura dos géneros*, which appeared first in Spanish, in the volume edited by Fernández Moreno, who included the fundamental exposition by Severo Sarduy, "El barroco y el neo-barroco." These studies formed part of a landmark UNESCO initiative, which was also issued in English. As for the Cuban writer in the poetic consciousness, an aesthetically sympathetic Brazilian poem is Donizete Galvão, "Lembrança de Severo Sarduy," *Mundo mudo*, 33.

63. See Echavarren, Kozer, and Sefami, *Medusario*, which is presented, in transamerican spirit, as "una tercera entrega, una ampliación considerable" [a third installment, a considerable enlargement] of two previous anthologies, a bilingual collection done in Brazil by a resident Argentine poet, Perlongher, and a collection of River Plate authors published in Mexico and edited by Echavarren. The prologues of each tome are reproduced in the third volume. The Brazilian selections in *Medusario* are all experimental prose rather than poetry per se. A more recent collection widens the scope with the inclusion of new Spanish American voices and Brazilian poets: Daniel, *Jardim de cama-*

leões. The extensive foreword by José Kozer, "O neobarroco: Um convergente na poesia latino-americana," was originally in English.

64. Perlongher, in Echavarren, Kozer, and Sefami, 20, 23.

65. Daniel, "A escritura como tatuagem," 20. On the musical angle suggested by Daniel, see Perrone, "De Gregório."

66. See Pen. Larkosh analyzed the unusual fiction in wide angle, proposing translation strategies consistent with a critical understanding of transgender performance. North America's leading Hispanist linguists have also pondered Bueno's remarkable text. An especially alert reflection is Milton Azevedo's. In a more general study, the writing is considered by John Lipski. A Paraguayan blog expressed gratitude to Wilson Bueno for his use of Guarani but saw fit to correct the language mistakes, oblivious to the macaronic and parodic literary intentions. For hybrid aggressive Brasiguayo language in lyric, see Douglas Diegues, *Dá gusto*, reviewed by Ferraz. Diegues's odd and sui generis adventures in "portunhol selvagem" have appeared in various internet blogs.

67. W. Bueno, "Fábulas."

68. *Inimigo rumor* 16 (2006): 3.

69. *Sibila—An International Journal of Poetry*. "Expanding the poetic meridian of Tordesillas." English portal at www.sibila.com.br. On this and other recent poetry magazines, see Cisneros, "Novos olhos."

70. At www.revista.agulha.nom.br/ag32martins.htm, for example, the indefatigable Floriano Martins encourages Spanish American exploration beyond the Borges-Paz-Neruda triad. See, in conjunction, F. Martins, *O começo da busca*, and Leyva, *Versos comunicantes*, dialogues and interviews with current Latin American poets. An additional volume, despite its title, is not just an Ibero- or Latin American collection but a transamerican job, with English and French examples: F. Martins, *Un nuevo continente*.

71. Raúl Antelo, "Surpresa ou assombro," *Diário catarinense*, Florianópolis, 29 October 2005, an appreciation of the Joca Wolff–Ricardo Corona translation in *Oroboro* of the *poema-galáxia* "Momento de simetria" by Arturo Carrera (Argentina, b. 1948). On periodicals, see Perrone, "De *Noigandres*."

72. Carlos Augusto Lima, "Revista 'Oroboro' representa o Mercosul literário," *Jornal do Brasil*, Idéias section, 17 September 2005.

73. Recondo, *Identidad, integración y creación cultural*, 20; following quotes, 416. See also Recondo, *Mercosur*, which considers ethnic backgrounds, colonizations, education, historical antecedents to the South American common market, and institutional cultural dimensions, including *arte concreta* and museums. See as well Recondo, *El sueño de la patria grande*; among the historical and editorial looks at Ibero-Americanist projects, he includes a roll of poets (including songwriters), authors of fiction, and the better-known essayists who have explicitly written of unity.

Chapter 6. Scions of Tropicália

1. From late 2005 to early 2007, museums in Chicago, London, and New York exhibited a multimedia retrospective that encompassed visual arts (installations, painting,

sculpture), popular music, underground periodical literature, stagecraft, and visual poetry. See essays of diverse character in the catalogue and introduction by Basualdo.

2. The standard English-language source is Dunn, *Brutality Garden*. A more compact synthesis and assessment of the movement is Perrone, "*Topos* and Topicalities." To be be somewhat more exact, the term *Tropicália*, the name preferred by the founding artists themselves, could be used to refer exclusively to pertinent musical events between late 1967 and early 1969. In practice, a new Brazilian *-ismo* was born with this tendency, and *tropicalismo,* as a sensibility manifested in writing as well, can be extended into the first half of the 1970s.

3. The main sources for this topic in English are Perrone, *Seven Faces*, chapter 4, and *Masters*, chapters 2 and 3.

4. Bonvicino and Ascher, 27–28.

5. For a detailed discussion, see Perrone and Dunn, introduction.

6. The coeditors in fact took their title *Tropicalizations* from a volume of poetry by US Puerto Rican poet Víctor Hernández Cruz, *Tropicalization* (New York: Reed, Cannon & Johnson, 1976).

7. *Tropical Truth* is a somewhat abridged translation of *Verdade tropical*. Therein Veloso explains how the idea of a full-length book emerged in the wake of an article about Carmen Miranda that he published in the leading New York daily, which is fully reconstituted (including parts left out by *The New York Times*) in Perrone and Dunn.

8. The critical opinion is that of Buarque de Hollanda in *Impressões de viagem*, 84.

9. Dunn, "The Tropicalista Rebellion," 128.

10. An interesting essay-biography in this regard is Mendonça, *Carmen Miranda foi a Washington*.

11. *Pasquim* (Rio de Janeiro) no. 135 (8 February 1972), quoted in Rasec, 244.

12. Collected works in Mautner, *Mitologia do Kaos*. See Web presentation at www.jorgemautner.com.br.

13. Jorge Mautner, press release, Polygram, 1974.

14. Mautner, *Mitologia*, vol. 3, n.p., includes a photograph of a notarized 1968 letter from Lowell to authorities in an effort to help get a visa for the Brazilian artist.

15. Rasec, 207–9.

16. "Mautner, a nova tragédia," *Minas Gerais suplemento literário* 7, no. 280 (8 January 1972), 11–12. Criticism of Mautner's output is limited; see the extended comments of Morais Jr. and items in Mautner, *Mitologia*, vol. 3.

17. Mautner, *Panfletos da nova era*, 100.

18. Veloso, *Tropical Truth*, 286–88. *Batuque* denotes African-derived drumming.

19. Caetano Veloso and Jorge Mautner *Eu não peço desculpa* (Universal 04400645192, 2003). From the first line of the latter's song "Todo errado" (All wrong), the album's title phrase translates as "I don't beg for forgiveness" or "I won't say I'm sorry" or "I don't regret it" or "I make no excuses," all applicable to the outlandish artist.

20. Mautner included "Maracatu atômico" on his own self-titled LP (Polydor 2451–051, 1974), for which Gil composed an item-numbered commentary, included in Mautner, *Mitologia*, vol. 3, n.p. Item 3 refers to the metamusical bossa nova classic "Desafinado"

as "a manifesto of the soul of the man of the history of that time," the fifties in Brazil; the same is said for "Tropicália" in the sixties and "Maracatu atômico" in the seventies.

21. The musical composition is © Warner-Chappell Edições Musicais Ltda. (Abramus). Exclusive print rights administered by Alfred Publishing Co., Inc. All rights reserved. A slightly different version of the song text appears in Mautner, *Mitologia*, vol. 3, n.p.

22. On the boom of the genre of *maracatu* and new music, see Crook, "Turned-Around Beat" and *Brazilian Music*; sections of Murphy, *Music in Brazil*; Galinsky, *Maracatu Atômico*. See also chapter 7, note 1.

23. For this quote and the next, Pedro Alexandre Sanches, "Chico Science busca maracatu psicodélico," *Folha de São Paulo*, 22 May 1996.

24. Risério, "Gil Brasil Bragil," 261.

25. Dunn, *Brutality Garden*, the final chapter of which treats of *mangue beat* and the lasting influence of Veloso and cohort.

26. José Teles, "Ele tinha um carinho raro entre os artistas," *Jornal do Comércio*, 4 February 1997; see also his *Do frevo ao manguebeat*.

27. See Moehn in Perrone and Dunn.

28. Walden, 185–94.

29. I owe this information to Reebee Garofalo. Personal communication 8 May 2000.

30. *Da lama ao caos* (Chaos 850.224/2-464476, 1994), especially the title track, links urban problems and environment, alluding to the theory of chaos in which order is located in disorder and vice versa (Galinsky, 25).

31. Teles, *Meteoro Chico*, 26.

32. Vários artists, *Red Hot + Rio* (Verve Antilles 314 533 183–2, 1996), with DJ Soul Slinger; *Afrociberdélia* (Chaos/Sony Music CDZ-81996 2-479255, 1996). A sample of "Maracatu atômico" closes the disc *CSNZ* (Chaos 789.125/2-490244), recorded in 1998 after the death of Chico Science.

33. See Harvey in Perrone and Dunn.

34. Salomão, "A praia tropicalista," 32.

35. Lenine, a singer-songwriter from Pernambuco, composed "Jack Soul Brasileiro," which plays with the international (*soul*) and comes close to a phonetically similar phrase involving cause and purpose: "já que sou brasileiro" [since I am Brazilian]. He recorded it on three occasions: various artists, *Jackson do Pandeiro revisto e sampleado* (BMG 7432155241, 1999); Lenine, *Na pressão* (BMG 7432171076, 1999); and as a guest on Fernanda Abreu, *Raio X* (EMI Odeon, 859283, 1996).

Chapter 7. (In-)Conclusion

1. Kaq, 49; next example, 55–56; his poems have no titles per se, these appear only in a table of contents for reference. The provocations of Chico Science were further verified in North American contexts by Idelber Avelar. In Brazilian criticism, the new musicological study by Herom Vargas considers again the metaphors of *mangue beat* and sources such as *antropofagia* and *tropicalismo*. As for poetry, a fresh intervention was made by

Amador Ribeiro Neto in the poem "Chico Science," published alongside the graphic interpretation of Roberto Coura. See the treatment in Perrone, "Harpas farpadas."

2. Kaq, 61, referring to Wisnik's macrostudy *O som e o sentido: Uma outra história das músicas* (Sound and sense: An other history of musics). Wisnik attributes a lot to the admired instrument and musician: "a harpa farpada, com a qual Jimmi Hendrix distorceu, filtrou, inverteu e reinventou o mundo sonoro dando a mais lancinante atualidade à força sacrificial do som" (43–44) [the barbed harp with which JH distorted, filtered, inverted and reinvented the world of sound, giving to its sacrificial force the most piercing sense of the present time].

3. P. Andrade, 50–51. The author's feeling of long-distance belonging via lyric is expressed in "A Light in San Francisco."

4. Antunes, *Palavra desordem*. Examples of all his books, especially poems with visual effects, are online at www.arnaldoantunes.com.br.

5. R. Lopes, in R. Corona, *Outras praias*, 180–81, translation by the poet and this author. "Boatswain" is employed for its English value, not as a rendering of "mar de lã" [wool sea], which is a metaphor for soft maritime conditions, and a vocalic rhyme. On the reception and uses of Shakespeare's last play, see Hulme and Sherman, eds. *"The Tempest" and its Travels*, especially Greene, "Island Logic" and Brotherston, "*Arielismo* and Anthropophagy: The Tempest' in Latin America."

6. R. Corona, *Corpo sutil*, 74–76.

7. Before the modern rendering cited in chapter 4, there was a historical translation by Lady Isabel Burton.

Bibliography

Accioly, Marcus. *Latinomérica*. Rio de Janeiro: Topbooks / Fundação Biblioteca Nacional, 2001.

———. *Poética: Pré-manifesto ou anteprojeto do realismo épico (época-épica)*. Recife: Editora Universitária da UFPE, 1977.

Aguilar, Gonzalo. *Poesia concreta brasileira: As vanguardas na encruzilhada modernista*. São Paulo: EDUSP, 2005.

———. *Poesía concreta brasileña: Las vanguardias en la encrucijada modernista*. Buenos Aires: Beatriz Viterbo, 2003.

Aguilar, José Roberto. *Hércules pastiche*. São Paulo: Iluminuras, 1994.

Ainsa, Fernando. *La reconstrucción de la utopía*. Mexico City: UNESCO, 1999.

Alcalá, May Lorenzo. *Vanguardia argentina y modernismo brasileño años 20*. Buenos Aires: Grupo Editor Latinoamericano, 1994.

Aleixo, Ricardo. *Trívio*. Belo Horizonte: Scriptum, 2001.

Alencar, José de. *Iracema: A Novel*. Translated by Clifford E. Landers. New York: Oxford University Press, 2000.

———. *Iracema, the Honey Lips: A Legend of Brasil*. Translated by Isabel Burton. London: Bickers and Son, 1886.

Allegrezza, William. "Politicizing the Reader in the American Lyric-Epic: Walt Whitman's *Leaves of Grass* and Pablo Neruda's *Canto general*." Ph.D. diss., Louisiana State University, 2003. etd.lsu.edu/docs/available/etd-1029103-145352/unrestricted/Allegrezza_dis.pdf.

Allen, Gay Wilson, and Ed Folsom, eds. *Walt Whitman and the World*. Iowa City: University of Iowa Press, 1995.

Alves, Vinícius. *See* Poe, Edgar Allan.

Alvim, Francisco. *Elefante*. São Paulo: Companhia das Letras, 2000.

Amado, Jorge. *A ronda das Américas*. Edited by Raúl Antelo. Salvador, Bahia: Casa das Palavras, 2001.

Amâncio, Moacir. *Ata*. Rio de Janeiro: Record, 2007.

———. *Colores siguientes*. São Paulo: Musa, 1999.

Amoreira, Flávio Viegas. *Escorbuto: Cantos da costa*. Rio de Janeiro: 7Letras, 2005.

———. *Maralto*. Rio de Janeiro: 7Letras, 2002.

Andrade, Mário de. *Macunaíma*. 1928. São Paulo: Martins, 1978.

Andrade, Oswald de. "Manifesto antropófago." In Rocha and Ruffinelli, 25–31.

————. "Manifesto of Pau-Brasil Poetry." Translated by Stella de Sá Rego. *Latin American Literary Review* 14, no. 27 (1986): 184–87.

Andrade, Paula Valéria. *Íris digital*. São Paulo: Escrituras, 2005.

Antelo, Raúl, ed. and trans. *Confluencia: Literatura argentina por brasileños e literatura brasileña por argentinos*. Buenos Aires: Centro de Estudios Brasileños, 1982.

————. "Modernismo brasileiro e consciência latinoamericana." *Contexto* 3 (1977): 75–90.

————. "*Na ilha de Marapatá*": *Mário de Andrade lê os hispano-americanos*. São Paulo: Hucitec, 1986.

Antunes, Arnaldo. *Como é que chama o nome disso*. São Paulo: Publifolha, 2006.

————. *Dois ou mais corpos no mesmo espaço*. São Paulo: Perspectiva, 1997.

————. *Palavra desordem*. São Paulo: Iluminuras, 2002.

————. *Psia*. São Paulo: Expressão, 1986.

————. *Tudos*. São Paulo: Iluminuras, 1990.

Antunes, Arnaldo, et al. *Nome*. CD-VHS-book. São Paulo: BMG, 1993. Reissued with DVD, 2007.

Aparicio, Frances R., and Susana Chávez-Silverman, eds. *Tropicalizations: Transcultural Representations of Latinidad*. Hanover, N.H.: University Press of New England, 1997.

Appadurai, Arjun. *Modernity at Large: Cultural Dimensions of Globalization*. Minneapolis: University of Minnesota Press, 1995.

Araújo, Ricardo, ed. *Edgar Allan Poe: Um homem em sua sombra*. São Paulo: Ateliê, 2002.

Ardao, Arturo. *Génesis de la idea y el nombre de América Latina*. Caracas: Centro de Estudios Latinoamericanos Rómulo Gallegos, 1980.

Artundo, Patricia. *Mário de Andrade e a Argentina: um país e sua produção cultural como espaço de reflexão*. Translated by Gênese Andrade. São Paulo: EDUSP, 2004.

Ascher, Nelson. "A poesia que nasce da negação e da dúvida." *Jornal da USP* 6, no. 251 (1993).

————. *O sonho da razão*. Rio de Janeiro: Editora 34, 1993.

Ascher, Nelson, Régis Bonvicino, and Michael Palmer, eds. *Nothing the Sun Could Not Explain: 20 Contemporary Brazilian Poets*. 2nd ed. Los Angeles: Green Integer, 2003.

Assunção, Ademir. *Zona branca*. São Paulo: Altana, 2001.

Assunção, Ademir, Ricardo Corona, and Rodrigo Garcia Lopes. "Medusário: Uma abordagem sobre poéticas brasileiras contemporâneas." *Medusa* 2, no. 10 (2000): 2–5.

Assunção, Ronaldo. "Mário/Borges: Diálogos subterrâneos entre dois poetas vizinhos." *Fragmentos* 28–29 (2005): 67–76.

————. *Mário de Andrade e Jorge Luis Borges: Poesia, cidade, oralidade*. Campo Grande: Editora da UFMS, 2004.

————. "Mário de Andrade y Jorge Luís Borges: Poesía urbana y vanguardia en la década de 1920." *Variaciones Borges* 19 (2005): 243–58.

Augusto, Eudoro. *Olhos de bandido*. Rio de Janeiro: 7Letras, 2001.

Augusto, Ronaldo. *Confissões aplicadas*. Porto Alegre: Ameop, 2004.

Avelar, Idelber. "Brazilian and 'Afrocyberdelic': The Mangue Beat Musical Scene and the Performance of Nationhood in Sound." Keynote address at "Performing Brazil," University of Wisconsin–Madison, 20 April 2007.

Ávila, Affonso. *Discurso da difamaçaõ do poeta*. São Paulo: Summus, 1978.

Ávila, Carlos. "*Invenção*—uma reedição necessária." In "Dossiê 50 anos da poesia concreta," special issue, *O eixo e a roda: Revista de literatura brasileira* 13 (2006): 95–101.

Azevedo, Beatriz. *Idade da pedra*. São Paulo: Iluminuras, 2002.

Azevedo, Carlito. *Collapsus linguae*. Rio de Janeiro: Lynx, 1991.

———. "Uma vez humano sempre acrobata." Idéias. *Jornal do Brasil*, 30 July 2005, 5.

Azevedo, Milton M. "Language Hybridity: Portunhol as a Literary Device in Wilson Bueno's *Mar paraguayo*." *Revista portuguesa de humanidades* 8 (2004): 267–78.

Bandeira, Manuel, ed. *Apresentação da poesia brasileira*. Rio de Janeiro: Casa do Estudante do Brasil, 1942.

Barbosa, Frederico. *Louco no oco sem beiras: Anatomia da depressão*. São Paulo: Ateliê, 2001.

———. *Nada feito nada*. São Paulo: Perspectiva, 1993.

———. *Rarefato*. São Paulo: Iluminuras, 1990.

———. "Vacamarela: Receita para calar apocalípticos." Foreword to *Antologia Vacamarela*, 4–7. São Paulo: Associação Vacamarela, 2007.

Barros, Jayme de. *Espelho dos livros*. Rio de Janeiro: José Olympio, 1936.

Barroso, Gustavo. *O Brasil na lenda e na cartografia antiga*. Rio de Janeiro: Companhia Editora Nacional, 1941.

Bary, Leslie. "Oswald de Andrade's Cannibalist Manifesto." *Latin American Literary Review* 19, no. 38 (1991): 35–47.

Basualdo, Carlos, ed. *Tropicalia: A Revolution in Brazilian Culture (1967–1972)*. São Paulo: Cosac Naify, 2005.

Bauer, Ralph. "Hemispheric Studies." *PMLA* 124, no. 1 (2009): 234–50.

Bejel, Emilio. *José Lezama Lima, Poet of the Image*. Gainesville: University Presses of Florida, 1990.

Berg, Stephen. "An Introduction to Oswald de Andrade's 'Cannibalist Manifesto.'" *Third Text* 46 (1999): 89–96.

Berger, Peter L. "Introduction: The Cultural Dynamics of Globalization." In *Many Globalizations: Cultural Diversity in the Contemporary World*, edited by Peter L. Berger and Samuel P. Huntington, 1–16. New York: Oxford University Press, 2002.

Bernstein, Charles, ed. "99 Poets / 1999: An International Poetics Symposium." Special issue, *Boundary 2* 26, no. 1 (1999).

———. "Our Americas: New Worlds Still in Progress." www.bc.edu/research/xul/5+5/bernstein.htm. Published in Portuguese as "Nossas Américas: Novos mundos ainda em processo," *Sibila* 6, no. 10 (2006): 82–91.

———. "Poetics of the Americas." *Modernism/Modernity* 3, no. 3 (1996): 1–23.

Bernucci, Leopoldo M. "Justiça poética na épica latino-americana moderna." *Revista USP* 50 (2001): 238–46.

———. "Os pecados do lado debaixo do equador: Notas sobre a épica sacra na América Latina." In Bernucci and Costigan, 107–15.

————. "That Gentle Epic: Writing and Elegy in the Heroic Poetry of Cecília Meireles." *Modern Language Notes* 112, no. 2 (1997): 201–18.

Bernucci, Leopoldo, and Lúcia Helena Costigan, eds. "O Brasil, a América Hispânica e o Caribe: Abordagens comparativas." Special issue, *Revista iberoamericana* 64, nos. 182–183 (1998).

Bishop, Elizabeth, and Emanuel Brasil, eds. *An Anthology of Twentieth-Century Brazilian Poetry*. Middletown, Conn.: Wesleyan University Press, 1972.

Bloom, Harold. *The Anxiety of Influence: A Theory of Poetry*. New York: Oxford University Press, 1973.

————. *A Map of Misreading*. New York: Oxford University Press, 1975.

Bonvicino, Régis. *Outros poemas*. São Paulo: Iluminuras, 1993.

————. *Página órfã*. São Paulo: Martins Fontes, 2007.

————. *Sky-Eclipse*. Los Angeles: Green Integer, 1999.

————. *Sósia da cópia*. São Paulo: Max Limonad, 1983.

————, ed. *Together: Um poema, vozes*. São Paulo: Ateliê, 1996.

Bonvicino, Régis, and Nelson Ascher. Introduction to Ascher, Bonvicino, and Palmer, 25–35.

Borges, Celso. *Vinte e um poemas*. Book with CD. São Paulo: ACB Araújo, 2000.

Borim, Dário. "Crepúsculos de utopias: Brasil e América Latina em Fernando Gabeira." *Ellipsis* 4 (2006): 7–48.

Bosco, Francisco. *Da amizade*. Rio de Janeiro: 7Letras, 2003.

Bowra, C. M. *From Virgil to Milton*. New York: St. Martin's, 1945.

Braga, Thomas. "Castro Alves and the New England Abolitionist Poets." *Hispania* 67, no. 4 (1984): 585–93.

Brasil, Emanuel, and William Jay Smith, eds. *Brazilian Poetry (1950–1980)*. Middletown, Conn.: Wesleyan University Press, 1983.

Brennan, Timothy. "The Cuts of Language: The East/West of North/South." *Public Culture* 13, no. 1 (2001): 39–63.

Brickhouse, Anna. *Transamerican Literary Relations and the Nineteenth-Century Public Sphere*. Cambridge: Cambridge University Press, 2004.

Brito, Mário da Silva. *O modernismo*. Vol. 6 of *Panorama da poesia brasileira*. Rio de Janeiro: Civilização Brasileira, 1959.

Britto, Paulo Henriques. *The Clean Shirt of It*. Translated by Idra Novey. Rochester, N.Y.: BOA Editions, 2007.

————. *Liturgia da matéria*. Rio de Janeiro: Civilização Brasileira, 1982.

————. *Macau*. São Paulo: Companhia das Letras, 2003.

————, ed. and trans. *Poemas do Brasil*, by Elizabeth Bishop. São Paulo: Companhia das Letras, 1999.

Brotherston, Gordon. "*Arielismo* and Anthropophagy: *The Tempest* in Latin America." In Hulme and Sherman, 212–19.

————. *Latin American Poetry: Origins and Presence*. Cambridge: Cambridge University Press, 1975.

Brown, Nicholas. *Utopian Generations: The Political Horizon of Twentieth-Century Literature*. Princeton: Princeton University Press, 2005.

Buarque de Hollanda, Heloísa, ed. *Esses poetas: Uma antologia dos anos 90*. Rio de Janeiro: Aeroplano, 1998.

———. *Impressões de viagem: CPC, vanguarda e desbunde, 1960/70*. São Paulo: Brasiliense, 1980.

———. "Two Poetics, Two Moments." In J. C. Rocha, 245–54.

Bueno, Alexei. *Os resistentes*. Rio de Janeiro: Francisco Alves, 2001.

Bueno, Wilson. "Fábulas." Interview by Claudio Daniel. *Suplemento Literário Minas Gerais*, n.s. 68 (2001): 8–9.

———. *Mar paraguayo*. São Paulo: Iluminuras, 1992.

Butterman, Steven F. "BRA-SILLY-DADE in the Poetry of Glauco Mattoso." Paper presented to the American Association of Teachers of Spanish and Portuguese, San Francisco, 8 July 2001.

———. *Perversions on Parade: Brazilian Literature of Transgression and Postmodern Anti-Aesthetics in Glauco Mattoso*. San Diego: San Diego State University Press, 2005.

Cabral, Astrid. *De déu em déu: Poemas reunidos, 1979–1994*. Rio de Janeiro: Sette Letras, 1998.

Caetano, Ana. *Quatorze*. Belo Horizonte: Poesia Orbital, 1997.

Caiafa, Janice. *Cinco ventos*. Rio de Janeiro: 7Letras, 2001.

———. *Fôlego*. Rio de Janeiro: Sette Letras, 1998.

———. *Neve rubra*. Rio de Janeiro: Sette Letras, 1996.

———. *Ouro*. Rio de Janeiro: 7Letras, 2005.

Calado, Carlos. *O jazz como espetáculo*. São Paulo: Perspectiva, 1990.

Calin, William. *Minority Literatures and Modernism: Scots Breton, and Occitan, 1920–1990*. Toronto: University of Toronto Press, 2000.

Campos, Augusto de. *O anticrítico*. São Paulo: Companhia das Letras, 1986.

———. "Cage: Chance: Change." Preface to *De segunda a um ano*, by John Cage, translated by Rogério Duprat, revised by Augusto de Campos, ix–xxiii. São Paulo: Hucitec, 1985.

———. *Despoesia*. São Paulo: Perspectiva, 1994.

———, trans. *Invenção de Arnaut e Raimbaut a Dante e Cavalcanti*. São Paulo: ARX, 2003.

———, trans. *Não sou ninguém: Poemas*, by Emily Dickinson. Campinas, São Paulo: Unicamp, 2008.

———, trans. *Porta-retratos*, by Gertrude Stein. Florianópolis: Noa Noa, 1990.

———, trans. *Quase-Borges + 10 Transpoemas: Traduções de poemas de Jorge Luis Borges*. São Paulo: Memorial da América Latina, 2006.

———. "Sousândrade." In *Pequeno dicionário de literatura brasileira*, edited by José Paulo Paes and Massaud Moisés, 241. São Paulo: Cultrix, 1967.

Campos, Augusto de, and Haroldo de Campos. *Revisão de Sousândrade*. 3rd ed. São Paulo: Perspectiva, 2002.

Campos, Augusto de, et al. *Balanço da bossa e outras bossas*. 2nd ed. São Paulo: Perspectiva, 1974.

Campos, Haroldo de. *Crisantempo: No espaço curvo nasce um*. São Paulo: Perspectiva, 1998.

————. *A educação dos cinco sentidos*. São Paulo: Brasiliense, 1985.

————. *Galáxias*. São Paulo: Ex Libris, 1984.

————. "A nova estética de Max Bense." 1959. In *Metalinguagem*, 3rd ed., 9–20. São Paulo: Cultrix, 1976.

————. *Ruptura dos gêneros na literatura latino-americana*. São Paulo: Perspectiva, 1976. Translated as "Superación de los lenguajes exclusivos" in Fernández Moreno, 279–300, and as "Beyond Exclusive Languages" in Fernández Moreno, Ortega, and Schulman, 221–43.

————. "Serafim: Um grande não-livro." In Oswald de Andrade, *Obras completas—2 Memórias sentimentais de João Miramar—Serafim Ponte Grande*, 99–127. Rio de Janeiro: Civilização Brasileira, 1975.

————. "Texto e história." 1967. In *A operação do texto*, 13–22. São Paulo: Perspectiva, 1976.

————. "The Trans-American Pilgrimage of Sousândrade's *Guesa*." In *Novas: Selected Writings of Haroldo de Campos*, edited by Antonio Sérgio Bessa and Odile Cisneros, 194–200. Evanston, Ill.: Northwestern University Press, 2007.

Cantarino, Geraldo. *Uma ilha chamada Brasil: O paraíso irlandês no passado brasileiro*. Rio de Janeiro: MAUAD, 2004.

Capelato, Maria Helena. "O 'gigante brasileiro' na América Latina: Ser ou não ser latino-americano." In *Viagem incompleta: A experiência brasileira, 1500–2000: A grande transação*, edited by Carlos Guilherme Mota, 285–316. São Paulo: SENAC, 2000.

Cardenal, Ernesto, ed. *Poesía cubana de la revolución*. Mexico City: Extemporáneos, 1976.

Cardoso, Fernando Henrique, and Enzo Faletto. *Dependency and Development in Latin America*. Translated by Marjory Mattingly Urquidi. Berkeley and Los Angeles: University of California Press, 1979.

Carneiro, Rosane. "Non line." In *Poesia sempre* 9, no. 14 (2001): 105.

Carvalho, Júlio. "Ronald de Carvalho." In *Poetas do modernismo: Antologia crítica*, edited by Leodegário A. de Azevedo Filho, 2:223–78. Brasília: INL, 1972.

Carvalho, Ronald de. *Pequena história da literatura brasileira*. 3rd ed. Rio de Janeiro: F. Briguiet, 1925.

————. *Toda a América*. Rio de Janeiro: B. de Mello, 1926.

————. *Toda la América*. Translated by Francisco Villaespesa. São Paulo: Editora Hispano-Brasileña, 1935.

Castor, Grahame. *Pléiade Poetics: A Study in Sixteenth-Century Thought and Terminology*. Cambridge: Cambridge University Press, 1964.

Castro, Ney Leandro de. *Musa de verão*. Natal: Clima, 1984.

Castro Alves, Antônio F. de. *The Major Abolitionist Poems*. Translated by Amy A. Peterson. New York: Garland, 1990.

————. *Navio negreiro*. Salvador, Bahia: Livraria Progresso, 1959.

Cevasco, Maria Elisa. "The Political Unconscious of Globalization: Notes from the Periphery." In *Fredric Jameson: A Critical Reader*, edited by Douglas Kellner and Sean Homer, 94–111. New York: Palgrave, 2004.

Chacal. *Drops de abril*. São Paulo: Brasiliense, 1983.

Chanady, Amaryll. "Latin American Imagined Communities and the Postmodern Challenge." Introduction to *Latin American Identity and Constructions of Difference*, ix–xlvi. Minneapolis: University of Minnesota Press, 1994.

Chevigny, Bell Gale. "'Insatiable Unease': Melville and Carpentier and the Search for an American Hermeneutic." In *Reinventing the Americas: Comparative Studies of Literature of the United States and Spanish America*, edited by Bell Gale Chevigny and Gari Laguardia, 34–59. Cambridge: Cambridge University Press, 1986.

Cisneros, Odile. "Entre *O Novo Mundo* e o 'Inferno': Sousândrade em Nova York." *Sibila* 1, no. 1 (2001): 64–73.

———. "Novos olhos sobre a poesia: Brazilian Poetry Journals of the 21st Century." *Aufgabe* 6 (2007): 13–21. Originally in *Sibila* 15 (2006).

———, trans. "The Wall Street Inferno," by Sousândrade. *Circumference—Poetry in Translation* 1 (2003): 94–105.

Coelho, Haydee Ribeiro. "Cuba e os escritores mineiros: Uma interlocução latino-americana." In *Trocas culturais na América Latina*, edited by Luis Alberto Brandão Santos and Maria Antonieta Pereira, 113–22. Belo Horizonte: FALE-NELAM-UFMG, 2000.

Colón, David. "'Now what the DEFFIL can that mean!': The Latin American Roots, Rhetoric, and Resistance of Concrete Poetry." *Journal of Latino-Latin American Studies* 1, no. 1 (2003): 34–45.

Corona, Ignacio. "Vecinos distantes? Las agendas críticas posmodernas en Hispanoamérica y el Brasil." In Bernucci and Costigan, 17–38.

Corona, Ricardo. *Cinemaginário*. São Paulo: Iluminuras, 1999.

———. *Corpo sutil*. São Paulo: Iluminuras, 2005.

———. *Ladrão de fogo*. Curitiba: Medusa, 2001. CD + booklet.

———, ed. *Outras praias: 13 poetas brasileiros emergentes = Other Shores: 13 Emerging Brazilian Poets*. São Paulo: Iluminuras, 1998.

Corona, Ricardo, and Paulo Henriques Britto. "Jim Morrison: O poeta do rock 'n' roll." *Medusa* 2, no. 9 (2000): 28–31.

Costa, Daniel, and Renato Negrão. *Dragões do paraíso*. Belo Horizonte: Poesia Orbital, 1997.

Costa, Horácio. *Mar abierto: Ensayos sobre literatura brasileña, portuguesa e hispanoamericana*. Mexico City: Fondo de Cultura Económica, 1998.

———, ed. *A palavra poética na América Latina: Avaliação de uma geração*. São Paulo: Memorial da América Latina, 1992.

———. "Poesia mexicana e brasileira modernas: Interfaces." In *Literaturas em movimento: Hibridismo cultural e exercício crítico*, edited by Rita Chaves and Tânia Macedo, 147–54. São Paulo: Via Atlântica, 2003.

———. *Quadragésimo*. São Paulo: Ateliê, 1999.

Costa, Horácio, and Charles A. Perrone, eds. and trans. Brazil issue. *Tigertail: A South Florida Poetry Annual* 6. Miami: Tigertail Productions, 2008.

Costa, Walter Carlos. "Emily Dickinson Brasileira." *Ilha do Desterro: A Journal of Language and Literature* 17, no. 1 (1987): 76–92.

Coura, Roberto, and Amador Ribeiro Neto. *Imagens e poemas*. João Pessoa, Paraíba: Editora Univeritária UFPB, 2008.

Coutinho, Eduardo F. *Literatura comparada na América Latina: Ensaios*. Rio de Janeiro: EDUERJ, 2003.

Creeley, Robert. Afterword to *A um*, edited and translated by Régis Bonvicino, 151–63. São Paulo: Ateliê, 1997.

Crook, Larry. *Brazilian Music: Northeastern Traditions and the Heartbeat of a Modern Nation*. Santa Barbara, Calif.: ABC-CLIO, 2005.

———. "Turned-Around Beat: *Maracatu de baque virado* and Chico Science." In Perrone and Dunn, 233–44.

Cuccagna, Cláudio. *A visão do ameríndio na obra de Sousândrade*. Translated by Wilma Katinsky Barreto de Souza with Cláudio Cuccagna. São Paulo: Hucitec, 2004.

Cvetkovich, Ann, and Douglas Kellner, eds. *Articulating the Global and the Local: Globalization and Cultural Studies*. Boulder, Colo.: Westview, 1997.

Daghlian, Carlos. "Poe in Brazil." In *Poe Abroad: Influence, Reputation, Affinities*, edited by Lois Davis Vines, 130–34. Iowa City: University of Iowa Press, 1999.

———. "A recepção de Poe na literatura brasileira." *Fragmentos* 17 (1999): 7–14.

Daghlian, Carlos, José Lira, and Walter Carlos Costa, eds. "Emily Dickinson." Special issue, *Fragmentos* 34 (2008).

Daniel, Claudio. "A escritura como tatuagem." Introduction to *Jardim de camaleões*, 17–22.

———. "Uma escritura na zona da sombra." Preface to Daniel and Barbosa, 23–31.

———. "Galáxia barroca: Um breve guia de viagem." *Revista Critério*. www.revista.criterio.nom.br/Folder_Galaxia_Barroca.pdf (accessed 15 May 2006).

———. *Jardim de camaleões: A poesia neobarroca na América Latina*. São Paulo: Iluminuras, 2004

———. "A poética sincrônica de Sousândrade." *Zunái*. www.revistazunai.com/ensaios/sousandrade_claudio_daniel.htm.

———. "O tumulto poético de Horácio Costa." Interview. *Coyote* 10 (2004): 26–33.

Daniel, Claudio, and Frederico Barbosa, eds. *Na virada do século: Poesia de invenção no Brasil*. São Paulo: Landy, 2002.

Dassiê, Franklin Alves. "Miles Davis, lado b" and "Monk solo." *Inimigo rumor* 17 (2005): 185.

Demarchi, Ademir. "Devaneios no altiplano: Duas visões da América Latina." *Agulha: Revista de cultura* 13–14 (2001). www.secrel.com.br/jpoesia/ag1314demarchi.htm.

———. "Sintomas e remédios da poesia contemporánea." www.germinaliteratura.com.br/literatura5.htm.

Diegues, Douglas. *Dá gusto andar desnudo por estas selvas: Sonetos salvajes*. Curitiba: Travessa dos Editores, 2002.

Dolhnikoff, Luis. "Loa à toa a um *loser*." In "Anatomia da metáfora," 20. *Coyote* 5 (2003): 18–21.

Dorfman, Ariel, and Armand Mattelart. *How to Read Donald Duck: Imperialist Ideology in the Disney Comic*. Translated by David Kunzle. 3rd ed. New York: International General, 1991.

Driver, David Miller. *The Indian in Brazilian Literature*. New York: Hispanic Institute in the United States, 1942.

Duarte, José, and Ricardo António Alves, eds. *POEZZ: Jazz na Poesia de Língua Portuguesa*. Coimbra: Almedina, 2004.

Dunn, Christopher. *Brutality Garden: Tropicália and the Emergence of a Brazilian Counterculture*. Chapel Hill: University of North Carolina Press, 2001.

———. "The Tropicalista Rebellion: A Conversation with Caetano Veloso." *Transition* 70 (1996): 116–38.

Echavarren, Roberto, ed. *Transplatinos: Muestra de poesía rioplatense*. Mexico City: El Tucán de Virginia, 1990.

Echavarren, Roberto, José Kozer, and Jacobo Sefami, eds. *Medusario: Muestra de poesía latinoamericana*. Mexico City: Fondo de Cultura Económica, 1996.

Echevarría, Roberto González. "Latin American and Comparative Literatures." In *Poetics of the Americas: Race, Founding, and Textuality*, edited by Bainard Cowan and Jefferson Humphries, 47–62. Baton Rouge: Louisiana State University Press, 1997.

Ellison, Fred P. *Alfonso Reyes e o Brasil: Um mexicano entre os cariocas*. Rio de Janeiro: Topbooks, 2003.

———. *Alfonso Reyes y el Brasil*. Mexico City: Sello Bermejo, 2000.

Espínola, Adriano. *Beira-sol*. Rio de Janeiro: Topbooks, 1997.

———. *Praia provisória*. Rio de Janeiro: Topbooks, 2006.

———. *Taxi, or Poem of Love in Transit*. Translated by Charles A. Perrone. New York: Garland, 1992.

———. *Táxi, ou Poema de amor passageiro*. São Paulo: Global, 1986.

Espinosa, César, ed. *Corrosive Signs: Essays on Experimental Poetry (Visual, Concrete, Alternative)*. Translated by Harry Polkinhorn. Washington, D.C.: Maisonneuve, 1990.

Feinstein, Sascha, and Yusef Komunyakaa, eds. *The Jazz Poetry Anthology*. Vol. 1. Bloomington: Indiana University Press, 1991.

———, eds. *The Second Set: The Jazz Poetry Anthology*. Bloomington: Indiana University Press, 1996.

Félix, Moacyr, ed. *41 Poetas do Rio*. Rio de Janeiro: FUNARTE, 1998.

Fernández Moreno, César, ed. *América Latina en su literatura*. Mexico City: Siglo XXI, 1972.

Fernández Moreno, César, Julio Ortega, and Ivan A. Schulman, eds. *Latin America in Its Literature*. Translated by Mary G. Berg. New York: Holmes and Meier, 1980.

Fernández Retamar, Roberto. *Caliban and Other Essays*. Translated by Edward Baker. Minneapolis: University of Minnesota Press, 1989.

———. "Calibán ante la antropofagia." In Rocha and Ruffinelli, 203–12.

———. *Todo Calibán*. La Habana: Letras Cubanas, 2000; San Juan, Puerto Rico: Callejón, 2003.

Ferraz, Paulo. "Novíssima poesia brasileira." *Sibila* 3, no. 4 (2003): 210–23.

Ferreira, Kiko. *Belo blue*. Belo Horizonte: Poesia Orbital, 1997.

Ferry, Anne. *The Title to the Poem*. Stanford, Calif.: Stanford University Press, 1996.

Figueira, Gaston. "Analogias e incompatibilidades entre la poesía estadounidense y la de América Latina." *Revista interamericana de bibliografía* 18 (1968): 280–94.

Fitz, Earl E. "From Blood to Culture: Miscegenation as Metaphor for the Americas." In

Mixing Race, Mixing Culture: Inter-American Literary Dialogues, edited by Monika Kaup and Debra J. Rosenthal, 243–72. Austin: University of Texas Press, 2002.

———. *Rediscovering the New World: Inter-American Literature in a Comparative Context*. Iowa City: University of Iowa Press, 1991.

———. "The Theory and Practice of Inter-American Literature." In *Beyond the Ideal: Pan Americanism in Inter-American Affairs*, edited by David Sheinin, 153–65. Westport, Conn.: Greenwood, 2000.

Fonteles, Bené. *Ney Matogrosso: Ousar ser*. São Paulo: SESC Imprensa Oficial, 2002.

Fortuna, Felipe. *Em seu lugar: Poemas reunidos*. Rio de Janeiro: Francisco Alves, 2005.

———. Interview by Augusto Massi. In *Artes e ofícios da poesia*, edited by Augusto Massi. Porto Alegre: Artes e Oficios; São Paulo: Secretaria Municipal de Cultura, 1991.

Franco, Jean. *The Decline and Fall of the Lettered City: Latin America in the Cold War*. Cambridge, Mass.: Harvard University Press, 2002.

———. *The Modern Culture of Latin America: Society and the Artist*. Rev. ed. London: Penguin, 1970.

Freitas Filho, Armando. *Máquina de escrever: Poesia reunida e revista*. Rio de Janeiro: Nova Fronteira, 2003.

Freyre, Gilberto. *Americanidade e latinidade da América Latina e outros textos afins*. Edited by Edson Nery da Fonseca. Brasília: UnB; São Paulo: Imprensa Oficial do Estado, 2003.

———. *O brasileiro entre os outros hispanos: Afinidades, contrastes, e possíveis futuros nas suas inter-relações*. Rio de Janeiro: José Olympio, 1975.

Furtado, Flora. *A morosa caligrafia*. Rio de Janeiro: Grupo Letra Itinerante, 2003.

Galinsky, Philip. *"Maracatu Atômico": Tradition, Modernity, and Postmodernity in the Mangue Movement of Recife, Brazil*. New York: Routledge, 2002.

Galvão, Donizete. *A carne e o tempo*. São Paulo: Nankin, 1997.

———. *As faces do rio*. São Paulo: Agua Viva, 1990.

———. *Mundo mudo*. São Paulo: Nankin, 2003.

Gama, José Basílio da. *The Uruguay: A Historical Romance of South America*. Translated by Richard F. Burton. Edited by Frederick C. H. Garcia and Edward F. Stanton. Berkeley and Los Angeles: University of California Press, 1984.

García Canclini, Néstor. *Hybrid Cultures: Strategies for Entering and Leaving Modernity*. Translated by Christopher L. Chiappari and Silvia L. López. Minneapolis: University of Minnesota Press, 1995.

Gardel, André. *Poemas de Nova York*. Rio de Janeiro: Ibis Libris, 2003.

Giamatti, A. Bartlett. *The Earthly Paradise and the Renaissance Epic*. Princeton: Princeton University Press, 1966.

Glazier, Loss Pequeño. *Digital Poetics: The Making of E-poetries*. Tuscaloosa: University of Alabama Press, 2002.

Glissant, Édouard. *The Indies*. Translated by Dominique O'Neill. Toronto: Éditions du GREF, 1992.

Goldstein, Laurence. *The American Poet at the Movies: A Critical History*. Ann Arbor: University of Michigan Press, 1994.

Gomes, Frederico. *Outono & inferno*. Rio de Janeiro: Topbooks, 2002.

Gomes, Maysa. *Zelo*. Belo Horizonte: Poesia Orbital, 1997.

Gonzalez, Mike, and David Treece. *The Gathering of Voices: The Twentieth-Century Poetry of Latin America*. London: Verso, 1992.

Grandis, Rita De, and Zilà Bernd, eds. *Unforeseeable Americas: Questioning Cultural Hybridity in the Americas*. Amsterdam: Rodopi, 2000.

Greene, Roland. "Anthropophagy, Invention, and the Objectification of Brazil." In Rocha and Ruffinelli, 115–28.

———. "Baroque and Neobaroque, History and Thistory." *PMLA* 124 (January 2009): 150–55.

———. "Inter-American Obversals: Allen Ginsberg and Haroldo de Campos Circa 1960." 5+5, 2009. www.bc.edu/research/xul/5+5/greene.htm.

———. "Island Logic." In Hulme and Sherman, 138–47.

———. "New World Studies and the Limits of National Literatures." In *Poetry & Pedagogy: The Challenge of the Contemporary*, edited by Joan Retallack and Juliana Spahr, 80–104. New York: Palgrave, 2006.

———. "Transamerican Poetics under the Sign of Globalization." Paper presented at the MLA convention, Chicago, 28 December 1999.

———. *Unrequited Conquests: Love and Empire in the Colonial Americas*. Chicago: University of Chicago Press, 1999.

———. "Wanted: A New World Studies." *American Literary History* 1–2 (2000): 337–47.

Gregory, Elizabeth. *Quotation and Modern American Poetry*. Houston: Rice University Press, 1996.

Grembecki, M. Helena, and Telê Jardim Porto. "Leituras hispano-americanas de Mário de Andrade." *Suplemento Literário do Estado de São Paulo*, 27 February 1965.

Grieco, Agrippino. *Obras Completas*. Vol. 6, *Gente nova do Brasil*. 2nd ed. Rio de Janeiro: José Olympio, 1948.

Grimson, Alejandro, Gustavo Lins Ribeiro, and Pablo Semán, eds. *La antropología brasileña contemporánea: Contribuciones para un diálogo latinoamericano*. Buenos Aires: Prometeo, 2004.

Gruesz, Kirsten Silva. *Ambassadors of Culture: The Transamerican Origins of Latino Writing*. Princeton: Princeton University Press, 2002.

Guillén, Nicolás. *La paloma de vuelo popular*. Buenos Aires: Losada, 1958.

———. Selection translated by Sérgio Milliet. *Revista brasileira de poesia* 1, no. 2 (April 1948).

Guimarães, Júlio Castañón. *Inscrições*. Rio de Janeiro: Imago, 1992.

Gullar, Ferreira. *Dirty Poem = Poema sujo*. Translated by Leland Guyer. Lanham, Md.: University Press of America, 1990.

Gunn, Giles. *Beyond Solidarity: Pragmatism and Difference in a Globalized World*. Chicago: University of Chicago Press, 2001.

———. Introduction to "Globalizing Literary Studies." *PMLA* 116, no. 1 (2001): 16–31.

Hanchard, Michael George. *Orpheus and Power: The Movimento Negro of Rio de Janeiro and São Paulo, Brazil, 1945–1988*. Princeton: Princeton University Press, 1994.

Handley, George B. *New World Poetics: Nature and the Adamic Imagination of Whitman, Neruda, and Walcott*. Athens: University of Georgia Press, 2007.

Harvey, John. "Cannibals, Mutants, and Hipsters: The Tropicalist Revival." In Perrone and Dunn, 106–22.

Hegel, G. W. F. *Philosophy of History*. New York: Dover, 1956.

Henriques Neto, Afonso. *Ser infinitas palavras*. Rio de Janeiro: Azougue, 2001.

Henríquez Ureña, Pedro. *Historia de la cultura en la América Hispánica*. Mexico City: Fondo de Cultura Económica, 1947.

Hoover, Paul. "What Is American About American Poetry?" www.poetrysociety.org/hoover.html.

Hoover, Paul, Régis Bonvicino, and Tarso M. de Melo, eds. "Lies About the Truth: An Anthology of Brazilian Poetry." *New American Writing* 18 (2000): 1–104.

Hopenhayn, Martin. "Globalization and Culture: Five Approaches to a Single Text." In *Cultural Politics in Latin America*, edited by Anny Brooksbank Jones and Ronaldo Munck, 142–56. New York: St. Martin's, 2000.

Hulme, Peter, and William H. Sherman, eds. *"The Tempest" and Its Travels*. Philadelphia: University of Pennsylvania Press, 2000.

Jameson, Fredric. "Notes on Globalization as a Philosophical Issue." In *The Cultures of Globalization*, edited by Fredric Jameson and Masao Miyoshi, 54–77. Durham, N.C.: Duke University Press, 1998.

Johnson, Randal, and Robert Stam. "The Shape of Brazilian Film History." In *Brazilian Cinema*, expanded ed., 15–51. New York: Columbia University Press, 1995.

Kadir, Djelal. "America and Its Studies." Introduction to "America, the Idea, the Literature," special issue, *PMLA* 118, no. 1 (2003): 9–24.

———, ed. Special issue on João Cabral de Melo Neto. *World Literature Today* 66, no. 4 (1992).

Kaq, Francisco. *Eu versus*. Rio de Janeiro: Sette Letras, 1999.

Kelsy, Harry. "American Discoveries Noted on the Planisphere of Sancho Gutiérrez." In *Early Images of the Americas: Transfer and Invention*, edited by Jerry M. Williams and Robert E. Lewis, 247–61. Tucson: University of Arizona Press, 1993.

Kenner, Hugh. *The Pound Era*. Berkeley and Los Angeles: University of California Press, 1971.

Keys, Kerry Shawn, ed. *Quingumbo: Nova poesia norte-americana*. São Paulo: Escrita, 1980.

King, Anthony D., ed. *Culture, Globalization and the World-System: Contemporary Conditions for the Representation of Identity*. 1991. Minneapolis: University of Minnesota Press, 1997.

Kozer, José. Interview by Claudio Daniel. *Suplemento Literário Minas Gerais*, n.s. 51 (September 1999): 8.

———. "O neobarroco: Um convergente na poesia latino-americana." Foreword to Daniel, *Jardim de camaleões*, 23–40. Originally presented as "The Neo-Baroque: A Converging in Latin American Poetry," at "The Pan-Hispanic World Today: Elements of Unity and Diversity," Texas A&M University, 15 November 2003.

Kuhnheim, Jill S. *Spanish American Poetry at the End of the Twentieth Century: Textual Disruptions*. Austin: University of Texas Press, 2004.

Kuss, Malena. "At Long Last, Someone Has Given Us a Name." Prologue to *Music in Latin

America and the Caribbean: An Encyclopedic History. Austin: University of Texas Press, 2003.

Kutzinski, Vera M. *Against the American Grain: Myth and History in William Carlos Williams, Jay Wright, and Nicolás Guillén.* Baltimore: Johns Hopkins University Press, 1987.

Lafer, Celso. "Conversaciones sobre Octavio Paz." *Cuadernos hispanoamericanos* 558 (1996): 7–27.

Lajolo, Marisa. "De palavras a linguagens." Preface to Vogt, *Ilhas Brasil*, 1–15.

Lara, Camilo, and Adriana Versiani. *Dentro Passa.* Belo Horizonte: Poesia Orbital, 1997.

Larkosh, Christopher. "Forms of A-Dress: Performances of the Foreign and S-Other-n Flows of Transnational Identity." In "Oceanic Worlds, Bordered Worlds," edited by Meg Samuelson and Shaun Viljoen, special issue, *Social Dynamics* 33, no. 2 (2007): 164–83.

Leão, Paulo. *A ordem do acaso.* Belo Horizonte: Poesia Orbital, 1997.

Leavell, Linda. *Marianne Moore and the Visual Arts: Prismatic Color.* Baton Rouge: Louisiana State University Press, 1995.

Leite, Sebastião Uchoa. *A uma incógnita.* São Paulo: Iluminuras, 1991.

———. *Crítica de ouvido.* São Paulo: Cosac-Naify, 2003.

———. *A ficção vida.* Rio de Janeiro: 34 Letras, 1993.

———. *Obra em dobras.* São Paulo: Duas Cidades, 1988.

Leminski, Paulo. *Caprichos e relaxos.* São Paulo: Brasiliense, 1983.

———. *Distraídos venceremos.* São Paulo: Brasiliense, 1987.

Leonardos, Ana Cristina. *Porto breve.* Rio de Janeiro: 7Letras, 2003.

Léry, Jean de. *History of a Voyage to the Land of Brazil Otherwise Called America.* 1578. Translated by Janet Whatley. Berkeley and Los Angeles: University of California Press, 1990.

Levitas, Ruth. *The Concept of Utopia.* Syracuse, N.Y.: Syracuse University Press, 1990.

Leyva, José Ángel, ed. *Versos comunicantes.* 3 vols. to date. Mexico City: Alforja, 2002.

Lezama Lima, José. *La expresión americana.* 1957. Madrid: Alianza, 1969.

Lima, Alceu Amoroso. *Cultura interamericana.* Rio de Janeiro: Agir, 1962.

Lima, Jorge de. *Antologia poética.* Rio de Janeiro: Sabiá, 1969.

Lima, Luiz Costa. "O campo visual de uma experiência antecipadora: Sousândrade." In Campos and Campos, 461–504.

Lima, Manoel Ricardo de. *Embrulho.* Rio de Janeiro: 7Letras, 2000.

Lipski, John M. "Too Close for Comfort? The Genesis of Portuñol/Portunhol." In *Selected Proceedings of the 8th Hispanic Linguistics Symposium*, edited by Timothy L. Face and Carol A. Klee, 1–22. Somerville, Mass.: Cascadilla Proceedings Project, 2006.

Livón-Grosman, Ernesto. "A Poetics of the Americas." *CiberLetras* 2 (2000). www.lehman.cuny.edu/ciberletras/v01n02/Livon-Grosman.htm.

———. "The Questing of the Americas." In Bernstein, "99 Poets," 129–30.

Lobo, Luiza. *Crítica sem juízo.* Rio de Janeiro: Francisco Alves, 1993.

———. *Épica e modernidade em Sousândrade.* Rio de Janeiro: EDUSP / Presença, 1986.

———. *Tradição e ruptura: "O guesa" de Sousândrade.* São Luís: SIOGE, 1979.

Lopes, Albert R., and Willis D. Jacobs. "Ronald de Carvalho." *Revista iberoamericana* 36 (1953): 391–400.

Lopes, Rodrigo Garcia, trans. *Folhas de relva*, by Walt Whitman. São Paulo: Iluminuras, 2005.

———. *Polivox*. Rio de Janeiro: Azougue, 2002.

———. *Solarium*. São Paulo: Iluminuras, 1994.

———. *Visibilia*. 2nd ed. Curitiba: Travessa dos Editores, 2005.

———, ed. *Vozes e visões: Panorama da arte e cultura norte-americanas hoje*. São Paulo: Iluminuras, 1996.

Lopez, Telê Porto Ancona. *Mário de Andrade: Ramais e caminhos*. São Paulo: Duas Cidades, 1972.

Lowe, Elizabeth, and Earl E. Fitz. *Translation and the Rise of Inter-American Literature*. Gainesville: University Press of Florida, 2007.

Lynn, Roa. *Brazil-USA: What Do We Have in Common?* 2nd ed. Washington, D.C.: Brazilian Embassy Cultural Section, 1999.

Maciel, Maria Esther. "América Latina reinventada: Octavio Paz e Haroldo de Campos." In Bernucci and Costigan, 219–28.

———. "Cartografia do presente: Poesia latino-americana no final do século." In *América em movimento: Ensaios sobre literatura latino-americana do século XX*, edited by Maria Esther Maciel, Myriam Avila, and Paulo Motta Oliveira, 33–48. Rio de Janeiro: Sette Letras, 1999.

———. "Sobre Octavio Paz: Conversa de Haroldo de Campos." *Nossa América / Nuestra América* 1 (1996): 20–29. In English at www.letras.ufmg.br/esthermaciel/withharold.htm.

———. *Vôo transverso: Poesia, modernidade e fim do século XX*. Rio de Janeiro: Sette Letras, 1999.

Mac Mathúna, Seán. "Is the Name Brazil of Celtic Origin?" *Flame* 7 (2001). www.fantompowa.net/Flame/brazil.htm.

Madureira, Luis. *Cannibal Modernities: Postcoloniality and the Avant-garde in Caribbean and Brazilian Literature*. Charlottesville: University of Virginia Press, 2005.

Magaldi, Cristina. "Adopting Imports: New Images and Alliances in Brazilian Popular Music of the 1990s." *Popular Music* 18, no. 3 (1999): 309–30.

Maranhão, Salgado. *Mural de ventos*. Rio de Janeiro: José Olympio, 1998.

———. *Palávora*. Rio de Janeiro: Sette Letras, 1995.

———. *Punhos da serpente*. Rio de Janeiro: Achiamé, 1989.

———. *Sol sangüíneo*. Rio de Janeiro: Imago, 2002.

Mariano, Antônio. *Guarda-chuvas esquecidos*. Rio de Janeiro: Lamparina, 2005.

Mariátegui, José Carlos. "¿Existe un pensamiento hispanoamericano?" *Mundial* (Lima), 1 May 1925.

———. "El iberoamericanismo y panamericanismo." *Mundial* (Lima), 8 May 1925.

Marques, Fabrício. *Dez diálogos com poetas contemporâneos*. Belo Horizonte: Gutenberg, 2004.

Martins, Floriano. *Alma em chamas*. Fortaleza: Letra e Música, 1998.

———. *O começo da busca: O surrealismo na poesia da América Latina*. Rio de Janeiro: Escrituras, 2002.

———, ed. *Un nuevo continente: Antología del surrealismo en la poesía de nuestra América*. San José, Costa Rica: Andrómeda, 2004.

Martins, Luciana. *Espetáculo das sensações alheias*. Curitiba: Medusa, 2003.

Martins, Wilson. *The Modernist Idea: A Critical Survey of Brazilian Writing in the Twentieth Century*. Translated by Jack E. Tomlins. New York: New York University Press, 1970.

Mata, Rodolfo. "Haroldo de Campos y Octavio Paz: Del diálogo creativo a la mediación institucional." *Anuario de estudios latinoamericanos* 32 (2001): 131–54.

———. "Tensões e vertentes da poesia mexicana, 1966–2004." *Sibila* 4, no. 6 (2004): 75–131.

Mautner, Jorge. *Fragmentos de sabonete: Notas sobre o renascimento americano do norte e do sul*. Rio de Janeiro: Ground, 1976.

———. *Mitologia do Kaos: Obras Completas*. 3 vols. + CD. Rio de Janeiro: Azougue, 2002.

———. *Panfletos da Nova Era*. São Paulo: Global, 1980.

Máximo, Ricardo. *Cantos erectos*. Rio de Janeiro: UAPE, 1999.

Maxwell, Kenneth. "Why Was Brazil Different?" In *Naked Tropics: Essays on Empire and Other Rogues*, 145–70. New York: Routledge, 2003.

McCabe, Susan. *Cinematic Modernism: Modernist Poetry and Film*. Cambridge: Cambridge University Press, 2005.

McCann, Bryan. "Black Pau: Uncovering the History of Brazilian Soul." In *Rockin' las Américas: The Global Politics of Rock in Latin/o America*, edited by Deborah Pacini Hernández, Héctor Fernández-L'Hoeste, and Eric Zolov, 68–90. Pittsburgh: University of Pittsburgh Press, 2004.

Meira, Caio. *Coisas que o primeiro cachorro na rua pode dizer*. Rio de Janeiro: Azougue, 2003.

———. *Corpo solo*. Rio de Janeiro: Sette Letras, 1998.

Mello, Heitor Ferraz. *Coisas imediatas*. Rio de Janeiro: 7Letras, 2004.

Melo, Tarso M. de. "Tradução da tradição—Anotações sobre os motores da poesia de Paulo Leminski." www.elsonfroes.com.br/kamiquase/ensaio2.htm.

Melo e Castro, E. M. de. "Poesia/transpoesia/repoesia: Alguns tópicos atuais nas poesias brasileira e portuguesa." *Revista USP* 36 (1997): 117–27.

Mendes, Emília. *Cantigas de amores a ilustres senhores*. With *Noturnos*, by José Pereira Júnior. Belo Horizonte: Poesia Orbital, 1997.

Mendonça, Ana Rita. *Carmen Miranda foi a Washington*. Rio de Janeiro: Record, 1999.

Merquior, José Guilherme. "The Brazilian and Spanish American Literary Traditions: A Contrastive View." In *The Cambridge History of Latin American Literature*, edited by Roberto González Echevarría and Enrique Pupo-Walker, 3:363–82. Cambridge: Cambridge University Press, 1996.

Mignolo, Walter D. "Afterword: Human Understanding and (Latin) American Interests: The Politics and Sensibilities of Geocultural Locations." *Poetics Today* 16, no. 1 (1995): 171–214.

———. *The Idea of Latin America.* Oxford: Blackwell, 2005.

———. "Loci of Enunciation and Imaginary Constructions: The Case of (Latin) America." Editor's introduction. *Poetics Today* 15, no. 4 (1994): 505–21.

———. "Putting the Americas on the Map: Geography and the Colonization of Space." *Colonial Latin American Review* 1 (1992): 25–65.

Milán, Eduardo. "El odiseo brasileño: La poesía de Haroldo de Campos." In *Justificación material: Ensayos sobre poesía latinoamericana,* 145–55. Mexico City: Universidad de la Ciudad de México, 2004.

Miller, James E. *Leaves of Grass: America's Lyric-Epic of Self and Democracy.* New York: Twayne, 1992.

Moehn, Frederick. "'Good Blood in the Veins of this Brazilian Rio' or a Cannibalist Transnationalism." In Perrone and Dunn, 258–70.

Moniz Bandeira, Luiz Alberto. "¿América Latina o Sudamérica?" www.clarin.com/diario/2005/05/16/opinion/o-01901.htm.

———. *Conflito e integração na América do Sul: Brasil, Argentina e Estados Unidos, da Tríplice Aliança ao Mercosul, 1870–2003.* 2nd ed. Rio de Janeiro: Revan, 2003.

Montaner, Carlos Alberto. *Los latinoamericanos y la cultura occidental.* Bogotá: Norma, 2003.

Monteiro, George. "Emily Dickinson's Brazilian Poems." *Revista interamericana de bibliografía* 22, no. 4 (1972): 404–10.

———. "Privileged and Presumptious Guests: Emily Dickinson's Brazilian Translators." *Luso-Brazilian Review* 8, no. 2 (1971): 39–53.

Montenegro, Delmo, and Pietro Wagner, eds. *Invenção Recife: Coletânea poética.* 2 vols. Recife: Fundacão de Cultura Cidade do Recife, 2004.

Morais, Claudio Nunes de. *Xadrez via correspondência.* Rio de Janeiro: Sette Letras, 1997.

Morais Júnior, Luis Carlos de. *Proteu, ou, A arte das transmutações: Leituras, audições e visões de Jorge Mautner.* Rio de Janeiro: HP Comunicação, 2004.

Moreira, Luiza Franco. "An American Life." *Inimigo rumor* 17 (2005): 54–55.

———. Introduction to translations of Robert Creeley. *Inimigo rumor* 17 (2005): 7–10.

———. *Meninos, poetas e heróis: Aspectos de Cassiano Ricardo do modernismo ao Estado Novo.* São Paulo: EDUSP, 2001.

———. "The Poet at the Window: Manuel Bandeira and Borges; Translation and Journalism." Paper presented at the University of Texas at Austin, 11 April 2006.

Moriconi, Ítalo. *Quase sertão.* Rio de Janeiro: Diadorim, 1996.

Morse, Richard M. *New World Soundings: Culture and Ideology in the Americas.* Baltimore: Johns Hopkins University Press, 1989.

———. "Triangulating Two Cubists: William Carlos Williams and Oswald de Andrade." *Latin American Literary Review* 14, no. 27 (1986): 175–83.

Mota, Carlos Guilherme. "Prefácio, nas asas da Panair." Preface to Santiago, *Crescendo,* 11–14.

Murphy, John P. *Music in Brazil: Experiencing Music, Expressing Culture.* New York: Oxford University Press, 2006.

Nascimento, Evando. "Uma leitura nos trópicos: A 'idéia' de América Latina." In *Leitura e experiência: Teoria, crítica, relato*, edited by Evando Nascimento and Maria Clara Castellões de Oliveira, 1–12. São Paulo: AnnaBlume, 2008.

Nist, John. *The Modernist Movement in Brazil*. Austin: University of Texas Press, 1967.

Nolan, James. *Poet-Chief: The Native American Poetics of Walt Whitman and Pablo Neruda*. Albuquerque: University of New Mexico Press, 1994.

Noll, João Gilberto. "Ilhas de Culminância." Preface to Moriconi, [5–6].

O'Dougherty, Maureen. *Consumption Intensified: The Politics of Middle-Class Daily Life in Brazil*. Durham, N.C.: Duke University Press, 2002.

O'Gorman, Edmundo. *The Invention of America: An Inquiry into the Historical Nature of the New World and the Meaning of its History*. Bloomington: Indiana University Press, 1961.

Oliveira, Solange Ribeiro de. "A literatura e as outras artes, hoje: O texto pop e a poesia brasileira contemporânea." *Revista de letras* (São Paulo) 48, no. 1 (2008): 101–15.

Ornellas, Sandro. *Simulações*. Salvador, Bahia: Fundação Casa de Jorge Amado, 1998.

O'Shea, José Roberto, ed. *Antologia de poesia norte-americana contemporânea*. Florianópolis: UFSC, 1997.

Paiva, Joaquim. *Aos pés de Batman*. São Paulo: Iluminuras, 1994.

Palattella, John. "Atlas of the Difficult World: The Problem of Global Poetry." *Lingua Franca* 9, no. 4 (1999): 52–58.

Palmer, Michael, and Régis Bonvicino, *Cadenciando-um-ning um samba, para o outro*. São Paulo: Ateliê, 2001.

Paro, Maria Clara Bonetti. "A América de Sousândrade e a América de Whitman: Marám nhan e Manhattan." In *Literaturas estrangeiras e o Brasil: Diálogos*, edited by Laura P. Zuntini de Izarra, 177–200. São Paulo: Associação Editorial Humanitas, 2004.

———. "Ronald de Carvalho e Walt Whitman." *Revista de letras* 32 (1992): 141–51.

———. "Whitman in Brazil." In *Walt Whitman and the World*, edited by Gay Wilson Allen and Ed Folsom, 128–36. Iowa City: University of Iowa Press, 1995.

Patiño, Roxana. "Identidad, territorios, diversidad: Para pensar la integración cultural en el Mercosur." In *Declínio da arte, ascensão da cultura*, edited by Raúl Antelo et al., 55–62. Florianópolis: Letras Contemporâneas, 1998.

Paz, Octavio. *Corriente alterna*. Mexico City: Siglo XXI, 1967.

———. *Obra poética, 1935–1988*. Madrid: Seix Barral, 1988.

———. *El signo y el garabato*. Mexico City: Joaquín Mortiz, 1975.

———. "The Word as Foundation." *Times Literary Supplement*, 14 November 1968.

Paz, Octavio, and Haroldo de Campos. *Transblanco: Em torno a "Blanco" de Octavio Paz*. Rio de Janeiro: Guanabara, 1986. 2nd ed., São Paulo: Siciliano, 1994.

Pedrosa, Célia, ed. *Mais poesia hoje*. Rio de Janeiro: 7Letras, 2000.

Peixoto, Marta. *Poesia com coisas: Uma leitura de João Cabral de Melo Neto*. São Paulo: Perspectiva, 1983.

Pen, Marcelo. "Decassílabo perfeito para nação imperfeita." pphp.uol.com.br/tropico/html/textos/2484,1.shl.

Pereira, Antonio. *Folhas do Carmim*. Belo Horizonte: Poesia Orbital, 1997.

Pereira, Edimilson de Almeida. *Zeosório Blues*. Belo Horizonte: Mazza, 2002.

Pereira Júnior, José. *Noturnos. See* Mendes, Emília.

Perloff, Marjorie. *The Poetics of Indeterminacy: Rimbaud to Cage*. Princeton: Princeton University Press, 1981.

———. "Writing as Re-writing: Concrete Poetry as Arrière-Garde." www.lehman.edu/ciberletras/v 17/perloff.htm.

Perlongher, Néstor, ed. *Caribe trasplatino*. São Paulo: Iluminuras, 1991.

Perrone, Charles A. "ABC of AdeC: Reading Augusto de Campos." *Review: Latin American Literature and Arts* 73 (2006): 236–44.

———. "De Gregório de Matos a Caetano Veloso e 'Outras palavras': Barroquismo na Música Popular Brasileira contemporânea." *Revista iberoamericana* 50, no. 126 (1984): 77–99. Reprint, *Barroco* 13 (1985): 107–23.

———. "De *Noigandres* & *Navilouca* a *Coyote* & *Oroboro*: Las revistas brasileñas de invención y las antologías antinormativas." *Nerter* 10 (2007): 77–81. Reprint, *Zunái* 4, no. 14 (2008). www.revistazunai.com/ensaios/charles_perrone_revistas_brasileiras.htm.

———. "*Harpas farpadas*: Casos singulares de interlocução interamericana." *Graphos* (Universidade Federal da Paraíba) 10/11, no. 2/1 (2009): 11–16.

———. "João Cabral de Melo Neto." In *Encyclopedia of World Literature in the Twentieth Century*, rev. ed., 3:247–48. Farmington Hills, Mich.: St. James Press, 1999.

———. *Masters of Contemporary Brazilian Song: MPB, 1965–1985*. Austin: University of Texas Press, 1989.

———. "*Pau-Brasil, Antropofagia, Tropicalismo*: The Modernist Legacy of Oswald de Andrade in Brazilian Poetry and Song of the 1960s–1980s." In *One Hundred Years of Invention: Oswald de Andrade and the Modern Tradition in Latin American Literature*, edited by K. David Jackson, 133–54. Austin: Abaporu Press, 1992.

———. "Presentation and Representation of Self and City in *Paulicéia Desvairada*." *Chásqui: Revista de literatura latinoamericana* 31, no. 1 (2002): 18–27.

———. "Resource and Resonance: A Story of Transamerican Poetics and Brazilian Song in Global and Cultural Perspective." *Luso-Brazilian Review* 38, no. 2 (2001): 75–85.

———. *Seven Faces: Brazilian Poetry Since Modernism*. Durham, N.C: Duke University Press, 1996.

———. "Signs of Intercourse: Material Poetry and Erotic Imperatives." *Gragoatá* 14 (2003): 197–218.

———. "*Topos* and Topicalities: The Tropes of Tropicália and *Tropicalismo*." *Studies in Latin American Popular Culture* 19 (2000): 1–20. Online at tropicalia.uol.com.br/site_english/internas/visestr_10.php.

Perrone, Charles A., and Christopher Dunn, eds. *Brazilian Popular Music and Globalization*. Gainesville: University Press of Florida, 2001.

Pignatari, Décio. *Poesia pois é poesia, 1950–2000*. São Paulo: Ateliê, 2004.

———. *Vocogramas*. Salvador, Bahia: Código, 1985.

Pike, Fredrick B. *The United States and Latin America: Myths and Stereotypes of Civilization and Nature*. Austin: University of Texas Press, 1992.

Pinto, Júlio Pimentel. "Borges and His Contemporaneous Streets." *História* 22, no. 2 (2003): 121–32.

———. "Ruas de Borges e de seus contemporâneos." At www.scielo.br/scielo.php?pid=0101-907420030002&script=sci_issuetoc.

Pinto, Manuel da Costa. *Antologia comentada da poesia brasileira do século 21*. São Paulo: Publifolha, 2006.

Pizarro, Ana. "Hispanoamérica y Brasil: Encuentros, desencuentros, vacíos." Keynote for the section "Relaciones Hispanoamérica y Brasil" at the 14th Congreso de la Asociación Alemana de Hispanistas, University of Regensburg, 6 March 2003. *Acta Literaria* 29 (2004): 105–20. At www.scielo.cl/scielo.php?pid=S0717-68482004002900007&script=sci_arttext.

Poe, Edgar Allan. *O corvo, corvos e o outro corvo*. Edited and translated by Vinícius Alves. Florianópolis: UFSC, 2000.

Pound, Ezra. *ABC of Reading*. 1934. New York: New Directions, 1951.

Pucheu, Alberto. "Apresentação." Foreword to "Poesia brasileira e seus encontros interventivos," special issue, *Terceira margem* (UFRJ) 8, no. 11 (2004): 5–8.

Raab, Josef. "El gran viejo: Walt Whitman in Latin America." *CLCWeb: Comparative Literature and Culture: A WWWeb Journal* 3, no. 2 (2001).

Ramalho, Christina. *Elas escrevem o épico*. Florianópolis: Editora Mulheres; Santa Cruz do Sul: EDUNISC, 2005.

———. "O híbrido lirismo brasileiro dos anos 90: Injunções históricas, políticas e econômicas." *Cerrados* 13, no. 1 (2005): 89–100.

Rasec, César. *Jorge Mautner em movimento*. Salvador, Bahia: C. Rasec, 2004.

Recondo, Gregorio. *Identidad, integración y creación cultural en América Latina: El desafío del Mercosur*. Buenos Aires: UNESCO / Belgrano, 1997.

———, ed. *Mercosur: Una historia común para la integración*. Buenos Aires: CARI, 2000.

———. *El sueño de la patria grande: Ideas y antecedentes integracionistas en América Latina*. Buenos Aires: CICCUS, 2001.

Reed, Ishmael, ed. *From Totems to Hip-Hop: A Multicultural Anthology of Poetry Across the Americas, 1900–2002*. New York: Thunder's Mouth Press, 2003.

Rennó, Carlos, ed. *Cole Porter: Canções, Versões*. São Paulo: Paulicéia, 1991.

Resende, Beatriz. "Cyberspace, South: Internet and Cultural Studies in Brazil." Paper presented at ICLA Congress, Pretoria, August 2000. acd.ufrj.br/pacc/beatriz.html.

Rezende, Renato. *Leaves of Paradise*. São Paulo: 100 Leitores, 2000.

Ribeiro, Ana Elisa. *Æ*. Belo Horizonte: Poesia Orbital, 1997.

Ribeiro, Darcy. *Las Américas y la civilización: Proceso de formación y causas del desarrollo desigual de los pueblos americanos*. Caracas: Biblioteca Ayacucho, 1992.

Ribeiro Neto, Amador. "Bom dia, melancolia." Preface to Barbosa, *Louco*, 11–20.

Risério, Antonio, ed. *Bahia invenção: Anti-antologia de poesia baiana*. Salvador, Bahia, 1974.

———. *Ensaio sobre o texto poético em contexto digital*. Salvador, Bahia: Fundação Casa de Jorge Amado, 1998.

———. "Gil Brasil Bragil: Uma apreciação didática." In *Gilberto Gil: Expresso 2222*, 254–87. Salvador, Bahia: Corrupio, 1982.

———. "O nome mais belo do medo." *Minas Gerais Suplemento Literário* 8, no. 360 (1973): 4–5. www.letras.ufmg.br/websuplit/exbGer/exbSup.asp?Cod=080360071973 04-08036007197305.

Rizzo, Ricardo. *Cavalo marinho e outros poemas*. São Paulo: Nankin, 2002.

Rocha, Flávia. *A Casa Azul ao meio-dia = The Blue House around Noon*. Curitiba: Travessa dos Editores, 2005.

Rocha, Flávia, and Edwin Torres, eds. "New Brazilian and American Poetry." Special binational issue, *Rattapallax* 9 (2003).

Rocha, João Cezar de Castro, ed. "A Revisionary History of Brazilian Literature and Culture." Special issue, *Portuguese Literary and Cultural Studies* 4–5 (2000).

Rocha, João Cezar de Castro, and Jorge Ruffinelli, eds. "Anthropophagy Today?" Special double issue, *Nuevo texto crítico* 12, nos. 23–24 (1999).

Rodríguez Monegal, Emir. *Mário de Andrade / Borges: Um diálogo dos anos 20*. Translated by Maria Augusta da Costa Vieira Helene. São Paulo: Perspectiva, 1978.

Romero, Sílvio. *História da literatura brasileira*. 2nd ed. 2 vols. Rio de Janeiro: H. Garnier, 1903.

Rostagno, Irene. *Searching for Recognition: The Promotion of Latin American Literature in the United States*. Westport, Conn.: Greenwood, 1997.

Rothenberg, Jerome, and Jeffrey C. Robinson, eds. *The University of California Book of Romantic and Postromantic Poetry*. Vol. 3 of *Poems for the Millennium*. Berkeley and Los Angeles: University of California Press, 2009.

Rouquié, Alain. *Amérique Latine: Introduction à l'Extrême-Occident*. Paris: Éditions du Seuil, 1987.

Ruiz, Ricardo Muniz de, and Thereza Christina Rocque da Motta, eds. *Ponte de versos: Uma antologia carioca*. Rio de Janeiro: Ibis, 2003.

Sá, Lúcia. *Rain Forest Literatures: Amazonian Texts and Latin American Culture*. Minneapolis: University of Minnesota Press, 2004.

Salomão, Waly. *Algaravias: Câmera de ecos*. São Paulo: 34 Letras, 1996.

———. *Lábia*. Rio de Janeiro: Rocco, 1998.

———. *Pescados vivos*. Rio de Janeiro: Rocco, 2004.

———. "A praia tropicalista." In *Tropicália: 20 anos*, edited by José Saffiotti Filho, 32–35. São Paulo: SESC, 1987.

Salomon, Jean-Jacques, Francisco R. Sagasti, and Céline Sachs-Jeantet. *The Uncertain Quest: Science, Technology, and Development*. New York: United Nations University Press, 1994.

Salvino, Romulo Valle. "Nada que o sol não explique: *Nothing the sun could not explain*." *Sibila* 3, no. 4 (2003): 188–209.

Sandmann, Marcelo. *Lírico renitente*. Rio de Janeiro: 7Letras, 2000.

Sant'Anna, Affonso Romano de. "The Great Speech of the Guarani Indian Lost to History, and Other Defeats," *Dactylus* 8 (Fall 1987): 31 ff.

Santí, Enrico Mario. "The Accidental Tourist: Walt Whitman in Latin America." In *Do the Americas Have a Common Literature?* edited by Gustavo Pérez Firmat, 156–76. Durham, N.C.: Duke University Press, 1990.

Santiago, Silviano. *Crescendo durante a guerra numa província ultramarina*. Rio de Janeiro: Francisco Alves, 1978.

——. *Salto*. Belo Horizonte: Imprensa Oficial, 1970.

——. *The Space In-between: Essays on Latin American Culture*. Edited by Ana Lúcia Gazzola. Durham, N.C.: Duke University Press, 2001.

Sarduy, Severo. "El barroco y el neo-barroco." In Fernández Moreno, 167–84. Translated as "The Baroque and the Neobaroque" in Fernández Moreno, Ortega, and Schulman, 115–32.

Saul, Scott. *Freedom Is, Freedom Ain't: Jazz and the Making of the Sixties*. Cambridge, Mass.: Harvard University Press, 2003.

Schwartz, Jorge. "Down with Tordesillas!" In J. C. Rocha, 277–93. Translation of "Abaixo Tordesilhas!" *Revista de estudos avançados* 7, no. 17 (1993): 185–200; also "¡Abajo Tordesillas!" *Casa de las Américas* 191 (1993): 26–35.

——. *Vanguarda e cosmopolitismo na década de 20: Oliverio Girondo e Oswald de Andrade*. São Paulo: Perspectiva, 1983.

Secchin, Antonio Carlos. *Escritos sobre poesia & alguma ficção*. Rio de Janeiro: Topbooks, 2003.

Sefami, Jacobo. *El destierro apacible y otros ensayos*. Mexico City: Premia, 1987.

Silva, Anazildo Vasconcelos da. *Formação épica da literatura brasileira*. Rio de Janeiro: Elo, 1987.

——. "Semiotização épica do discurso." Unpublished essay. 2005.

——. "Vertente épica do *Pau-Brasil*." In *Oswald plural*, edited by Gilberto Mendonça Teles et al., 187–99. Rio de Janeiro: Editora da UERJ, 1995.

Silva, Anazildo Vasconcelos da, and Christina Ramalho. *História da epopéia brasileira: Teoria, crítica e percurso*, vol. 3. Rio de Janeiro: Garamond, in press.

Silva, José Asunción. *Obras completas*, vol. 1. Buenos Aires: Plus Ultra, 1968.

Sklodowska, Elzbieta, and Ben A. Heller, eds. *Roberto Fernández Retamar y los estudios latinoamericanos*. Pittsburgh: Instituto Internacional de Literatura Iberoamericana, University of Pittsburgh, 2000.

Slavitt, David R., trans. *Selected Poems*, by Manuel Bandeira. Riverdale-on-Hudson, New York: Sheep Meadow Press, 2002.

Solt, Mary Ellen, ed. *Concrete Poetry: A World View*. Bloomington: Indiana University Press, 1970.

Sommer, Doris. *Foundational Fictions: The National Romances of Latin America*. Berkeley and Los Angeles: University of California Press, 1991.

Sorá, Gustavo. *Traducir el Brasil: Una antropología de la circulación internacional de ideas*. Buenos Aires: Zorzal, 2003.

Sousândrade [Joaquim de Sousa Andrade]. *Poesia e prosa reunidas de Sousândrade*. Edited by Frederick G. Williams and Jomar Moraes. São Luís: AML, 2003.

Sovik, Liv. "Globalizing Caetano Veloso." In Perrone and Dunn, 96–105.

Strand, Mark, ed. and trans. *Looking for Poetry: Poems by Carlos Drummond de Andrade and Rafael Alberti and Songs from the Quechua*. New York: Knopf, 2002.

Süssekind, Flora. "Deterritorialization and Literary Form: Brazilian Contemporary Literature and Urban Experience." Working Paper CBS-34-02, Centre for Brazilian Studies, University of Oxford, 2002. www.casaruibarbosa.gov.br/dados/DOC/artigos/o-z/ FCRB_FloraSussekind_UOC_brazilian_studies.pdf.

Szeman, Imre. "Globalization." In *Encyclopedia of Postcolonial Studies*, edited by John Hawley, 209–17. Westport, Conn.: Greenwood, 2001.

———. "Globalization." In *Johns Hopkins Guide to Literary Theory and Criticism*, 2nd ed., edited by Michael Groden, Martin Kreiswirth, and Imre Szeman, 458–65. Baltimore: Johns Hopkins University Press, 2005.

Szklo, Gilda. "A modernidade em *Paulicea desvairada* e *Fervor de Buenos Aires*." *Minas Gerais Suplemento Literário* 706 (12 and 19 April 1980).

Teles, José. *Do frevo ao manguebeat*. São Paulo: Editora 34, 2000.

———. *Meteoro Chico*. Recife: Bagaço, [1998?].

Tomlinson, John. *Globalization and Culture*. Chicago: University of Chicago Press, 1999.

Torres Filho, Rubens Rodrigues. *Novolume*. São Paulo: Iluminuras, 1997.

———. *Poros*. São Paulo: Duas Cidades, 1989.

Torres-Ríoseco, Arturo. *The Epic of Latin American Literature*. 1942. Berkeley and Los Angeles: University of California Press, 1961.

Toumson, Roger. *L'Utopie perdue des Îles d'Amérique*. Paris: Honoré Champion, 2004.

Treece, David. *Exiles, Allies, Rebels: Brazil's Indianist Movement, Indigenist Politics, and the Imperial Nation-State*. Westport, Conn.: Greenwood, 2000.

Unruh, Vicky. *Latin American Vanguards: The Art of Contentious Encounter*. Berkeley and Los Angeles: University of California Press, 1995.

Valente, Luiz Fernando. "O traço apolíneo de Salgado Maranhão." *Alceu* 4, no. 7 (2003): 141–49.

Vargas, Herom. *Hibridismos musicais de Chico Science & Nação Zumbi*. São Paulo: Ateliê, 2008.

Vasconcellos, Affonso Ivo Vieira de, and Ana Adelaide de Souza Vasconcellos. *Madrugada*. Belo Horizonte: Poesia Orbital, 1997.

Vassallo, Lígia. "A literatura brasileira e a América Hispânica." *Brasil Brazil* 16, no. 30 (2003): 47–64.

Veloso, Caetano. *Letra só*. Edited by Eucanaã Ferraz. 2 vols. São Paulo: Companhia das Letras, 2003.

———. *Tropical Truth: A Story of Music and Revolution in Brazil*. Translated by Isabel de Sena. New York: Knopf, 2002. Originally published as *Verdade tropical* (São Paulo: Companhia das Letras, 1997).

Veríssimo, José. *Cultura, literatura e política na América Latina*. Edited by João Alexandre Barbosa. São Paulo: Brasiliense, 1986.

Vilar, Bluma W. *Álbum*. Rio de Janeiro: Sette Letras, 1996.

Vogt, Carlos. *Ilhas Brasil*. São Paulo: Ateliê, 2002.

———. *Metalurgia*. São Paulo: Companhia das Letras, 1991.

Walcott, Derek. *Omeros*. New York: Farrar, Straus and Giroux, 1990.

Walden, Stephen T. "*Brasilidade*: Brazilian *Rock Nacional* in the Context of National Cultural Identity." Ph.D. diss., University of Georgia, 1996.

Weber, Adele. *Tipos de rua e alguns recados*. Rio de Janeiro: Grupo Letra Itinerante, 2003.

Weinberger, Eliot. "Ninguém fala português." Interview. *Sibila* 2 (2002): 13–19.

Weintraub, Fábio. *Baque*. São Paulo: Editora 34, 2007.

Whitener, Brian. "Brazilian Poetry." *Chicago Review* 47, no. 2 (2002): 91–93.

Williams, Emmett. *An Anthology of Concrete Poetry*. New York: Something Else Press, 1967.

Williams, Frederick G. "Sousândrade em Nova Iorque: Visão da mulher americana." *Hispania* 74, no. 3 (1991): 548–55.

———. "The Wall Street Inferno: A Poetic Rendering of the Gilded Age." *Chásqui: Revista de literatura latinoamericana* 5, no. 2 (1976): 15–32.

Williams, William Carlos. *The Collected Poems of William Carlos Williams*. Edited by A. Walton Litz and Christopher MacGowan. 2 vols. New York: New Directions, 1986–88.

Willis, Bruce Dean. *Aesthetics of Equilibrium: The Vanguard Poetics of Vicente Huidobro and Mário de Andrade*. West Lafayette, Ind.: Purdue University Press, 2006.

Wisnik, José Miguel. *O som e o sentido: Uma outra história das músicas*. São Paulo: Companhia das Letras, 1989.

Wolff, Joca. *Pateta em Nova Yorque*. Florianópolis: Letras Contemporâneas, 2002.

Xavier, Luiza. *Save As*. Rio de Janeiro: 7Letras, 2002.

Yúdice, George. *The Expediency of Culture: Uses of Culture in the Global Era*. Durham, N.C.: Duke University Press, 2003.

Zenith, Richard, trans. *Education by Stone: Selected Poems*, by João Cabral de Melo Neto. New York: Archipelago, 2005.

Index

ABC folk form, 40
abolitionist poetry, 150
Accioly, Marcus: committed writing, 102–3; globalization in, 131; historical awareness, 103; *Latinomérica*, 127–35; manifesto, 130; "poetic justice," 100
activism in the arts, 20–21
Adderly, Cannonball, 81
African-American poets, 77
African-American solidarity, 89–92
Aguilar, José Roberto, 71
Ainsa, Fernando, 153, 163
Aleixo, Ricardo, 78
Alfonso X (the Wise), 141
Alma América (Santos Chocano), 100
Almanak (São Paulo), 53*f*, 54
Alves, Antônio F. de Castro. *See* Castro Alves, Antônio F. de
Alvim, Francisco, 93
Amado, Jorge, 146, 206n25
Amâncio, Moacir, x, 194n6
Amazonian area, 156
America: as all-encompassing whole, 125; as ideological construction, 30; as assemblage of "indisciplines," 126; Carvalho on, 126; early mapmakers on, 11, 26–27; as metaphor for surprise and invention, 32; as name of continent, 9; post-1800 titles, 99; prerepublican use in Brazil, 101; singular US usage, 26, 185, 189n2; three Americas, 97–98; use of term, 26, 191n30
América Latina, historical roots of name, 27–28
America(n), use of terms, 26, 185, 189n2
Americanism: Carvalho's approach, 124; ideal, 113
Americanization, less pernicious view of, xv
Americanness, 94, 141, 184

americano, ambivalence of term, 70
Americas: inclusive use of, 3; plurality of, xiv
"America-scape," xvi
Amoreira, Flávio Viegas, 94, 197n74
"amorse" (Augusto de Campos), 146, 147*f*, 148; versions, 207n28
Andean nations, 125
Andrade, Carlos Drummond de, 40, 61
Andrade, Mário de, 102, 123; Amado on, 206n25; Borges contrasted, 144–45; as figure of modernism, 143–44
Andrade, Oswald de: "Cannibalist Manifesto," 25–26, 70–71, 102, 168, 173, 198n9, 201n58; Carvalho compared, 120–21; compared to Williams, 58, 61; dedication to, 21; Fernández Retamar on, 25; on film, 70–71; Girondo meeting, 145; influence of, 67, 167; landmark contributions, 18–19; "Manifesto of Pau-Brasil Poetry," 18–19, 121, 167–68; musical homage, 114; Noigandres poets linked, 20; old/new juxtaposition, 175; *Poesia Pau-Brasil*, 102; screenplays, 198n8; Sousândrade compared, 112
Andrade, Paula Valéria, 181
animal-rights outlook, 112
Antelo, Raúl, 144, 161
anti-acculturation, agents of, 96
anti-imperialism: in Accioly, 134; impact on poetry, 48, 153; postwar changes in, 33; in song, 155; versus Pan-Americanism, 29
Antilles, 118, 120
Antunes, Arnaldo: x; "A utopia continua," 182; "Céu-Hell," 41*f*, 42; "Dentro," 56*f*, 56; on film, 72; "Gertrudiana," 56, 57*f*, 58; "Ilha," 14, 15*f*; influence of, 182; influence of popular music, 86; "Now/Nowhere/Here" installation, 36, 194n10; on Stein, 55; US appearances, 36–37, 194n10

Charles A. Perrone is professor of Portuguese and Luso-Brazilian literature and culture in the Department of Spanish and Portuguese Studies and is coordinator of Brazilian Studies in the Center for Latin American Studies at the University of Florida, Gainesville.